AFTER THE LOST GENERATION

After the Lost Generation

A CRITICAL STUDY OF THE WRITERS OF TWO WARS

BY JOHN W. ALDRIDGE

THE NOONDAY PRESS
A division of Farrar, Straus, and Company
NEW YORK

To my mother and father and Leslie

PREFACE TO NEW EDITION

I HAVE DECIDED, in the face of some impulse to the contrary, to forego the labor of revision which the republication of this book might seem to demand of me. Today, six years after its original appearance, the book seems to me still to have value as a pioneering commentary—itself already faintly historical —upon an historical moment of perhaps abiding interest in recent American literary affairs. It may also be instructive as an inquiry into the literary situation which was just emerging at the time I began writing. I have, at any rate, often been surprised to see how the passage of time has confirmed insights which initially seemed conjectural, and certain tendencies which then seemed merely potential. I have also concluded that the place and scope of the book as it stands have already in a small way been defined, and that the book has perhaps had as much to do with fixing the historical character of the circumstances it describes as they have had to do with fixing its place and scope. To revise now, therefore, so as perhaps to include discussion of newer writers and more recent developments than those of 1950, would seem to me to risk violating both its own autonomous character as an historical work and that of the situation it attempts to define. At the time of composition of course that situation was current fact and not history. But it is clearly history now, and I should prefer to let it remain so.

J.W.A.

Princeton: January, 1958

PREFACE TO THE FIRST EDITION

ONE CANNOT SPEAK of fiction without sooner or later speaking of values. The process by which a writer selects, out of the vast store of undigested experience which is himself, the material that is to go into his novel is a process of assigning value to certain portions of that experience. One might in fact say that the quality which most clearly distinguishes literary material from mere experience is the value the writer has been able to give to it within a dramatic or narrative framework. In much the same way, a reader will respond to the meaning of a novel and find it dramatic to the extent that he is able to realize it in terms of his own values. Ideally, the writer and the reader should share the same values, so that the material which the writer selects as valuable enough to write about will automatically be valuable to the reader. But this would depend upon the existence of a society based on certain stable moral assumptions, the sort of society to which, perhaps, Richardson and Smollett belonged, to which, in a different way and to a lesser extent, even Scott Fitzgerald and Ernest Hemingway belonged, but to which we obviously do not belong today.

I have not intended in this book to trace down the causes for the disappearance of such a society, or the changes which have consequently occurred in literature, since the time of Richardson and Smollett. That would be the aim of a far better and maturer book than this one can pretend to be. But I have been interested in tracing down such of these changes as have become evident since the time of Fitzgerald and Hemingway, particularly in the work of their newest successors, the younger novelists of the 1940's. In doing so, I have also inevitably written another book, a book about the two wars and their contrasting effects on the writing which the two American war generations have produced. In the main, however, the book about the disappearance of a stable society and a common set of values and the book about the two generations form a single unit and, I hope, one commentary on the same dilemma. It is impossible to be aware of the differences between the work of Hemingway and Gore Vidal or between the work of Fitzgerald and Paul Bowles (differences which might be represented in degrees on the falling barometer of diminishing literary returns) without also being aware of the differences between the moral resources which these writers had at their disposal.

In the section devoted to the literary generation of the first war I have discussed only those writers who seem to me most illustrative of the artistic preoccupations of their age and whose work has had the most lasting influence on the young writers of today. When I refer to Hemingway, Fitzgerald, and Dos Passos as "war" writers, I obviously do not mean to suggest that they all wrote war novels or even that they were primarily concerned in their work with a description of war. I mean simply that they all wrote under the influence of the climate of war and were profoundly affected by it as well as by the literary movement which it stimulated.

Since I have taken the two wars as the focal points of this study, I have not discussed the work of the writers of the 1930's. Besides, I know of none, with the exception of Thomas Wolfe, who had an influence on the young writers of the 1940's comparable to that of the three Lost Generation writers I have chosen to discuss. For some reason, those of us who began to take a serious interest in literature in the first years of the second war felt an immediate kinship with the Lost Generation. We acknowledged them as our true literary forebears, even though a whole new generation had grown up since their time and stood between them and us. To be sure, we read the novels of Steinbeck, Farrell, and Saroyan written in the Thirties, just as we read those of Wilder, Cather, Lewis, and Dreiser who belonged, roughly, to the generation of Hemingway; but they simply did not touch us, did not seem to be confronting the same issues or operating in the same spheres. As for Wolfe, who most certainly did touch us, I feel that the most important attitudes reflected in his work are reflected more satisfactorily, with far less distortion, in the work of Hemingway, Fitzgerald, and Dos Passos.

The writers I have selected for discussion in the second part of the book are nearly all *younger* writers who have appeared since the end of the second war and who form, because of the war and the interval of more than twenty years, the first *completely new* literary generation since the generation of the 1920's. Norman Mailer, Robert Lowry, Vance Bourjaily, Merle Miller, Truman Capote, Gore Vidal, and Frederick Buechner are all close to or under thirty and, therefore, about the same age that Hemingway and the others were when they wrote their early novels. Paul Bowles, Irwin Shaw, John Horne Burns, and Alfred Hayes are slightly older; but I have included them because they have written either serious war novels or novels that are particularly suitable as illustrations of new developments in fiction. Once again I wish to make it clear, however, that these writers were not chosen because they have all written war novels or even because they have all devoted some part of their novels to the war, although most of them have. They were chosen because they all grew up and began to write in the atmosphere of war, because they form, in fact, a distinct "war" generation, and because the marks of the war and of the tensions of its aftermath are clear in their work.

Finally, of course, I have fallen back on my own capricious taste. I have discussed these writers simply because they seem to me the most interesting of the younger literary group. There are many others whom I might have discussed and whom someone other than they will most certainly feel I should have discussed. Those who hold to the imprecise belief that writers are young writers until they have reached the age of fifty will wish I had included Robert Penn Warren, James Gould Cozzens, Tom Lea, Nelson Algren, Walter Van Tilburg Clark, and Lionel Trilling. I have not included them because I believe they are not young enough to belong to the newest literary generation or to have been affected in the same way by the experiences that generation endured. Other readers will insist that I should at least have included Jean Stafford, Mary McCarthy, Shirley Jackson, Howard Nemerov, Eudora Welty, Carson McCullers, and a dozen more. While I have made brief comments on the work of a few, I found most of them less relevant to my purpose than those I have discussed in detail.

The point of view from which I have examined the younger writers should be evident in the material itself. I have written out of my own experience and out of what seems to me to be the typical experience of my contemporaries. I have not wished and I am not equipped to write about the experience of the writers and readers who came to maturity before 1920 or before 1940. They have no more reason to ask that I tell their story than to criticize Malcolm Cowley for failing in his *Exile's Return* to tell the story of the writers who did not take part in the expatriate movement or who had already gone into their dotage when the movement began. But I should be surprised if anyone who lived through the years leading up to the second war did not find something in this book that is true for him.

The idea on which the book is based has grown out of a time almost eight years past when a lot of us were younger than we now are by considerably more than eight years and still able to think about tomorrow as if it were absolutely sure to come. There was no war then, at least not for my friends and me, but the excitement of war was everywhere; and it gave a special brightness and clarity to all that we saw, did, and thought. We were all about nineteen and beginning our second year of college; and looking back, it seems to me that we were very much like the young men Vance Bourjaily writes about in *The End of My Life* with perhaps a touch of the Stephen Dedalus of Joyce's *Stephen Hero* and of Buck Mulligan in *Ulysses*. I remember that there was nothing quite like the taste of the black coffee we drank in the late nights and early mornings of that time, or the green of the trees in the summers, particularly when we had gone for days without sleep, or the sadness of the leaves blowing over the streets in the falls, particularly when we had been reading Thomas Wolfe, which was most of the time, or the parties we went to where we learned to drink and make love, or the poems and stories we wrote that were full of such sincerity and hope. It seemed to us—at least the assumption was implicit in everything we said and did—that we were coming of age in an era of singular crisis and upheaval. The natural excitement of awakening to life, the normal college experience, was reinforced and heightened by our impending participation in a great world war. The books that were going to be written after that war, the books that we would help to write, would be more magnificent and wise than any ever written in the past. We had read a great deal about the Lost Generation: we could quote pages of Cowley's *Exile's Return;* we knew Hemingway, Dos Passos, Fitzgerald, Eliot, Stein, and Joyce even better than we knew one another; and we were sure that our age would be like theirs—a time of discovery, transition, and revolt. It was not merely that we had the sense of youth, although we had that in abundance. We had as well a genuine sense of inevitability and of new energy getting set to explode.

When my friends and I left college and went to war, we carried with us this feeling about tomorrow; and when we came back from the war we found we had preserved it almost intact. But it was not long before we began to realize that somewhere along the way tomorrow had been lost. Not only had the new age not arrived but there seemed little likelihood that it was going to; and we concluded, not without some bitterness, that we had been keeping alive and making love to an illusion.

During the years that followed, we tried over and over again to discover exactly what had happened. In the letters we wrote to one another and in the conversations we had together, we thought of countless possibilities but never arrived at a final answer. We always had too many emotional associations whenever we tried to reconstruct the past and our memories began playing tricks, so that after a while we couldn't be sure if something had really happened, if that was the way we had really felt, or if we had only read about it somewhere. Finally I think most of us decided we had been partly deluded and partly right, that what we had sensed was true at the time but was no longer true, and that the healthiest thing to do was forget about it.

But in tracing my own steps back to the enchantment of those years and in reviewing all that has taken place since then, I have come to certain tentative conclusions which I have tried to set down in this book. The struggle to understand a vivid personal experience has led me quite naturally to consider the larger problem of which it is a part; and I am aware that in doing so I have removed all but the emotional core of the original experience and that, as a result, it may seem to my friends that I have written about something else altogether. However this may be, I should like them to know that this is my contribution to the running discussion we have been engaged upon so long. And to them, particularly to Grant Genung and Paul Ramsey, who have been as deeply concerned to understand as I, I should like to acknowledge a debt of gratitude. Without their understanding, guidance, and support, extended to me over the years of our friendship and the period of difficult growth and struggle during which the idea for this book was being formed, I should never have been able to write it down, nor indeed have had the slightest inclination to do so.

I am also indebted to Malcolm Cowley not only because his *Exile's Return* has helped me considerably in my understanding of the 1920's but because he has been in every way a stimulus and guide in the development of my thinking about literature. I also wish to thank Theodore S. Amussen for his friendly encouragement and assistance on the early drafts of the manuscript; Ed Kuhn for his unfailing understanding and patience and his keen editorial advice on the writing of the final drafts; and the University of Vermont and the sponsor of the Grant for Studies in Creative Criticism for providing me with the time and funds necessary to complete the book.

J.W.A.

ACKNOWLEDGMENTS

The author wishes to thank the following publishing firms for permission to quote from the books listed below:

Crown Publishers, for *All Thy Conquests* by Alfred Hayes; Doubleday & Company, Inc., for *Three Soldiers* by John Dos Passos; E. P. Dutton & Co., Inc., for *The Season of Comfort* and *A Search for the King* by Gore Vidal; Harper and Brothers, for *The Gallery* by John Horne Burns and *The Girl on the Via Flaminia* by Alfred Hayes; Houghton Mifflin Company, for *Manhattan Transfer* and *U.S.A.* by John Dos Passos; Alfred A. Knopf, Inc., for *A Long Day's Dying* by Frederick Buechner; New Directions, for *The Sheltering Sky* by Paul Bowles and *The Crack-Up* by F. Scott Fitzgerald; W. W. Norton & Company, Inc., for *Exile's Return* by Malcolm Cowley; Philosophical Library, Inc., for *First Encounter* by John Dos Passos; Random House, for *Other Voices, Other Rooms* by Truman Capote and *The Young Lions* by Irwin Shaw; Rinehart & Company, Inc., for *The Naked and the Dead* by Norman Mailer; Charles Scribner's Sons, for *The End of My Life* by Vance Bourjaily, *The Beautiful and the Damned*, *The Great Gatsby*, *The Last Tycoon*, *Tender Is the Night*, *This Side of Paradise* by F. Scott Fitzgerald, and *A Farewell to Arms*, *For Whom the Bell Tolls*, *The Sun Also Rises*, *To Have and Have Not* by Ernest Hemingway; William Sloane Associates, for *That Winter* by Merle Miller.

Sections of this book have appeared in a different form in *Harper's Magazine*, *The Saturday Review of Literature*, *Penguin New Writing*, and *Neue Auslese*.

CONTENTS

Part I

THE LOST GENERATION

CHAPTER I

Disillusion and Separate Peace

MOST OF THE WRITERS who began moving into Montparnasse in the early Twenties had been through the war. In one capacity or another, whether with the volunteer transport units working with the French, the Red Cross ambulance sections on the Italian front, or in the various branches of the combat army after America entered the war, they had undergone the same experiences and had the similar emotional responses that were to distinguish them as a generation. They were a generation in the purest sense, perhaps, as Malcolm Cowley said, the first real one in the history of American letters, and they had chosen to be a "lost" generation, the specially damned and forsaken, lost from all others and themselves by the unique conviction of their loss, the conviction by which they lived, wrote, and perceived the life of their time.

Like most of their contemporaries who came to maturity before 1918, these young aesthetes, of whom such an amazing number were destined to make their mark in the literary world, were deeply and sentimentally affected by the patriotic slogans and catchwords that are so much the vogue of wartime. They left college and jobs to find, in what seemed a glorious adventure, escape from boredom and a cause worthy of belief. Behind them, as their transports moved out of the harbors of New York and Boston, they left conventional training in high schools and colleges, where they had been equipped with standard attitudes and prejudices. Further back still were the farmhouses and tenements where they had been born, the fields in Pennsylvania, the streets

3

and back lots in Chicago and St. Paul where they had first played, the woods in upper Michigan, the Big Two-Hearted River, the blue Juniatas; the unreal, only truly real world of childhood from whi h they had escaped, been lost, to which they could never return. Ahead of them lay Europe with its promises of love, excitement, freedom—the Europe they knew for its women, its paintings, its books, its Paris; the Europe they knew only from novels, steamship folders, and picture postcards.

It was no accident that so many of these young men chose to volunteer with the Norton-Harjes and the other motor units then recruiting in Paris rather than go directly into a combat service. They were still tentative, uncertain about the war and their place in it. They were attracted by the romance of serving in a foreign country with a foreign army; they had made a sportsman's decision, committed themselves to hardship and danger with the recklessness of big-game hunters and with as little compulsion beyond the thrills they expected to encounter along the way. But they wanted, at the same time, to remain disinterested and aloof; they wanted to experience the excitement of death without the pain of it. They wanted above all to be free to move on whenever their jobs stopped paying off in thrills.

Fortunately their status as American gentlemen volunteers gave them exactly what they came for. As strangers among strangers, they were treated with respect. They were outside the petty restrictions imposed upon the officers and men of a regular military organization, and owing to the nature of their work and a relaxed, almost nonexistent discipline, they were able to mix in comparative freedom with the civilian population. They were fed, clothed, and commanded by a government to which, since it was not their own, they owed no allegiance. They were onlookers at a struggle in which, at the time, they had no personal stake. They learned the etiquette without the experience of war, the extravagance and fatalism, the worship of courage and the fear of boredom that men ordinarily learn as the price of survival; and they lost, almost by proxy, the illusions they once had had. But if the war taught them bitterness, it was a bitterness tinged with longing and detached regret, a romantic distillation of other men's despair. They were still capable of being excited by danger and the prospect of sacrificing themselves for a noble cause, stricken to exultation by the simple poignancy of death among the poppies, melted by the spectacle of love amid the ruins of a French château. They were special observers, immunized by their nationality and the good fortune of their service from all but the most picturesque aspects of the war.

In his book, *Exile's Return*, Malcolm Cowley, one of the most honest historians of the time, describes how this sense of non-participation grew into what he calls "the spectatorial attitude." While watching a column of men belonging to many Allied armies moving through a French village, he and other members of his transport unit felt that they "could never be part of all this. The long parade of races was a spectacle which it was our privilege to survey, a special circus like the exhibition of Moroccan horsemen given for our benefit on the Fourth of July, before we all sat down at a long table to toast *la France héroique* and *nos amis américains* in warm champagne. In the morning we should continue our work of carrying trench-mortar bombs from the railhead to the munition dumps just back of the Chemin des Dames—that too would be a spectacle." *

To such observers the war was something apart. In the words of one of Dos Passos' Grenadine Guards, it wasn't a war at all, it was "a goddam madhouse . . . a goddam Cook's tour." It was an exhibition in violence and destruction, a gigantic bullfight one was privileged to view from the stands. And when it became a bit too rough or too bloody or just too dull, there were always new

* From *Exile's Return* by Malcolm Cowley, published and copyright, 1934, W. W. Norton and Company, Inc., New York.

and exciting places to go, new and exciting drinks to sample, new and exciting girls to fall in love with.

But if the war experience of the Harvard aesthetes and the Grenadine Guards set the emotional pattern of the Lost Generation, gave it its nerves and its capacity for excess, it remained for those other young men who served longer and more dangerously, who were forced out of their spectatorial role and into a role of active participation, to give it character and a formal philosophy. The two together—the sentimental and essentially immature longing of the observer that expended itself in bitter, riotous play and the premature disillusion of the participant who saw too much too soon—seem to me to account for the duality of so much of the literature that generation produced, its blend of tenderness and violence, innocence and numbness; its women with the shatter-proof hearts and the broken souls; its tough young men with the look of punch-drunk boxers and the fears of being left alone in the dark; all its sad and forsaken, beautiful and damned.

Perhaps in no other novel can the twin personality of lostness be so clearly seen as in Hemingway's *A Farewell to Arms.* The love story of Frederick Henry and Catherine Barkley is, in the largest sense, the story of how the Lost Generation earned its name, how the character of its loss was revealed in its philosophical outlook, and how the spectatorial attitude proved to be inadequate to cope with the real issues of the war.

Frederick Henry is an American serving with an Italian ambulance unit. As a spiritual nonparticipant, he is able to hold himself aloof from the war and its politics. Even when his job requires him to go to the battle areas and bring back the wounded, he preserves his detachment. The war is always outside, something in which "they" are engaged, never himself— "This war . . . did not have anything to do with me. It seemed no more dangerous to me . . . than war in the movies." * Yet the war is always there, just over the mountains, just down the road. For Frederick Henry it serves as a permanent frame in which his own private chaos is somehow mitigated. It relates to him as belief in God relates to the priest and being a good surgeon relates to Rinaldi. Without the war he would have no tangible assurance that beyond his personal identity, the self he protects so carefully from all jars and shocks, the universe did not rush in all directions, vast and purposeless.

The retreat from Caporetto may be said to divide *A Farewell to Arms* into two parts. Up to the retreat Frederick Henry's relations with the war are primarily spectatorial, but with this difference: that after nearly two years at the front the attitudes and responses of the gentleman volunteer have been raised in him to the next higher power and become formulated into a distinct philosophical code. Onto the background of incessant war he must project an artificial system of checks and balances that will serve as a discipline for himself and his environment. Within the area of his sensibility, which he keeps tightly focused so that only the essentials of experience can come through, he feels relatively secure. But the world beyond the range of his will constitutes a perpetual threat to his safety. It is peopled with strange, violent gods and governed by a primitive jungle law. Those who do not keep themselves at all times self-hypnotized and numb it kills. "It kills the very good and the very gentle and the very brave impartially. If you are none of these you can be sure it will kill you too but there will be no special hurry." His only salvation lies in the faithful performance of the little ceremonies he has invented for himself, for it is through these that he wins the favor of the gods who hold the power of life and death.

* From *A Farewell to Arms* by Ernest Hemingway, published and copyright, 1929, Charles Scribner's Sons, New York.

/ Life for him is thus a matter of continual propitiation and restraint. He is a man walking on the edge of a bottomless abyss; the slightest misstep will send him plunging to destruction. Everything he does must be done in slow motion so as not "to rush his sensations any." What cannot be broken down to simplicity under his clenched will must be cast out. Too much thinking, particularly on an abstract level, is dangerous. Abstract thoughts, like abstract words, seduce his mind away from essential experience, the true nature of things, and make him uncomfortably aware of the shadow world outside that sometimes haunts him in sleep. It is only when the weather is clear (the rain, too, is dangerous), the war is going well, and he can concern himself exclusively with his own sensations and with the objects which arouse them, that he is entirely at ease. If at one time the emotions of war had excited him, increased his appetite for life, they now constituted the whole of life and served him as a drug against the thought of his possible death.

Within the magic circle Frederick Henry has drawn around himself, love is inadmissible. Love, like the formal religion which the priest represents, requires an emotion which is basically unselfish and beyond the control of the will. While the quick oblivion of sex is desirable because it renews the body and nerves without complicating the mind, the oblivion of love is synonymous with the oblivion of sleep and death and leads to the total extinction of the personality. Love is thus improper for a man whose existence depends on preserving a tight hold over himself and the war. /

But with the introduction of Catherine Barkley, this hold is loosened, and we see the beginning of a reversal which is later realized in the Isonzo bombardment and the retreat from Caporetto. Until the moment in the garden when he and Catherine are alone together for the first time, Frederick Henry has been completely absorbed in his relation to and control over the war as fact, as objective reality. From that moment on, however, the fact of love begins to dominate the fact of war; and in the bombardment during which he is wounded, love emerges as the single certainty and the war recedes into nightmare. "I tried to breathe but my breath would not come and I felt myself rush bodily out of myself and out and out and out . . . and I knew I was dead. . . . Then I floated, and instead of going on I felt myself slide back. I breathed and I was back." Where the war had once stood as an objective order upon which he could project and give meaning to his private confusion while at the same time losing nothing of himself, it was now a destructive force that threatened to rob him of himself altogether.

The retreat from Caporetto, if viewed in this sense, is an externalization of Frederick Henry's personal withdrawal from a philosophical position which is no longer tenable. As he moves back over the congested roads with his ambulances and men toward the plains of the Tagliamento, it is as if some giant spring has been released and reality has been shifted out of context. Everything is larger than life, swollen beyond the proportions of sense. The normal processes of war are in reverse, making courage insubordinate and cowardice the rule. To him the whole affair is madness. The only thing left in the world is Catherine.

If the retreat is symbolic of Frederick Henry's separate peace, his plunge into the Tagliamento to escape the *carabinieri* is, as Malcolm Cowley suggested, an act of purgation symbolizing the death of the war and the beginning of a new life of love. "You had lost your cars and your men as a floorwalker loses the stock of his department in a fire. You were out of it now. . . . You had no more obligation . . . it was not my show anymore. I was made to . . . eat and drink and sleep with Catherine." But the removal of that love to Switzerland really prepares us for another death, for suddenly all the little signs and portents that have gone unheeded until now come together to fulfill the tragic

prophecy with which the book began. There have been the lost
Saint Anthony, Catherine's pregnancy and fear of the rain because, she said, "sometimes I see me dead in it," the priest's disillusion, Rinaldi's imaginary syphilis. They have all, in one way
or another, been hurt by the war, and it is as if they had been
released from it only to die or be lost in the peace.

When Catherine Barkley dies, the collapse of all reality is
complete. Frederick Henry had believed in the war, and the
war had wounded him. He had then believed in love because it
promised to pay back all the war had taken away. Now love was
dead, as cold and lifeless as if it had never been. "But after I
had got them out and shut the door and turned off the light it
wasn't any good. It was like saying good-by to a statue. After a
while I went out and left the hospital and walked back to the
hotel in the rain."

And that, it seems to me, was the final effect of the war upon
the Lost Generation, the thing that in the end made their loss
more than a loss of inhibition and gave a desperate sadness to
everything they did. The war wrenched them away from the land
of their childhood. It carried them forward in the long process
of disinheritance which began in school, when they were divested
of their local customs and beliefs, and continued through their
college years when they each took on the stamp of fragile aestheticism that eventually made them more at home in Gertrude Stein's
salon than on Main Street. As spectators, guests of the war by
courtesy of the management, they were infected with irresponsi-
bility, thrilled at second hand by danger, held to a pitch of excitement that made their old lives seem impossibly dull and
tiresome. As participants, they learned to view all life, all human
emotion, in terms of war, to pursue pleasure with an intensity
made greater by the constant threat of death, and to hold tight
to themselves and to the concrete simplicities (until the simple

and concrete seemed to be all there was, all that was worth knowing) when the world around them seemed to be breaking to pieces. If the war hurt them, as it hurt Frederick Henry, they became numb and stopped thinking and believing. It was not their war any more. If love died they stopped believing in love too and began believing in sex. If everything collapsed and they were left with nothing, that too was all right. They began believing in nothing.

CHAPTER II

Exile

FROM THIS SENSE of physical isolation and spiritual emptiness, it was easy for the young men to take the next logical step— active, conscious revolt and self-exile from a country which was neither gay enough nor cultured enough to deserve their presence. The idea of exile, like the idea of the religion of art, grew out of their need to sustain the emotions which the war had aroused in them, to keep up the incessant movement, the incessant search for excitement, and to find another faith to replace the one they had lost in the war.

Conveniently, a formal philosophical structure for such ideas had been shaping itself both before and during the war years in the writings of certain prominent social-literary critics, among them H. L. Mencken and Van Wyck Brooks. For a number of years these men had been expressing grave concern for the plight of the sensitive artist in a machine-made, standardized society. It seemed to them that life in America was tawdry, cheap, color- less, and given over to the exclusive worship of wealth and machinery; that for a young writer to do his best work in such a society was impossible. In 1921, Harold Stearns's symposium, *Civilization in the United States,* gave these ideas detailed and scholarly expansion. The thirty intellectuals whom Stearns had gathered together examined in essay form as many phases of American life and came up with the same conclusions: life in America is not worth living. If the young artist is to preserve his talent, he must leave the country. He must, as Stearns urged in his own essay, go to Europe where the creative life is still possible. To show that he meant it, Stearns left for France soon after his book was delivered to the publisher, and, whether because of his example or not, hundreds of the young men followed.

The story of what happened during those years abroad has been written and rewritten many times over. The process of exile was complete. The young men came to Paris. With their wives and children, cats and typewriters, they settled in flats and studios along the Left Bank and in the Latin Quarter. They took jobs as foreign correspondents for American newspapers, sent back social gossip and racing news; wrote book reviews, magazine articles, and stories; bet on horses, gambled, borrowed, and begged; did anything to keep alive and to prolong the show. If we can believe the stories, they were drunk much of the time, traveled considerably, and had a great many love affairs. They also managed to get an impressive amount of good writing done. The early work of Hemingway, Fitzgerald, Dos Passos, Cummings, and others bears witness to the fact. Betweentimes, when they were not drinking at the cafés, partying, or making love, they talked a lot and did a certain amount of thinking. At about this time, some of them discovered Gertrude Stein, and she, in turn, discovered among them talents worthy of her guidance. It was she, perhaps more than any other, who taught them how to make the most of their "lostness," how to develop, as had Sherwood Anderson, an idiom that would be true of their time and truly their own.

Then, as the new writing began to appear, new little magazines began springing up to accommodate it. Their titles, *Broom, transition, This Quarter, Secession,* were indicative of their editorial policies. Fresh currents of energy were breaking out everywhere, everywhere the accent was on the new and different, the departure from old forms and techniques, the rebellion. The years of European apprenticeship were paying off in a vigorous new literature, a literature written so compellingly, with such a tragic sense of loss, that it seemed to describe the predicament of all contemporary humanity. For writers like Hemingway, Dos Passos, and Cummings, the experience of their generation—the bitterness, the monumental disbelief which the war had taught— was the only tradition. They had been uprooted from the world of their childhood with its unwavering ideals and trusts and plunged into the world of Caporetto, the Western front, the "enormous rooms" of the war; and they had awakened from the war only to find themselves in another and even more fantastic world—that of Dada, surrealism, and Gertrude Stein. If they understood only the immediate present and past, if they worshiped only the gods of sex, liquor, violence, and art, it was because they had known nothing else. Life for them would forever after be perceived and lived within the frame of the war and the emotions of war.

Thus, while Mencken and Lewis were still discovering the banalities of life back home, the young men who had acted on their indictments and fled to Europe were discovering a new language which would express themselves and their own unique experience. In Gertrude Stein the demands of a persistent originality had led to greater and greater indulgence in pure technique. Hers was an art deprived of its objective basis, lost somewhere in the convolutions of its careless meaning. The search for ever-widening suggestiveness carried the older Joyce into the limbo of dream, the ultimate subjective state beyond the necessity of words. But the young Hemingway's search for the "real thing," "the exact sequence of motion and fact which made the emotion," ended in a prose that was as crystal-clear as brook water, that was written "without tricks and without cheating," with nothing that would "go bad afterwards." Hemingway in those years was the American compromise with Dada. He was everybody's example of an American who combined the best that was in America with the zeal and discipline of the French. He was coarsely, robustly healthy in the tradition of Mark Twain and Sherwood Anderson, but he was never vulgar, almost never naïve; and in his passion for exactitude, *le mot juste,* he could only be compared with Flaubert.

This is not to say that Hemingway's was the only or even the most typical new style in the exile literature. E. E. Cummings's nervous, syncopated prose in *The Enormous Room* caught as accurately the sensibility of a world stunned by a prevailing sense of defeat; but his was a less restrained, though equally self-conscious; approach. Cummings had a more acute sense of rebellion than Hemingway. He was breaking the same ground stylistically, but he was doing it with a self-conscious violence and consequently a less steady hand. The result was a prose that struck through the pretensions of the past at the same time that it parodied them, a prose that suited itself instantly to the quick-reflexed life it was describing, and that contained the stomping discords and tingling minor harmonies of an intricate jazz symphony. If it bore little resemblance to Hemingway's prose, its purpose was nonetheless the same: to express the truth of the thing as it was at the moment it occurred, the truth stripped down to such an ultimate nakedness that, as Hemingway put it, it would be "as valid in a year or ten years or, with luck and if you stated it purely enough, always." Both men succeeded so well in conveying this exact truth, the precise emotions of despair and loss as they had known them, that these emotions were given a special currency and validity and seemed to explain the entire generation to itself and the world. Gertrude Stein had given the key to Hemingway when she had said, "You are all a lost generation," and Hemingway had written a novel around it. Now her words became the slogan of the new literature, and all the young men were trying to live up to them.

One could of course as easily make a god of lostness—and thus be saved—as one could be lost. One could think of it as an intellectual fashion rather than a condition of life and adopt its values in place of having no values at all. Besides, if one believed in nothing one was obliged to practice the rituals of nothingness, and these were good and pleasurable. One could drink and make love all night and still be holy. Yes, and if one carried it far enough, one could even reduce one's art to a deliberate exercise in futility. It was one of the ironies of art, as it was one of the ironies of the doctrine of loss, that beyond a certain point it merged with and became its opposite: the religion of art became irreligion and the lack of values became itself a value.

In the exile colony the process really began with Stein and Joyce when they renounced their native traditions and took on the traditions of pure art. It began, in other words, as it began for Hemingway and Cummings, with a search for absolutes; but it carried beyond them, and in the work of other, less dedicated writers it was turned into a process of general rebellion and misdirected defiance—rebellion against the ends which art was intended to serve and defiance of the public which would not understand those ends. If Stein and Joyce had been victimized by the idiot world and driven into the temple of art, then art would be devoted exclusively to the befuddlement of the world, and the purpose which Stein and Joyce had determined to preserve would be cast down. Art in the hands of the Dadaists was an instrument of confusion; and the obscurity which was once only the accidental by-product of an isolated, religiously fervid talent became in them the sole aim of the artist.

Dada might be said to have contained in the extremest form nearly all the attitudes on which the exile literary movement was based. If, as Malcolm Cowley has suggested, the reader of Joyce was expected to master a dozen languages, be familiar with the mythology of all races, and memorize the map of Dublin, in order to comprehend him, if the reader of Stein was helpless without her personal key to understanding, the reader of a Dada poem or novel could not hope, either through learning or a lifelong acquaintanceship with the author, to unravel a meaning. Dada, according to its adherents, had no meaning. It was dedicated to "pure" and "absolute" art. "Art," the Dada Manifesto read, "is a private matter; the artist does it for himself; any work of art that can be understood is the product of a journalist."

Dada was thus the extreme of individualism. It coupled an open rejection of audience with the belief that all communication between men was impossible. But perhaps in no other respect was Dada more typical of the tendencies of exile than in its active defiance of the world. Defiance, contemptuous rebellion, had been the motive power behind the entire expatriate movement as it had been the first principle of the religion of art. A generation of priests had defied the old commandments: a generation of Stephen Dedaluses had borne their chalices "safely through a throng of foes." But where the defiance of the chosen had led to flight, the defiance of Dada led to open war. The world, said Dada, "left in the hands of bandits, is in a state of madness, aggressive and complete madness." . . . "Let each man cry: there is a great labor of destruction and negation to perform. We must sweep and clean." . . . "What there is within us of the divine is the awakening of anti-human action." The duty of the artist was clear: he must expend upon the world the full measure of his contempt, and he must "protest with all the fists of his being" all assertions of humanity and life. And what of his duty to his art? Art was the weapon of his disgust. Its needs were always subordinate to the destructive function it was set to perform. Art, therefore, was anti-art, dedicated to its own eventual suicide.

Armed with such a view Dada marched upon the helpless world. To the accompaniment of ringing electric bells and deafening shouts and laughter from the audience, meetings were held, poems and articles were read that no one could hear, drawings done in chalk were exhibited and erased on the stage. At one meeting Tristan Tzara, the founder of Dada, recalls "thousands of people of all classes manifested very uproariously it is impossible to say exactly what—their joy or their disapproval, by unexpected cries and general laughter, which constituted a very pretty accompaniment to the manifestoes read by six people at once. The newspapers said that an old man in the audience gave himself up to behavior of a character more or less intimate, that somebody set off some flash-light powder and that a pregnant woman had to be taken out." At another "twelve hundred people were turned away. There were three spectators for every seat; it was suffocating. Enthusiastic members of the audience had brought musical instruments to interrupt us. . . . I invented . . . a diabolical machine composed of a klaxon and three successive invisible echoes, for the purpose of impressing on the minds of the audience certain phrases describing the aims of Dada. . . . It was impossible to hear a single word. . . ." There were always meetings, demonstrations (sometimes in churches, once in a public urinal), "manifestations" of Dada policy. There were even Dada trials and theatrical performances that ended usually with fights on the stage and the intervention of the police. But even at the height of its bustling activity, there was something ineffectual about Dada. Its protests were directed against no specific injustice, toward no social reform. The freedom it fought for and finally won was used to no purpose. The most exciting of its gestures were merely phantom poundings on a wall that offered no resistance.

Yet beneath its monstrous wastefulness and hollow disdain, Dada was alive. If its achievements as a doctrine, as an extreme of art, were poor and few, its influence as a stimulus to action for others, for the entire age, was great. The phenomenon of Dada cannot, in fact, be separated from the whole restless spirit of the Twenties; for in it all the roads of exile converged and the best and worst possibilities of the exile ideal were realized. From Dada, it was only a short step to the "nada hail nada full of nada" of Hemingway, the sociological zero of Dos Passos, the romantic hopelessness of Fitzgerald, the "nothing again nothing" of Eliot, the "indefinite refusal to be anything whatsoever" of Valéry, the implicit denial of society in Stein and Joyce—even to the "lost, ah lost" of Wolfe. Dada was everywhere; its ghost in a hundred manifestations haunted the literature of a decade. If Dada had no meaning, it had an infinite capacity to suggest meaning. "If you must speak of Dada you must speak of Dada. If you must not speak of Dada you must still speak of Dada."

And I believe the final effect of Dada as well as of the religion of art and the doctrine of negation was a salutary one. The creative energy which was short-circuited in Dada found release elsewhere and spread through the writing of the Twenties like a prairie fire; protest and denial gave that writing a single point of view, a unified plan of attack, and the impetus of rebellion carried it away from the narrow traditions of the past and toward new and startling discoveries in form and technique. The indignation and sense of having been betrayed which the Lost Generation brought out of the war was expressed in a fearless realism that exploited until then forbidden subject matter; while the teachings of the religion of art, self-consuming though they were when fanatically carried out, gave those writers an awareness of artistic mission, a feeling of belonging to a special priesthood with special requirements which they were bound by holy order to live up to. If despair and disillusion were negative values, they were at least good values for the literature of the time, and they were better than no values at all.

But Dada was destined to die as the exile was destined to end. In the fall of 1929 when the machinery of art had been grinding away at full speed for nearly a decade, turning out new morals and literary mannerisms so bright and daring that they seemed to presage a magnificent long life for American art abroad, something in the mechanism snapped and the machine began running down. Back home in Wall Street, among the debris of ticker tape and ruined fortunes, lay the remnants of a broken promise, the promise everybody had made to everybody else—that the show would go on forever.

With the end of the roaring business boom of the Twenties came the end of the roaring exile of the artists. The small private incomes from securities, the monthly checks from the folks, the publisher's advances toward the writing of the next book, were abruptly sliced in half; then gradually they stopped coming altogether. Job contracts ran out and somehow failed to be renewed. For the first time the young men, and with them the actors, escape artists, clowns, and special guests who had come along to watch the fun and whose sole function was to be slightly amused, were faced with the choice of stopping the show or starving. Actually there was no choice: it had already been made for them. They began quietly packing their bags and drifting toward Marseilles and Cherbourg.

A few chose to remain, the ones whose investments in Paradise had grown too large to abandon. Harold Stearns stuck it out and was making the rounds of the cafés in search of his missing friends years after the friends had gone home. He took to wearing borrowed clothes and making bad bets on the horses. He became ill and for long periods was painfully and lonesomely blind. His story in his autobiography, *A Street I Know*, is the story of the end of an era and of one man's realization too late of his own folly. When compared with his bitter indictment of America in *Civilization in the United States* it becomes sad, embarrassing reading. One wishes that a better, more dignified end might have come to a man who felt so deeply and who wrote so well, and to a time that promised so much, gave only a little less than it promised, and made so much difference in our lives.

Yet it would be a mistake to assume that the expatriate movement died solely because of the collapse of the economic system on which it was based. It died as well from mass "over-extension of the flank," from drawing too long on resources which it did not possess. There had been signs as far back as 1927 when French workers had invaded the café terraces of Montparnasse to protest the Sacco and Vanzetti execution. There had been a series of suicides that year, and there were other suicides in the years that followed. "By 1927," wrote Scott Fitzgerald, "a wide-spread neurosis began to be evident, faintly signalled, like a nervous beating of the feet, by the popularity of cross-word puzzles . . . contemporaries of mine had begun to disappear into the dark maw of violence. A classmate killed his wife and himself on Long Island, another tumbled 'accidentally' from a skyscraper in Philadelphia, another purposely from a skyscraper in New York. One was killed in a speak-easy in Chicago; another was beaten to death in a speak-easy in New York and crawled home to the Princeton Club to die; still another had his skull crushed by a maniac's axe in an insane asylum where he was confined. . . ." * On December 10, 1929, Harry Crosby, wealthy expatriate poet and publisher, was found dead with a woman whom he had presumably loved and killed. On April 28, 1932, while his steamer was moving north through the Gulf of Mexico, Hart Crane jumped from the rail to his death.

The bankruptcy was spiritual as well as economic. The Lost Generation had learned the hard way that all roads, if they are followed far enough, lead back to zero. The religion of art, in

* From *The Crack-Up* by F. Scott Fitzgerald (edited by Edmund Wilson), published and copyright, 1945, New Directions, New York.

spite of the great heritage it left behind, had led ultimately to the negation of art. The ways of adventure, dream, and calculated futility that had promised escape from middle-class mediocrity had led to fanaticism, creative impotence, and anarchy. All the extreme courses of action had been tried and found wanting. Even the exile itself which had begun as an escape from the sterility of the American wasteland and as a self-styled grace period for young American talent had ended, in far too many cases, in another and greater sterility and a blind alley for that talent. If the ideals which had motivated the Lost Generation were good for literature, if in the end they produced many good writers, they were bad for life and they produced as many broken human beings. For every Hemingway, Fitzgerald, Dos Passos, Cummings, and Joyce, there was a Harry Crosby, a Hart Crane, and a Harold Stearns. And even for Joyce there was a *Finnegans Wake* and for Fitzgerald a *Crack-Up*. In fact, the clear line of exile influence runs through almost everything these men wrote; the strengths and weaknesses of the exile philosophy are in them all, and no matter how much they have tried to overcome it or how often some of them have succeeded in overcoming it, their common experience of exile and loss binds them all together and has helped to form them into the kind of writers they have become.

CHAPTER III

Hemingway

Nightmare and the Correlative of Loss

FOR MEMBERS of my generation, the young men born between 1918, roughly, and 1924, there was a special charm about Hemingway. By the time most of us were old enough to read him he had become a legendary figure, a kind of twentieth-century Lord Byron; and like Byron, he had learned to play himself, his own best hero, with superb conviction. He was Hemingway of the rugged outdoor grin and the hairy chest posing beside a marlin he had just landed or a lion he had just shot; he was Tarzan Hemingway, crouching in the African bush with elephant gun at ready, Bwana Hemingway commanding his native bearers in terse Swahili; he was War Correspondent Hemingway writing a play in the Hotel Florida in Madrid while thirty fascist shells crashed through the roof; later on he was Task Force Hemingway swathed in ammunition belts and defending his post singlehanded against fierce German attacks.

But even without the legend he created around himself, the chest-beating, wisecracking pose that was later to seem so incredibly absurd, his impact upon us was tremendous. The feeling he gave us was one of immense expansiveness and freedom and, at the same time, of absolute stability and control. We could put our whole faith in him and he would not fail us. We could follow him, ape his manner, his cold detachment, through all the doubts and fears of adolescence and come out pure and untouched.

The words he put down seemed to us to have been carved from the living stone of life. They were absolutely, nakedly true because the man behind them had reduced himself to the bare tissue of his soul to write them and because he was a dedicated man. And they told of strange countries we had never seen that were always white and clear in the sun, of savage, beautiful women and strong men, of good drinking, good companionship, plenty of lusty love. They also told of unforgettable horror and sadness: of dead women in the rain; dead soldiers surrounded by torn personal papers; sunken ships full of floating corpses; drowning mules with their legs cruelly broken; wounded hyenas eating their own entrails; horses gored by bulls; punch-drunk boxers waiting stolidly to be murdered; soldiers out of their minds with battle fatigue; nymphomaniacs, homosexuals, and broken-down prostitutes; and of times that might have been such damn good times (if only Jake had not been sexually incompetent, if only Brett had not been a compulsive bitch, if only Harry Morgan had had better luck, if only Catherine Barkley hadn't died), of fine sunny days of Alpine skiing that had to end, of nights in a farmhouse up in Michigan, nights of the kind of incomparable conversation that comes to young men once and once only and that can never come again. The words of Hemingway conveyed so exactly the taste, smell, and feel of experience as it was, as it might possibly be, that we began unconsciously to translate our own sensations into their terms and to impose on everything we did and felt the particular emotions they aroused in us.

I remember hikes we took in the country when we carried along with us the big loaf of hard bread, the wedge of sour cheese, and the dry red wine of those magnificent moments at Caporetto, the Swiss ski lodge, and the fishing stream in Spain. I remember nights of drinking in front of an open fire when everybody sooner or later began talking like Nick Adams and trying to seduce somebody else's girl with the practiced indifference of Harry Morgan.

I remember too the nice girls who came to those parties and drank too much and tried to live up to Brett's frantic example, and how some of them were never quite the same afterward. Then there were the stories we wrote that had no beginning and no real end, that usually stopped in the middle of some laconic, half-bitter, half-wistful sentiment, stories of men and women talking in bars with the women perhaps confessing Lesbian passions and the men coolly sipping Anis del Toro. I remember others that had to do with has-been prize fighters, dope peddlers, and several about prostitutes. They were not very good stories, but they seemed good at the time, maybe only for the reason that they sounded like Hemingway; and they represented something he had given us, a way of looking at life, perhaps, and of ordering and giving meaning to our experience. If it was not the best way, it was at least as good as most, and it was probably a lot better way than any we could have discovered for ourselves.

At any rate, the Hemingway time is dead now. It ended when the last echoes of the lost Twenties finally stopped reverberating in the early Forties, when the young men had to stop reminiscing about the first Great War (which none of them could remember) in order to start thinking about the second Great War, and when the young women gave up trying to be hard and sophisticated and began preparing themselves for jobs or marriage and motherhood. It ended too when the spell wore off, when, coming back from the war, we discovered that we had lost Hemingway and that the world he described was no longer the world we lived in.

Yet the Hemingway time was a good time to be young. It seems to me that we had much then which the war later forced out of us and that in the end what many of us lost was something far greater than Hemingway and his strong formative influence. There are young writers today who, in losing or getting rid of Hemingway, have been able to find nothing to put in his place, who have rejected his time as untrue for them only to fail at finding

themselves in their own time. There are others who, in their em-
barrassment at the hold he once had over them, have not profited
by the lessons he had to teach, and still others who were never
touched by him at all. These last are perhaps the real unfortunates,
for they have been denied access to a powerful tradition, one
that is as important and true as any my generation can ever have.

The Hemingway of those first stories—printed in the small de
luxe way by friends in Paris—had already staked out the dimen-
sions of his world. All the experience he was ever going to have
he seemed to have had already; all the emotions he or any of his
characters was ever going to feel he seemed to have already
felt and measured against the capacity of his art to express them.
It was as if he had arrived on the literary scene fully equipped for
the job he had set himself to do, with his mind already made up
about his chances of success and failure, and with a cynical conviction that nothing that might happen to him in the remainder
of his life could possibly compare in intensity and horror with
his first infant impressions of hell.

The boundaries of that world extend from the Michigan woods
to the battlefield at Caporetto and the bull rings of Spain around
to the studios along the Paris Left Bank; and the clear, never
wavering line they trace runs from brute violence to mass violence
to the obsessive recollection of violence. Nowhere else in our literature can such a systematic and chill-blooded series of rendings,
gorings, murders, suicides, and executions be found. And of the
world of no other modern writer can it be more truly said that it
is, at its best, a perfect synthesis in art of temperament and experience, private vision and public knowledge, or that its worst
is as consistently a defect of vision and experience as it is of art.

Hemingway's first professionally published book, *In Our Time*,
might as easily have been his last. It contained everything he had
learned about life up to that time and, as was later evident, every-

thing he was ever to learn. It was in many ways a slight, overly foreshortened book. The brief connecting chapters or episodes were almost too tightly drawn to convey the intended emotion; the famous sentences were often so pared that they seemed wooden; and what was later to become an absolute incisiveness was in them a second-grade primer simplicity. Yet it was an honest and original book, enhanced by vigor, clarity, and the odd nostalgia of many of its passages, and one was struck by the author's talent for avoiding the ordinary errors of apprenticeship.

But perhaps the real significance of *In Our Time* derived from the fact that in recording the shock effects of the modern age upon the forming character of a sensitive boy Hemingway wrote what amounted to a case history of the typical figure in Lost Generation literature. In Nick Adams he found his own first hero and demonstrated, by going back to childhood experiences, how that hero acquired the equipment which was to become standard for all the heroes of his world. Certainly Nick's early education in violence in the Michigan woods is the first and only education for them all, and from Nick on the procession of Nick-like figures does little more than confirm and enlarge upon it. Whether the background is an Indian camp or a bull ring, a trout stream or a European battlefield, growing up for Nick is a process of learning to endure; and when as a soldier or a middle-aged father he looks back later on to his childhood it is not peace or protection he remembers but a time when there was less call upon his endurance, when the threat was mainly to others and only indirectly to himself. Like his real-life contemporaries and his creator, he has no past more distant than the memory of violence. His awareness of his surroundings has always been proportionate to his opposition to them, and his well-being dependent upon his winning a victory, however momentary, over them.

Nick's development by violence is clearly marked out in the arrangement of the pieces that make up *In Our Time*. The short interchapters—originally published as the separate booklet, *in our time*—set the key for the whole. Each deals with a moment of extreme crisis, violence removed from all narrative context and given a maximum emotional charge; and together they form a sequence of highly effective studies in death. The stories themselves concern apparently unrelated incidents in Nick's boyhood, interspersed with glimpses of expatriate life abroad and one or two war anecdotes. Yet taken as a whole the vignettes and the stories add up to a single effect. From the idyllic landscape of the Michigan Indian country to a bloody Italian street and a wound in the spine may seem a fantastic leap for Nick, but it is immediately evident that he has merely traded one horror for another and that back home he was surrounded by as many, if not as imminent, dangers as he encountered in the war. They are really not separate worlds at all. The violence of war and peace, the recurrent protagonist, is the catalytic agent which brings out their true identity.

Now, reading about the simple and poetic life in which Nick grew up, the fishing trips, the nights of rowing on the bay, the hot loves of the Indian girls on the soft pine-needle floor of the forest, we are aware of dark faces in the water beneath the rippling of our oars; the swamp below the river of good fishing is somehow haunted; the sun does not come through the big cedars overhead, and fishing there is "a tragic adventure." Even among the trees at the very center of the forest hidden enemies are spying on our lust. In the Indian's cabin, while his squaw underwent a Caesarean operation, the Indian in the upper bunk had turned his face to the wall and cut his throat. On a fishing beach at night Nick had given up his girl. On another night down at Horton's Bay, Liz Coates had been raped. A great distance away but with an equal brutality, Nick had potted Germans as they came over the wall of a garden and had helped build a simply priceless barricade. Some time later, six cabinet ministers had been executed against the wall of a hospital; two Hungarians caught breaking into a cigar store had been shot down by police; and an outraged bull had charged a man across an arena in Spain.

The scene shifts, but violence remains the typical condition of life. And the boy too remains the same. He emerges from this background with the equipment with which he began. Having known nothing but violence, he now reacts to nothing but violence. Yet that reaction is not quite what it was. Too much pain has been endured. There have been too many dead bodies, too many executions and murders, too many terrors to haunt the sleep. The old sensitivity has disappeared, been hidden, and the other traits —the taciturnity, the casual dismissiveness—have been strengthened into a single determination to survive and made part of a code, a religion of safe conduct.

In the novels which follow *In Our Time* it is possible to trace the parallel development of this code and Hemingway's conception of violence on which it depends. If we look back to the most extreme moments of violence described in the vignettes, we find that they approach in their grotesqueness and horror .a kind of waking nightmare. The scene of the Greek evacuation, for example, with its jumble of carts, old men and women, cattle, household goods, all moving through the rain against a background of jutting minarets—a movement so like the other evacuation after Caporetto—belongs more to the fevered world of the drug addict than it does to the world of balanced sense. So also does the description of the gored white horse standing with the blood pumping between his front legs while the bull makes up his mind to charge. So particularly does the description of the simply priceless barricade and the shooting of the Germans as they come up over the wall. Even the relatively harmless fishing trip which Nick takes on Big Two-Hearted River becomes hallucinatory when, as a neurotic soldier, he reviews it in memory. Violence at its most terrible is always more unreal than real for Hemingway, always closer to sleep, dream, and death than to life; and as it is against violence that his characters' code is erected, so it is only so long as they can conceive of violence in concrete and impersonal terms that the code is effective.

I attempted to show in a previous chapter how Frederick Henry's code in *A Farewell to Arms* evolved directly out of his war experience, and how, in the Caporetto retreat, Hemingway found an exact equivalent in action for the unreality, the abstractness, which the war had assumed in Frederick Henry's mind. Up to the retreat he had been able to preserve himself by thinking continually of the war as something external to himself. But after he was wounded and had participated in the retreat, he became part of the war, and his code was rendered powerless. The war had entered the realm of the abstract, the nightmare horror, and as he, Frederick Henry, lost control over the war, he lost himself and all belief.

In *The Sun Also Rises* a similar loss occurs, only now the violence which the war represented has shifted to the peacetime world of Paris and Spain. Jake Barnes and Lady Brett are the logical consequences of Frederick Henry's and Catherine Barkley's experience. In fact, they *are* Frederick and Catherine, if Frederick's wound can be said to have been sexually incapacitating and Catherine's death spiritual instead of physical. Their worlds, too, are really the same: peace is no more than an extension of war; life is still a primitive jungle with all sorts of taboos restricting those who survive. The only difference is that where Frederick Henry and Nick Adams were solitary heroes pitted against a destructiveness from the outside and subject only to the laws they had invented for themselves, the people of *The Sun Also Rises* are threatened as well by a destructiveness which is within each of them and which they are capable at any moment of turning upon one another. Their allegiance is to the code of the group; and their sentence is as grave if it is handed down by the group as it is if it comes in a bolt of destruction from the hostile world outside.

It is important now to avoid making a "bad show" of oneself. One must know the rules at all times and play the game in strict observance of them. Jake and Brett are very old hands: they not only know all the rules, they invent them as they go along. As veterans who have proved their superiority by surviving, they realize the absolute necessity of the cold head, the clenched will, the machined coordination of mind and body. As lovers, they know the possibilities and remain carefully within them. They have managed to get this far because they respect the simple values—simple drinking, simple thinking, simple fornication— and because they are smart enough to keep themselves thoroughly insulated (Jake with alcohol, Brett with sex) so they will be unable to register pain or boredom or worry over their predicament. If they falter occasionally, as does Jake, it is only in the privacy of their rooms at night, and then a good cry settles everything.

The Pamplona fiesta, like the Isonzo bombardment in *A Farewell to Arms,* serves to precipitate this grasp of life and to prepare the way for the supreme trial by violence which came for Frederick Henry during the retreat and which comes for Jake, Brett, and the others toward the end of the festivities. As in the other novel, Hemingway here achieves "the exact sequence of motion and fact which made the emotion." For as the excitement of the Spanish holiday grows more intense, the drinking and the street dancing more frenzied, and as the visiting celebrants are swept along in a mounting tide of emotion, it becomes clear that the fiesta provides the key or parallel in action for the animal savagery which they loose upon one another.

A moment after a steer is gored in the bull ring, Robert Cohn, the man who behaved badly by daring to admit his feelings, is publicly humiliated in a café. As the Spaniard later in the story is accidentally killed by a bull, Cohn is socially and spiritually murdered by the unfeeling Brett; and while Jake watches the Spaniard's funeral procession go down the street, Cohn, equally dead, leaves Pamplona. After the fist fight with Cohn it seems to Jake for the first time that things are going badly; and it is as a moral and physical consequence of the fight that he begins to lose control of himself and to feel that the whole experience is unreal. Brett also begins to show signs of breaking up. She has lost faith in herself because of Cohn, and now she is anxious to have an affair with Romero, the young bullfighter. "I've got to do something I really want to do," she says to Jake. "I've lost my self-respect." * In each case the inner drama of the characters has found an object in the events which surround them, their lostness has been fully externalized in the terms of the action, and even Jake's sense of unreality is verified as the code which had held them all together disintegrates in the nightmare rush of fights, hangovers, and sex—each balanced and intensified by the violence of the bull ring.

Now it is in proportion as his people run out of code that Hemingway runs out of artistic resources with which to make them effective. The code has gradually become part of the magic formula which produces the emotion of his work; and in *To Have and Have Not* it is all too evident that without the code that formula breaks down. Harry Morgan is a comic-book intensification of all that his predecessors were. He is tough, numb, and simple-minded. But unlike Frederick Henry, Jake Barnes, even Nick Adams, he has no insides: the toughness, numbness, and simple-mindedness run straight through to the bone. He is of course above all a man "things are done to," but instead of becoming disillusioned he becomes angry; instead of suffering nobly, making a "good show"

* From *The Sun Also Rises* by Ernest Hemingway, published and copyright, 1926, Charles Scribner's Sons, New York.

of himself, he fights back; and in the process he betrays his creator and his purpose.

For when he made Morgan, Hemingway somehow failed to endow him with the old sure-fire ingredients. With his sheet-metal insides Morgan can have no tenderness, and all Hemingway's characters must have tenderness if only for the reason that they must become bitter. They must also be threatened by an environment which is basically alien to their natures, so that when they are finally destroyed they can be revealed as the pathetically lost and bankrupt souls they really were all the time. But Morgan is never more completely at home than when he is dodging bullets or beating up thugs. Even his drinking is not an opiate, but a rather superfluous bolster to his *cojones*. He was born as unscrupulous as the world he grew up in, and all his life he has fought violence with violence. He cannot, therefore, fall picturesquely apart. He must be destroyed wholly from the outside; and his destruction can take place only on the outside.

To offset the seemingly insuperable mistake of Morgan, Hemingway tries first to seduce us with a phony sociological issue and then, more subtly, to win our sympathy with such pseudoepic assertions as "No matter how a man alone ain't got no bloody f——ing chance." * Morgan is ostensibly the victim of the socially and economically privileged "Haves," who are or were Hemingway's conception of what is wrong with the world and particularly with good people like Morgan. But Morgan is not a justifiable object for the emotion we are intended to feel for him. He is not really underprivileged, and he is not really victimized. He comes through, rather, as a quaintly brutal, quaintly pigheaded man who has had the poor judgment to take one too many chances and who, if he arouses our interest at all, arouses our impatience and distaste.

* From *To Have and Have Not* by Ernest Hemingway, published and copyright, 1937, Charles Scribner's Sons, New York.

Hemingway tries further to divert us by introducing a group of alcoholic intellectuals, rummies, and punch-drunk veterans with the "old rale"; and by providing us with various portraits of the very rich in all the stages of dissipation and decay. He even attempts openly to pull off the old formula trick as when Richard Gordon is defeated in his marriage and knocked out in a bar brawl at the precise moment that Morgan is defeated by the Cubans on his launch. But where it worked before, it does not work now. The worlds of the two men do not really touch, and Richard Gordon's defeat, unlike Jake's and Brett's, does not rise out of the central action of the novel but is subsidiary and forced. Nor does the world of the rich, which artistically at least must be responsible for the injustice inflicted on Morgan and his kind, really have anything to do with him. Morgan's fate is scheduled from the very beginning, and nothing can prevent it. Hemingway cannot objectify his destruction because it does not come as a result of a moral failure, a failure of nerve or of code, but of a failure of luck. Morgan had no morals, no nerves, no code, and no more luck than he deserved.

In attempting to assert a social sympathy which he was apparently not ready to feel but thought he ought to feel, Hemingway stumbled into an area in which his artistic comprehension could not follow. Certainly *To Have and Have Not* must have afforded him ample evidence of what can happen when he loses touch with the genre which has always been most natural and effective for him and with the characters who, with their destructible code, their easy disillusion, and their happy indifference to the plight of men like Morgan, have served him so long and so well.

For Whom the Bell Tolls may have been Hemingway's attempt to destroy the bad by embracing the good; but the momentary slip of grasp which made the story of Harry Morgan a painful undertaking is, in the story of Robert Jordan, quite clearly revealed as a permanent and major weakening of Hemingway's sure control. For where Morgan may reasonably be passed off as an absurd caricature of all that Hemingway ever put into a man, but a caricature retaining, at the same time, all the essential elements which make up a fair resemblance to the original, Robert Jordan is the least Hemingwayish of all the heroes, and what elements of resemblance he has are obviously there by accident. Pilar, Maria, Pablo, Anselmo, and the others are also accidents. Pilar is the great old Earth Mother whose heavy breasts have overhung Hemingway's writing for two decades. She is sex, she is honor, she is fortitude, all the sterling virtues. Maria is just another lusty little Indian girl like Trudy who "did first what no one has ever done better." Pablo is a composite of Robert Cohn and Count Mippipopolous of *The Sun Also Rises*. Anselmo is very much like the old man at the bridge.

But the fact that they, like Jordan, belong to the same old band of "insiders" we have met before has nothing whatever to do with the point of the novel; in fact, it detracts persistently from it. We are reminded that however hungrily Hemingway may have been eying the drama of humanity's last stand in the Spanish Civil War he was nonetheless incapable of inventing new types with which to depict it. He was still limited by his standard character insights while the issues to which that drama gave rise demanded new insights. The result is that nearly all the people in the novel are by nature incompatible with its central problem and unsuited to the action which they are intended to carry through. They are designed for another context, and we habitually see them in another context. They live and breathe convincingly in the world of the earlier novels, and Hemingway does not justify their business in the world of this one. As accidents, perhaps as uneasy ghosts out of the novel Hemingway would have liked to write or thought he was writing, they remain to muddle the narrative and to offend us occasionally by all the ways in which they do not really resemble the old types at all.

Their code, for example, retains just enough of the original to be nearly convincing. A man is judged now by how well he comports himself in the face of danger. He is also judged by how well he is able to die. But no man is required to endure purely by fortitude, nor entrusted with the responsibility of his own survival alone. Two new props have been added: to supplement the old physical drugs, there are now the "orders" which must be carried out, and to make the stakes higher and the will more determined, there is the "cause," the thing that a man saves for others before he saves himself. But it is beyond this point that Hemingway gets into difficulties. Violence, instead of being the abstract nightmare force it was in *A Farewell to Arms* and *The Sun Also Rises,* has already become identified with the war and the fascists; and the code, instead of being set against violence, now arises directly out of it. It is physical death the characters face, not spiritual collapse nor moral degeneration; and they are already resigned to dying for the "cause." Since, therefore, they cannot be lost, there can be no moment in the action when their destruction is paralleled in the events that surround them or when violence becomes, or seems to them to become, abstraction. For the first time in Hemingway history his people attach no importance to themselves as individuals. For the first time they affirm life by collective action and collective sacrifice. But their gain in social maturity is achieved at the expense of Hemingway's dramatic formula, his perfected technique, conceived in negation and based on the principle of individual selfishness, for bringing to a climax and resolving in art the basic human failure of his time.

Now, cut off from that time and that technique and that failure, he is left with sacrifice; and sacrifice, as *To Have and Have Not* indicated, is an unwieldy motivation for Hemingway. To make Robert Jordan's action convincing he had somehow to make it concrete. But the requirement that the bridge be destroyed does not arise out of the facts of the situation as they appear. It is a requirement, rather, of military order and has bearing on an external condition, the conduct of the entire war and the eventual success of the "cause." It remains outside the drama of Jordan and the guerrilla band and cannot, therefore, be demonstrated within the limits of that drama. The result is that Hemingway is forced to editorialize Jordan's motive and to try to make up in rhetoric for what it lacks in inner necessity.

It is interesting to see, however, that Hemingway still falls occasionally into his old pattern. There is, for instance, the attempt to give Jordan's destiny a mystical twist, as if to restore the destructive element in the story to the abstract plane where it belongs. Pilar has presumably read the outcome of the mission in Jordan's hand; but she keeps the information to herself so that he will not be afraid. Similarly, a short time before he is injured and left to die, Jordan experiences a moment of uneasiness along with a feeling of nightmare unreality. "He had an unreal feeling about all of this now as though he had said it all before or as though it were a train that were going, especially as though it . were a train and he was standing on the platform of a railroad station." * This too is a premonition, a first foreshadowing of death by violence. Frederick Henry felt it during the Isonzo bombardment when he was wounded and again during the retreat. Jake Barnes felt it at Pamplona during the last days of the fiesta. But with Jordan there is no failure of code, nor is the feeling paralleled in the incidents outside him. He is going out to die now; and he has lost neither faith nor nerve, although, significantly, he has lost the flask of giant killer that might have made dying a little easier. He is Hemingway's new complete man facing death not as a weakling, an expatriate, or an irresponsible drunk, but as a

* From *For Whom the Bell Tolls* by Ernest Hemingway, published and copyright, 1940, Charles Scribner's Sons, New York.

courageous human being dying so that all humanity may live. It is a good death he is going to; and Hemingway approaches it with such assurance that we are almost willing to forget that the motive behind it is not altogether convincing.

A parallel slackening in Hemingway began to be evident as far back as *A Farewell to Arms,* although the excellence of the writing in that book and the idyllic nature of the circumstances with which it dealt did much to obscure its defects. The love story in particular was so lyricized and so universally appealing that for many years after its appearance any sort of critical examination was withheld as somehow profane. Yet it is precisely the love story which should engage our attention, for in it Hemingway reveals the extent of his dependency upon the limited emotional frame of war.

The flight of the lovers into Switzerland, it will be remembered, brought to a conclusion Frederick Henry's withdrawal from the war which began during the Isonzo bombardment and later achieved full objectivity when his sense of unreality was correlated by the nightmarishness of the retreat. It also signaled the emergence of love from what Edmund Wilson called "the alien necessities of which (it had up to then) been merely an accident," and prepared the way for the real intimacy which, by their persistent interference, those necessities demanded. Why then does the love, now that it is at last free to complete itself, seem so strangely inadequate, particularly when we realize that it must now become real to balance the unreality of the war?

Always before it was most intensely real, both to Frederick Henry and to us, when it was farthest from its object, when Frederick Henry was alone with it and pitted against the impediments which denied it fulfillment. It was most real, in other words, when, as it was set against and contrasted with the war, it showed itself to be the idealized emotion of an idyllic relationship. Even when Frederick and Catherine were together in Milan

it was real only by virtue of the hostility of the forces which surrounded it. But when the requirements of his story compelled
Hemingway to remove the lovers from the war altogether, he
found himself outside the violence which gave them significance.
Violence had set the key for the entire relationship. Outside it
Catherine, instead of emerging as a human personality and justi-
fying the emotion felt for her, became merely an abstraction of
that emotion; and Frederick, instead of emerging from nightmare and the dream of love into clear daylight and the reality of
love, merely traded his vision for its imperfect counterpart. Hemingway is at his best when he can intrude a barrier between his
characters and the full realization of their emotion. As long as it
is there, he is spared the difficulty of making them completely
real and their emotion dramatically effective.

In *The Sun Also Rises* Jake's sexual impediment hid the possible inadequacy of his affair with Brett. Because physical con-
summation was impossible, we were able to forget that the only
obstacle *was* physical and to imagine that genuine love would
flourish if only that phase of it were gratified. Brett's purely sexual
relations with other men, furthermore, only served to point up
the purity of her feeling for Jake, and Hemingway was careful
to see that no other proof was necessary. In *To Have and Have
Not* the relations of Morgan and his wife were required to be
nothing more than sexual. But the emotion Robert Jordan felt
for Maria had to be convincing as love. The story received its
entire tragic emphasis from the perfection of their three days
together and from the knowledge that those three days were all
there were going to be. It had to be a sublime, an idyllic emotion to stand against the war and the hazards of guerrilla life and,
particularly, to counterbalance the grimness of Jordan's mission.
But the war did not, as in *A Farewell to Arms,* actually impede
the lovers at any time during their relationship. The war was always in the background, never an "alien necessity," and they were

free to love as deeply as they were able in the time they had.

Hemingway was thus faced at the outset with the problem of dramatizing their emotion and giving it immediate objective reality as love. But the moment he tried to make it something more than a private emotion of Jordan's, he discovered he had no evidence for it beyond the purely sexual. The time limit set by the story gave no opportunity for love to develop naturally, and even if it had it was unlikely that the lovers could be made to demonstrate a capacity to sustain a genuine love relationship. But sex was plentiful, and sex was always easy. Maria might be a shade ludicrous as a faculty wife, but she had a "gold-brown smooth-lovely face," "small and firm" breasts, a long and passionate body, and an immense, if undeveloped, talent for the bed. To fortify these attributes, there were mystical touches with Maria that there had been with no one else. Like palm reading with Pilar, sex with Maria was an entrance into the unknown. In the frenzy of intercourse the earth moved. Sex even had something to do with Jordan's political convictions. Right after a "forever to nowhere, heavy on the elbows in the earth to nowhere, dark, never any end to nowhere" ecstasy it seemed to him that "continence is the foe of heresy."

But all these disguises are transparent. The mysticism is forced and the sex is only sex. Instead of being an aspect of love, it is all the love there can ever be for Hemingway—a drug to the senses, a momentary relief from the fear of death. From Caporetto and Pamplona to Loyalist Spain it is a shorter distance than one might have supposed, but in many ways it is still not short enough.

In those early stories and novels Hemingway was able to realize all he knew in terms of his first education at war. War was the common denominator to which the motive power of his world could always be reduced. It served him as a barricade against every emotion; and every emotion was given a special poignancy and truth as it was set against the war. The code of his best heroes was the code of war, of primitive courage and honorable death. Life, whether in the Michigan woods, the battlefield, or the bull ring, was a test of superhuman endurance and will power, a "good show" performed by giants on the verge of tears. But one was numb and one was tough. Things went "fine" or things went "badly." There was drinking and there was sex. These were the limits and they explained everything. If a man broke down in the war, if his nerves went to pieces under pressure and he disobeyed the rules, then he was lost. If he behaved badly in the peace, he was also lost. Lostness was the ultimate condition in both. In the end, something always collapsed. The war collapsed, you could not take the war any more, and Catherine died. You had been wounded a certain way, and there were never going to be those "damn good times" with Brett. The horse stumbled, your leg was broken, and the business with Maria, everything, was finished. There was all the fun you might have had, all the places you might have gone, all the women you might have slept with, if only things hadn't "gone badly."

Lostness was also the formula of art. In art you caught "the exact sequence," you described the thing as it actually happened. People breaking up in a moment of violence, their code and their courage going under—that was the central drama; and you got that by projecting the emotion onto the violence, by finding its key in the events around it, and by dramatizing the real thing "that made the emotion." Art was actually the essence of the good life. It required the same control, the same iron will, to write an absolutely true book that it took to kill a bull in the ring or lead a patrol under an artillery barrage. You even got rid of the bad times in art by the same process that you got rid of them in life. In art you wrote them down and they were no longer part of you. In life you got rid of them by doing something good afterward. Romero killed the bull well and got rid of the humiliation of

Cohn. Brett wiped out the time she slept with Cohn by sleeping with Romero. Good art, like good living, was something "you felt good after." Bad art, like bad living, was something "you felt bad after."

The confusion which resulted from Hemingway's attempt to depart from this formula is evident all through his last two novels. The struggle to affirm carried him beyond the limits of his education and away from the hard sure center of his art. His most recent stories, *The Short Happy Life of Francis Macomber* and *The Snows of Kilimanjaro,* represent the kind of success it is still possible for him to attain when he reverts to that old formula and to those first attitudes.

All the artistically favorable elements the Twenties possessed come together in the best of Hemingway. With the values which the war, exile, and his time provided him—his preoccupation with violence, his philosophy of denial, and his formula of loss—he is one of the finest writers of his generation. Without them, it is doubtful if he would have written at all.

Going back over Hemingway's work today is rather like going back to the house where you lived as a child and finding it smaller and somehow less substantial than you always remembered it. You wonder how it is that the crisp language, the clear descriptive passages, and the brittle dialogue that once—not so long ago— seemed so impressively right and so distressingly infectious can have become so suddenly stale, and why it is that you no longer feel the old excitement, the old sense of discovery, you had when you first read them. Perhaps it is because we are now far enough away from Hemingway to perceive the limitations of his art and world. The era out of which he wrote is almost thirty years behind us now; and the people he described, with their monosyllables, their perpetually clenched teeth, their pugilistic morals, and their primitive emotions, are more caricatures of the past than they are representative of the life we know. There are omissions that were charming before but that now rise up to trouble us: scenes that seem incomplete because we are aware now of all that they do not say, emotions that are reduced to a simplicity our experience will not allow us to approve.

It is not that we can no longer react to the sensations of Hemingway but that, having once reacted, our reaction can never be quite what it was. The talent that could, with a single turn of phrase, light up all the world we knew now lights only its portion; the rest is darker than we thought. And what is it that remains? First and always, the war—the courage, the hunger, the fear, and the pain of war. Men on the edge of death, jaws set, minds on the morning that will not come, all the mornings, remembering the flash of trout in a mountain stream, the cremation of ants in a camp fire, the Trudys and the Bretts. Bored women on the edge of love, stifling the fear that this will not be enough in the act of love, beautiful women with bobbed hair set against a backdrop of bulls pawing the Spanish earth, dying horses and hyenas with their entrails white and blue in the sun. People who in death achieve their only significance, for whom to die well is the only reward for a lifetime of drinking, sex, big-game hunting, and wars. What remains is a narrow world, a burly boy's world, made up of violence and bound by violence to the end.

CHAPTER IV

Fitzgerald

The Horror and the Vision of Paradise

"Amory saw girls doing things that even in his memory would have been impossible:" wrote the young Fitzgerald in *This Side of Paradise*, "eating three o'clock after-dance suppers in impossible cafés, talking of every side of life with an air half of earnestness, half of mockery, yet with a furtive excitement that Amory considered stood for a real moral let-down. But he never realized how widespread it was until he saw the cities between New York and Chicago as one vast juvenile intrigue." *

It was an oddly innocent intrigue that Amory-Fitzgerald reported. The girls almost always lost their curiosity after the first kiss. "I've kissed dozens of men," said one typically. "I suppose I'll kiss dozens more." The young men, even with the advantages of "sunk-down" sofas and innumerable cocktails, were usually content with shy claspings and sentimental poetry. It was an intrigue of manners merely, conducted by glittering children who could hardly bear to be touched; and it was the creation of a young man's innocence at a time when all things seemed larger than life and purer than a childhood dream.

This was the surface of Fitzgerald's world. Beneath it, almost undetectable even to Fitzgerald himself, was something else, something that the dawn light of eternal morning failed to pene-

* From *This Side of Paradise* by F. Scott Fitzgerald, published and copyright, 1920, Charles Scribner's Sons, New York.

trate and that stood between Amory Blaine, the enchanted voyager in Paradise, and the full possession of his enchantment. At Myra St. Claire's bobbing party he and Myra had slipped away from the others and gone to the "little den" upstairs at the country club. There they had kissed, "their lips brushing like young wild flowers in the wind." But "sudden revulsion seized Amory, disgust, loathing for the whole incident," and he "desired frantically to be away." Later at college he had gone with a classmate and two girls on a Broadway holiday. Toward the end of the evening when they arrived at the girls' apartment, he was repelled by the laughter, the liquor, and his partner's "side-long suggestive smile," and for a terrifying moment he saw a deathlike figure sitting opposite him on the divan. Still later, when he, a friend, and a girl were caught in a hotel room by house detectives, Amory saw above the figure of the girl sobbing on the bed "an aura, gossamer as a moonbeam, tainted as stale, weak wine, yet a horror, diffusely brooding . . . and over by the window among the stirring curtains stood something else, featureless and indistinguishable, yet strangely familiar. . . ."

Fitzgerald tells us that for Amory "the problem of evil . . . had solidified into the problem of sex." There are, to be sure, obvious sexual overtones to these visions, overtones that indicate a disturbing preoccupation with sexual guilt in Fitzgerald. But they indicate as well even deeper disturbances in Paradise itself; in fact, they are the same horrors which came to the older Fitzgerald in the night as he lay awake with insomnia, and they bring with them the same conviction of failure which prefigured his tragic "crack-up" and death. Indeed, they are horrors that touch at the core of Fitzgerald's work and are implicit in his vision, his "tragic sense," of the life of his time. For the beautiful there is always damnation; for every tenderness there is always the black horror of night; for all the bright young men there is sadness; and even Paradise has another side.

It is both an innocent and a haunted Paradise that Fitzgerald reveals in his first book; but it is not a perfect revelation of either. Amory's "enormous terrified revulsion" is an as-yet-uncentralized emotion. Amory is made to feel his horror, but at no time is it projected into the terms of the narrative. Perhaps it was a thing which Fitzgerald found inexpressible, which he could not understand in himself and could not, therefore, portray. But it is clear that in the very middle of his enchantment he was performing an act of exorcism, as if to free himself of ghosts that were even then speaking to him of the tragedy that was to be his and his time's.

The distance between Amory Blaine and Anthony Patch of *The Beautiful and Damned* is marked by Fitzgerald's growing comprehension of his theme and an increase in his power to detach from the personal and make dramatic the issues which were only imperfectly realized in the earlier novel. But more than anything else the novel is a record of Fitzgerald's emerging disenchantment with the Paradise ideal, a disenchantment which is paced so precisely by Anthony's drift toward ruin that it is almost as if Fitzgerald had been able to assert it finally only after Anthony had discovered it for him.

Through the entire first third of the book Anthony is merely a slightly older version of Amory. There are even signs that he might have come to nothing more than Amory's rather pompous realization of himself, the suffering, betrayed, but somehow purer young man who, at the end of *This Side of Paradise*, went forth to meet the world crying, "I know myself, but that is all." There is the difference, however, that where wealth for Amory was the gateway to the Paradise of his fancy, wealth for Anthony is a means of escaping the horror of life and of cheating the business system out of his soul. All of Anthony's sensibilities rebel at the thought that he might someday have to give up his notion of the utter futility of all endeavor and go to work. As long as he has wealth he can "divert himself" with pleasure, settle himself in that comfortable routine in which "one goes once a week to one's broker and twice to one's tailor," and hold himself aloof from that "air of struggle, of greedy ambition, of hope more sordid than despair, of incessant passage up and down, which . . . is most in evidence through the unstable middle class." * There is the further and very important difference that where Amory lost the girl he loved Anthony marries her.

Significantly, the disaster which overtakes this marriage is never actually centered in the marriage itself. Fitzgerald's acute "environmental sense" has by now become attuned to the destructive impulses of his time, with the result that the internal currents that sweep Anthony and Gloria along to greater and greater dissension are persistently less important than the disruptive circumstances which surround them. The spiritual breakdown, for example, which is represented in the wild parties, the furious drinking and spending of their class, counterpoints their failure to find in each other more enduring resources; but it is doubtful if without the attraction of the parties, the drinking, and the spending, they would have been quite so demoralized or so quickly damned. The horror is now on the exterior. It is a sense, vague and diffusive, of prevalent disaster; but the forms it takes, while indirectly the result of the increasing tensions within the marriage, stem from those other circumstances of which the marriage is merely an accident.

The summer house which Anthony and Gloria lease shortly after they are married becomes intolerable because of the poisonous associations that accumulate inside it. "Ah, my beautiful young lady," it seems to say to Gloria, "yours is not the first daintiness and delicacy that has faded here under the summer suns. . . . Youth has come into this room in palest blue and left it in the

* From *The Beautiful and Damned* by F. Scott Fitzgerald, published and copyright, 1924, Charles Scribner's Sons, New York.

grey cerements of despair. . . ." But despair is still only "a somber pall, pervasive through the lower rooms, gradually . . . climbing up the narrow stairs. . . ." The nightmare episode during the party when Gloria runs insanely through the darkness to escape a fear that is only partially identified with Joe Hull is another manifestation of that nameless dread which has come to reside at the Patches'. But Maury Noble, who discourses that same night on the meaninglessness of life and the nonexistence of God, is as much to blame. And what can be said of the songs—

> I left my blushing bride
> She went and shook herself insane
> So let her shiver back again

and

> The panic has come over us
> So ha-a-s the moral decline

—which rise above these phantasms like the chorus of death itself? The crumbling structure is not only a marriage. It is Fitzgerald's vision of Paradise as well, going down in the dissolution of an age.

With the destruction of this ideal Fitzgerald's Jazz Age romance comes to an end. He might well say now with Anthony who, having won his inheritance at the price of his sanity and youth, boards a ship for Italy—"I showed them. It was a hard fight, but I didn't give up and I came through!" There is deep significance for Fitzgerald in this embarkation, this new pursuit of his vision into another world. It is part of the recurrent cycle of his generation; and it is the direction of his own final development. But to Fitzgerald in his passage from golden illusion to the bitterness of loss to ultimate exile and return there is one more step to take—and he takes it in his story of Jay Gatsby and the failure of the American Dream.

The Great Gatsby is by all odds Fitzgerald's most perfect novel. The gain in dramatic power which began to be evident in *The Beautiful and Damned* is climaxed now in a moment of insight in which self-understanding strikes and discovers its revelation in art. All the channels of Fitzgerald's sensibility seem to have anticipated their end in Gatsby; and all the dissident shapes that obstructed the progress of his search seem to find their apotheosis in Gatsby's romantic dream.

This dream of a past recapturable, of a youth and a love ceaselessly renewed, contrasts oddly with the milieu in which it is placed; yet it is obviously Fitzgerald's intended irony that a man like Gatsby should carry the burden of his own earlier enchantment at the same time that Gatsby's fate should emphasize its futility. It is because his dream is unworthy of him that Gatsby is a pathetic figure; and it is because Fitzgerald himself dreamed that same dream that he cannot make Gatsby tragic. Gatsby has all Fitzgerald's sympathy and all Fitzgerald's mistrust. He is thus Fitzgerald's most potent assertion of Paradise at the same time that he is his most emphatic farewell to it.

The events leading up to the opening of the novel resemble Fitzgerald's typical Jazz Age story. Gatsby, the simple, Midwestern youth, falls in love with Daisy, the beautiful rich girl. There is the brief, wholly idyllic affair which is abruptly terminated by the war. There is Daisy's quiet and conventional marriage to Tom Buchanan and Gatsby's return to the memory of a love which, as it has fed on itself, has reached obsessive proportions and become more real than any obstacle time or circumstance can put in its way. There are the years of struggle during which Gatsby painfully constructs the personality and the fortune which will make him deserving of Daisy; and there is the final achievement—the magnificent house in West Egg looking across the bay to the green light at the end of the Buchanan's dock. It is at this point that Gatsby is introduced; and it is immediately afterward that the flaws in his calculations become clear.

Gatsby's plan depends for its success upon Daisy's discontent with her marriage and her willingness to exchange it for a life of love. But Daisy's discontent, like her sophistication, is a pose, something picked up from "the most advanced people," part of the sham and deception of her world. "The instant her voice broke off, ceasing to compel my attention, my belief, I felt the basic insincerity of what she had said," Nick Carraway tells us. "I waited, and sure enough, in a moment she looked at me with an absolute smirk on her lovely face, as if she had asserted her membership in a rather distinguished secret society to which she and Tom belonged." * Daisy was born into that society, and she has been corrupted by it. That fact, so early revealed to us but unknown to Gatsby, sets the key for the principal irony of the novel.

Gatsby's story is, in a sense, Fitzgerald's parody of the Great American Success Dream. Gatsby, surrounded by the tinsel splendor of his parties, dressed in his absurd pink suits, protected from social ostracism by the fabulous legend he has constructed around himself, is still the naïvely ambitious boy who wrote in that schedule of childhood the formula of success—"Rise from bed. . . . Study electricity. . . . Work. . . . Practice elocution, poise and how to attain it. . . . Study needed inventions." The purchase of love and happiness is part of that formula; and if Gatsby had not been destroyed by a corruption greater than his own, it is probable that he would have arranged that too. But it was his misfortune to have believed too strenuously and loved too blindly. "Gatsby believed in the green light, the orgiastic future that year by year recedes before us. It eluded us then, but that's no matter—tomorrow we will run faster, stretch out our arms farther.

* From *The Great Gatsby* by F. Scott Fitzgerald, published and copyright, 1925, Charles Scribner's Sons, New York.

. . . And one fine morning— So we beat on, boats against the current, borne back ceaselessly into the past."

Scott Fitzgerald also believed in the "green light." He believed in the Buchanans, and he believed in Gatsby; and it was inevitable that he should end by disavowing both. If *The Beautiful and Damned* saw the emergence of his disenchantment with Paradise, *The Great Gatsby* was the final projection in art of that disenchantment and the beginning of a new phase in his career. The man who wrote *Tender Is the Night* almost nine years later had left even disenchantment behind. There was no dream now. There was only horror and sickness. The destructive element had at last completely broken through the privacy of the haunted mind and become part of the larger spectacle of an entire age short-circuiting itself to ruin.

"It occurred to me," remarked Nick Carraway in *The Great Gatsby*, "that there was no difference between men, in intelligence or race, so profound as the difference between the sick and the well." In the years between that novel and *Tender Is the Night* Fitzgerald had ample opportunity to test the truth of this observation; for they were years of ebbing vitality and doubt for him as well as for his time. The interval was marked by Fitzgerald's growing identification of himself with the life around him, by a greater and greater immersion in its sickness, and a progressive failure of self-control. The "age of excess" had told on him from the start; a process of "over-extension of the flank," of "burning the candle at both ends," had begun as far back as Princeton, when he had been invalided out in his junior year, and had continued through the writing of his early books. There was always a hint of fever glow, of deep and excessive withdrawals at the bank of talent, about Fitzgerald's work. *Gatsby* may be said to have been a temporary recovery. But *Gatsby* was written during that fragile moment when the drive of youth meets with the intuitive wisdom

of first maturity and before either the diseases of youth or the
waverings of age begin to show through. Besides, *Gatsby* was
the kind of book that had to be written; and perhaps the energy
that went into the writing of it came to some extent from the book
itself. But something in Fitzgerald died with Gatsby; when
Gatsby's world fell to pieces and its glitter slowly dissolved, Fitzgerald was left with the pieces and the afterglow. He lived on in
the afterglow; but it was by now a glow of sickness; and the pieces,
when he fitted them back together, proved to be good only for
a world as sick and bankrupt as he.

Tender Is the Night, then, is what Fitzgerald himself called
"the novel of deterioration." It is written with a neurotic subtlety,
crammed with tortured images and involuted patterns. It is like
something out of a mental patient's diary and, by turns, like the
clinical report of a patient who is doubling as his own psycho-
analyst. The patterns of the earlier novels have now been broken
down, rearranged, and absorbed into a new narrative form. Again
the effect is a psychiatric formula—the mind unconsciously concealing the true object of its horror through a projection upon
other objects which may or may not have originally pertained to
that horror. But Fitzgerald fails to complete the process. Gloria
Gilbert and Daisy Buchanan have become Rosemary Hoyt with
her "virginal emotions" and her peculiarly American immaturity;
but they have also become Nicole Diver, the enchanting and half-
demented Jazz Daughter of Fitzgerald's new dissolute Paradise.
Amory Blaine, Anthony Patch, and Tom Buchanan are all to be
found in Dick Diver, but so too is Jay Gatsby. On all sides of
these principals Fitzgerald has scattered the evidence of the general decay which he set out to depict. There is Nicole's incestuous
relationship with her father; the corruption of the English
Campions and Lady Carolines; the anarchism of Tommy Barban,
who must be perpetually at war; the exhibitionism of Yale Man
Collis Clay; the literary degeneracy of Albert McKisco; the self-

indulgence of Abe North, whose moral suicide anticipates Dick Diver's own. But these forces, while satisfactorily realized in themselves, are not drawn together in the main situation of the novel, which is the story of the Divers.

Rosemary Hoyt takes over the "infatuation" element from the long line of deluded Fitzgerald males. She is delighted and fascinated by the Divers; their "special gentleness" and "far-reaching delicacy," their effortless command of the richness of life, seem to Rosemary to contain a purpose "different from any she had known." They exert over her the kind of magic Thomas Wolfe glorified in the people "who have the quality of richness and joy in them . . . and communicate it to everything they touch." But Rosemary cannot penetrate the secret horror—that revolting scene which Violet McKisco came upon in the bathroom that night at the party—which is at the core of the Divers' relationship, nor can she know the price Dick has had to pay for his "amusing world" and his "power of arousing a fascinated and uncritical love." Rosemary is perhaps too hypnotized to care; her principal emotion is one of relief at having escaped through the Divers "the derisive and salacious improvisations of the frontier."

Yet Rosemary has come to Fitzgerald's last frontier, to the Divers who are "the last of their line" and whose ancestral curse it is to drift steadily but unaware toward ruin. Fitzgerald's familiar contrast between outward splendor and inner disintegration is particularly apt now to point up the Divers' underlying ambivalence: the glamour which is the thinnest sugar-coating of evil, the surface glitter which is the reflection of an incurable sickness of heart. Dick, the generous giver of his strength, first to the neurotic Nicole, then to all who demand it, is the shell of an illusion, the "exact furthermost evolution" of Fitzgerald's dream of the rich and the caricature of the emptiness he found at the center of that dream. At one time in his life Dick was faced with a choice between "the necessary human values," which he had learned from his father, and Nicole, whom he could not have without accepting her world of "charm, notoriety, and good manners." In the beginning, and in Dick's position as a doctor, Nicole was, as Arthur Mizener observed, a "professional situation"; it was his need to express his best impulses that made it a "human situation"; "wanting above all to be brave and kind, he . . . wanted, even more, to be loved." * So, as a doctor, he accepted the responsibility of Nicole's care, and, as a man, he accepted the responsibility of her love. And to her world and its increasing demands, to all the people who came to depend on him for all that they lacked in themselves, he gave his humanity. He was gay, charming, and polite. He gave until there was nothing left in him to give, until the impulses of his humanity were turned destructively upon himself and Nicole. Then, in a final act of will, realizing that Nicole's love for him was inseparable from her psychological dependence upon him, he broke that dependence and watched Nicole drift away from him forever. What he had failed to treat as a professional situation had been just that all along. The human situation had never existed outside himself.

This irony is deepened by the irony of the novel's setting. Europe, particularly the European Riviera, had been the last refuge of Fitzgerald's heroes. It was Amory Blaine's promise of the good life. It was Anthony Patch's escape from the vulgarity of the economic order. It was the hope of Paradise for Fitzgerald himself. But it was characteristic of Fitzgerald that he should find even this last oasis corrupt; and it was fitting that he should have Dick Diver renounce the scene of his corruption and return to America. Doctor Diver, uprooted and lost, seeking his sources through a succession of small, and progressively more obscure towns—Buffalo, Batavia, and Geneva, New York; and Scott Fitz-

* From *Tender Is the Night* by F. Scott Fitzgerald, published and copyright, 1934, Charles Scribner's Sons, New York.

gerald, turning his back on the East for the last time, facing west to Hollywood, the place of all our lost illusions.

The Last Tycoon is a brilliant fragment of the book Fitzgerald was writing when he died. Even with Edmund Wilson's scholarly interpretation of the notes that were left with the manuscript, we are given no more than an intimation of Fitzgerald's purpose; and even after we have read his synopsis and the opening chapters, we have always to bear in mind that both the plan and the writing would have been altered considerably in the final version. Yet it is possible to visualize from the material at hand the scope and promise of Fitzgerald's intention and to weave *The Last Tycoon* at least partially into the context of the earlier novels.

There is, first of all, the figure of the tycoon himself, Monroe Stahr. Stahr, the last frontiersman, the embodiment of Fitzgerald's search for values beyond all frontiers, has come to rest at last in Hollywood, where the frontier has become a thing of cardboard and tinsel and the American Dream a corporation dedicated to the purveyance of dreams. In Hollywood, Stahr's empire is as magnificent and powerful as the one Gatsby envisioned; it is also as corrupt. But corruption has now become an acceptable part of the social order. In fact, it is inevitable in a nation "that for a decade had wanted only to be entertained." Yet, because Stahr is wholly committed to his dream of power, he is, like Gatsby, basically incorruptible.

To be incorruptible in Fitzgerald's world, however, is to be destroyed by a larger corruptive force. Men like Gatsby and Stahr who subordinate everything to their ambition have only one fear—the collapse of the system on which their ambition is based; and as the novel develops, it becomes clear that some such collapse is occurring around Stahr. As in *Tender Is the Night*, the prophecy of doom is carried in the minor figures who remain, for the most part, on the periphery of the action. There is the ruined producer Manny Schwartz, whose suicide introduces the tragic theme in the opening section; Mr. Marcus, the industrial magnate who has lost his powers; the has-been actors and actresses, all haunting the scene of their last triumphs; even Cecilia, who, in all her innocence and youth, is somehow tainted. Then, too, there are the debilitating effects on Stahr himself of the struggle which made him a king—his fanatical disregard of his failing health, his morbid preoccupation with his dead wife, his almost deliberate "perversion of the life force," as if he were consciously intent on death. Stahr, like the Divers, is "the last of his line," and, like them, he embodies all the strengths and weaknesses of a dynasty.

"Is *this* all?" asks Brimmer, the Communist organizer, as Stahr loses his control. "This frail half-sick person holding up the whole thing?" * And Fitzgerald himself might well have asked the same question; for Stahr comes as a pathetic climax to his lifelong search for Paradise. Looking back over the novels, however, we can see how the pattern of this search resolves itself in Stahr; indeed, how there can be no other possible resolution. Amory Blaine's infatuation with wealth set the key for Anthony Patch's corruption by wealth. In Gatsby, Fitzgerald sounded the futility of his dream only to reembrace the rich in Dick Diver and discover the real futility of the spiritually bankrupt; and as Anthony, Gatsby, and Dick were destroyed, so Stahr prepares us for the final destruction, that ultimate collapse of self which comes after all dreams have died.

We can see too by what an inescapable process of disenchantment Fitzgerald arrived at Hollywood and his own crack-up. There have been his wanderings east from the "barbarian" St. Paul to the Princeton of *This Side of Paradise;* the New York parties of *The Beautiful and Damned;* the East Egg society of

* From *The Last Tycoon* by F. Scott Fitzgerald (edited by Edmund Wilson), published and copyright, 1941, Charles Scribner's Sons, New York.

The Great Gatsby; and still east to the Paris and Riviera of *Tender Is the Night;* until Dick Diver's repatriation brings him abruptly back to the West once more. And as each place is left behind and the possibilities of place are diminished, the horrors accumulate until finally there is only enough will left for one last act of self-immolation—the return to the supreme lie of Monroe Stahr's world.

In completing the cycle of his life and art, Fitzgerald reproduced the design of an entire literary movement. But Fitzgerald was more than merely typical of that movement: he was its most sensitive and tormented talent and the prophet of its doom. With a sense of the destructive impulses of his time that can only be compared with Hemingway's, he yet lacked Hemingway's stabilizing gift—the ability to get rid of the bad times by writing of them. Fitzgerald never got rid of anything; the ghosts of his adolescence, the failures of his youth, the doubts of his maturity plagued him to the end. He was supremely a part of the world he described, so much a part that he made himself its king and then, when he saw it begin to crumble, he crumbled with it and led it to death.

But the thing that destroyed him also gave him his special distinction. His vision of Paradise served him as a medium of artistic understanding. Through it he penetrated to the heart of some of the great illusions of his time, discovering their falsity as if he were discovering his own. If that vision—like Hemingway's correlative of loss which it so much resembles—was limited, it was at least adequate to Fitzgerald's purpose; and it was a means of contact between his art and the experience of his time.

There is a certain quaintness about Fitzgerald's work today as there is about Hemingway's. But in Fitzgerald one has the sense of such a literal contemporaneity that it is almost impossible to read him without giving more attention to his time than to what he had to say about it. Mah-jongg, crossword puzzles, Freud, bathtub gin, Warren G. Harding, and Fitzgerald are inextricably one; the time amounts to a consistent betrayal of the man. Yet the distance that separates his time from ours enables us to rediscover him in a fresh focus and to see in the important things he wrote that other dimension, always there, but obscured until now by the glitter of his surfaces. The emphasis now is on Fitzgerald's acutely penetrative side, his ability to manipulate the surfaces as if they were mirrors that reflect not only the contents of a room, the splendor of its occupants, but the concealed horrors of its essence—the ghosts hidden just behind the swaying arras, the disenchantment behind the bright masks of faces, the death to which everyone in the room has been spiritually mortgaged. The sense of impending catastrophe is never more deeply or terribly felt than when we are immersed, and seem almost destined to be drowned, in the welter of life with which Fitzgerald presents us: the end of the big party is always implicit in its beginning, the ugliness of age is always visible in the tender beauty of youth.

With this awareness, this assurance that Fitzgerald penetrated to the truth beneath his vision, it ceases to matter that his vision was, in many ways, frivolous and unbecoming or that, with all his insight, he often failed to perceive the implications of what he saw. What matters and will continue to matter is that we have before us the work of a man who gave us better than any one else the true substance of an age, the dazzle and fever and the ruin.

CHAPTER V

Dos Passos

The Energy of Despair

JOHN DOS PASSOS' first novel, *One Man's Initiation*, was originally published in England in 1920, and then reissued, under the title of *First Encounter*, in this country in 1945. In the preface which he added to the later edition Dos Passos drew certain comparisons between the experience of the first war, in which, at the time he wrote the book, he was serving as a Norton-Harjes ambulance driver, and the experience of the second war, in which he was now, twenty-five years later, serving as a middle-aged traveling correspondent. It seemed to him that his own generation had entered the first war full of high hopes and illusions: the future, illuminated by the speeches of Woodrow Wilson and the figure of Lenin, was "a blank page to write on," and the revolutions that "the working people of the world could invent out of their own heads" were going to end in "a reign of peace and justice." But it was clear to him that the generation of the second war had no such illusions and that the most they seemed able to hope for was that "what they would return to after the war would not be worse than what they had left." * In pointing out these differences Dos Passos was apparently trying to suggest simply that the young men of the second war would not be writing books like *One Man's Initiation.* But what he may or may not have sensed

* From *First Encounter* by John Dos Passos, published and copyright, 1945, John Dos Passos and Philosophical Library, Inc., New York.

was that, because of these differences, they would also have little patience with anyone who had.

To those of us who read it for the first time in 1945 and who saw it, as we saw everything that year, in terms of the war we had just survived, the novel seemed impossibly romantic and naïve. It had been written, of course, in a time of illusions, just as Dos Passos said it was; but even though we knew that and tried to allow for it, it still stood in our way. There was entirely too much wide-eyed wonder about the book, too much ohing and ahing over scenes and events of wartime which we had long been hardened to. The main character, Martin Howe, seemed to us the palest and most precious of young Harvard aesthetes. He was the eternal poseur perpetually hypnotizing himself with the splendor of his own emotions. And when we came to the section in which, after months of alleged front-line duty, he virtuously renounced a woman who invited him to bed and went off to dream of an imaginary dancing girl, we began to have grave doubts about his masculinity. But the thing that bothered us even more was Dos Passos' own innocence of the craft of writing. Here was a man who had become a symbol of all that was modern in American literature, whose imaginary U.S.A. had seemed to epitomize, in terms as cold and passionless as steel, the nightmare horror from which an entire generation was struggling to awaken, and yet who had written his first book in a style that seemed scarcely to belong to the twentieth century at all and that certainly did not belong to the kind of material it was being used to describe. It was a style full of exotic overtones and lush images, complicated by a thousand romantic impressions and pseudo impressions. There was hardly a scene that had not been spoiled by verbal theatrics and self-indulgence. The young Dos Passos had set everything off with great peals of rhetoric; and all that was mundane and typical in the life he was describing, all that could not be presented with a flourish and a crash, seemed to have escaped him utterly. The result was that the book read like a series of disconnected dramatic climaxes. It had no narrative continuity and no bottom. Events followed other events by the merest chance; and one could never be sure that a character who happened to leave the room in the middle of a crucial scene might not disappear forever.

This was an initial impression drawn from a first reading of a book that had been written at the end of one war and reissued at the end of another. It was an honest and inevitable impression at the time. In 1945, we were all unable to see beyond the limits of our immediate experience and much too full of ourselves to feel more than passing contempt for a book that dealt in unfamiliar and, to us, unrealistic terms with an aspect of life which we had long since decided was our own special and private property.

Yet if we go back over *One Man's Initiation* now that five years have passed and the memory of the war has begun to fade and reread it in terms of the whole of Dos Passos' work, perhaps we shall have to admit we were wrong. I do not mean that the book seems any better as a novel than it did when we first read it or that it seems any better written. But I do mean that we can see it now in relation to the experience with which it deals and not exclusively in relation to our own experience. And, having seen it more clearly for what it is, we can begin to recognize it as part of a pattern, a grand design, that holds Dos Passos' work together. We can, in fact, find in it, now that we are less blinded by the superficial awkwardnesses of style, tone, and structure, the source of his special power, that inverted lyricism and protest which is behind his best later books and which finally explains why he has become the writer he is.

Like Frederick Henry in *A Farewell to Arms,* and like Dos Passos himself, Martin Howe is an American gentleman volunteer serving as an ambulance driver with a foreign army. But one soon learns that he is, in most respects, a much younger man than Frederick and that he has not begun to have Frederick's experience. Frederick, by the time his story opened, had been at the front for nearly two years and had seen enough of the war to come to some sort of terms with it. He had long since lost his illusions, the fine words had become abhorrent to him, and he had found it possible to survive only by formulating for himself a special philosophical code which allowed him to believe that the war had nothing to do with him. But Martin, at the beginning of his story, comes to the war chock-full of illusions and fine words: the war has everything to do with him and he can hardly get enough of it. Like his real-life counterparts, those naïve and adventurous young men just out of Harvard who volunteered for service with the Norton-Harjes and the other American ambulance units recruiting in Paris, he has left college in boredom and arrived in France eager to take part in what he is still able to think of as a great and exciting crusade to "save the world for democracy." To him, in the beginning, the issues are clear and ridiculously simple: on one side there is civilization and decency; on the other side there are the dirty Huns who have left behind them, in their barbaric drive across Europe, a bloody trail of impaled babies and ravished virgins.

At the outset his service seems ideal. He has time and money, he is in France, and the season is spring. His senses are alive with what Malcolm Cowley described as that "keen, precarious delight" that comes with wartime and the prospect of death, when it seems that the trees are green, "not like ordinary trees but like trees in the still instant before a hurricane," that the sky is "a special and ineffable blue," and that the grass smells of "life itself." But for Martin the prospect of death is comfortably remote: he is destined to be near enough to the fighting to experience the maximum excitement with the minimum risk; his work will require him to evacuate the wounded and dying but not share their pain. He will always have the special immunity of the outsider, the onlooker, the sensitive, detached guest who, even though he might imagine it, must never be allowed to face the creeping horror in the house.

Martin's exact relation to the war is made clear in a scene very early in the book. He and a friend are sitting in a garden drinking wine with a French schoolmaster and his wife. A French army convoy passes on the road beside them; and the men in the trucks call out to them: "Get to the front!" "Into the trenches with them!" "Down with the war!" But Martin merely stares at them, "noting intelligent faces, beautiful faces, faces brutally gay, miserable faces like those of sobbing drunkards." To him, sitting in the cool of the garden casually sipping his wine, the faces of the men are merely part of a spectacle to be observed. They are not faces of men who, as the old French woman says, "know they are going to death"; they are items that can be classified into types and filed away, perhaps to be written about later on. In another scene, very reminiscent of one Cowley describes in his book,* Martin is sitting at dusk on the steps of a dugout listening to the sound of shells in the air overhead. "It was like battledore and shuttle-cock, these huge masses whirling through the evening above his head, now from one side, now from the other. It gave him some-how a cosy feeling of safety, as if he were under some sort of a bridge over which freight-cars were shunting madly to and fro." Once again he is the detached observer, watching the war from

---

* "On a July evening, at dusk, I remember halting in the courtyard of a half-ruined château, through which zig-zagged the trenches held by the Germans before their retreat two miles northward to stronger positions. Shells were harmlessly rumbling overhead: the German and the French heavy bat-teries, three miles behind their respective lines, were shelling each other like the Brushton gang throwing rocks at the Car Barn gang; here, in the empty courtyard between them, it was as if we were underneath a freight yard where heavy trains were being shunted back and forth." (*Exile's Return,* 49–50)

the ringside. His position gives him "a cosy feeling of safety"; the movement of the shells reminds him of a mild garden game; he knows they are meant for someone else.

But by a process of gradual indoctrination and baptism that is very similar to the one Frederick Henry experienced, Martin loses his detachment, and with it his illusions, and begins to identify himself with the suffering that surrounds him. It is not easy to tell exactly when this occurs, for the book is constructed in such a way that one sees Martin only in single, isolated episodes that are often considerably separated in time. But one begins to be aware, somewhere in the middle of the book, that what was up to then a lyrical and romantic account of the general emotional atmosphere of war as perceived from a distance has suddenly become a passionately indignant exposé of the horrors of war as perceived at close range. The excitement which Dos Passos seems to have felt when he conceived of war as a great adventure and crusade has apparently been transformed, by some process of emotional electrodynamics, into an immense energy for denunciation. It is as if the force of his idealism had been so great that, once it had been thwarted and disappointed, he had turned it upon the thing he had originally idealized and sought to destroy it. Certainly, the intense negation one senses in the last half of the book does not spring from a different kind of power from that which was behind the lyricism in the first half. It is the same kind of power: it has simply been reinforced now by hurt feelings and has changed directions.

One sees this change in Martin at the same time that one sees it in Dos Passos but in different ways. Dos Passos begins to concentrate less on Martin's poetic responses to the beauties of the countryside and more on single episodes of war violence—the burial of the dead, the tragic death of a German prisoner, the look of maimed bodies. His writing becomes hard and choppy. Martin begins to speculate on the meaning of all the waste and bloodshed and to see the men on both sides of the fighting as helpless victims of the same evil. He talks passionately to his French anarchist friends of the possibility of a people's revolution that will bring about the overthrow of the capitalist system and make an end of wars. "First we must burst our bonds, open our eyes, clear our ears. No, we know nothing but what we are told by the rulers. Oh, the lies, the lies, the lies, the lies that life is smothered in! We must strike once more for freedom, for the sake of the dignity of man. Hopelessly, cynically, ruthlessly we must rise and show at least that we are not taken in; that we are slaves but not willing slaves. Oh, they have deceived us so many times. We have been such dupes, we have been such dupes!"

The illusions that the war has destroyed in Martin are momentarily replaced by illusions of social reform, but only momentarily. For in the closing scene of the book, just as he has begun to dare to hope once more, Martin learns that his anarchist friends have been killed in action; and it seems to him that with their death the promises of the cause they represented have been lost forever.

Like all of Dos Passos' characters, whether they have struggled to survive in the midst of war, the capitalist system, or the great despairing emptiness of the U.S.A., Martin Howe is defeated in the end. And, as always, his defeat is made clear to us in the protest of an outraged sensibility against a world that is too big, too powerful, and too chaotic to be understood. As always, too, it is the protest of an aesthetic sensibility, one in which the strength of a former idealism has been short-circuited into hate. The energy that enlivens Dos Passos' best work always has its source in the conflict created by this sensibility as it takes its revenge upon the established social order for failing to keep the faith.

One Man's Initiation, then, is more than simply a record of Martin Howe's loss of illusions. It is a sort of preview as well of the kind of novel that is to become standard for Dos Passos. In it, he found the answer and the formula which, twenty years and a dozen books later, he could still only reiterate: illusions must always be destroyed, protest must always prove ineffectual, the natural condition of modern man, particularly aesthetic man, under the present social and economic system must always be defeat. It is perhaps strange that, having learned this at the time he wrote his first novel, Dos Passos should have been able to devote the rest of his career to producing novels of profound social condemnation. Yet if we look closely at those novels, we shall be able to see in them a gradual decline in Dos Passos' power to condemn. Those he wrote before *Adventures of a Young Man* (1938) are all enlivened and enriched by this power because his sensibility continued to protest long after his intelligence realized the futility of protest. But in those which follow *U.S.A.*, the energy of youthful disillusion has died out, and all that remains is a listless and heartsick negation. The change really began to be evident, however, in the novels which came immediately after *One Man's Initiation;* for even though Dos Passos' indignation continued to be strong, he now knew what the outcome of his characters' struggles must inevitably be. Never again could he write with the simple faith and conviction with which he created Martin Howe. Now, for the first time, he was above his characters, watching them from the vantage point of superior knowledge, allowing them to enjoy for a moment their petty hopes and desires, but standing ready always to inflict upon them the punishment which he had learned was the unavoidable end of all their striving.

It was perhaps this very knowledge in Dos Passos that gave his second novel, *Three Soldiers,* its special charm, at least for those of us who read it for the first time in the early days of the second war. Martin Howe's idealism, to a generation brought up on Hitler, Eliot, and Hemingway, had seemed to belong to another century; it had embarrassed us by its failure to anticipate our own despair. But in the suffering of John Andrews we found a strictly contemporary emotion, one we could readily understand, respect, and admire. Andrews was a member of that great lost battalion of doomed men to which we assigned all our best heroes—Jake Barnes, Frederick Henry, the nameless protagonist of *The Waste Land*, Studs Lonigan, Eugene Gant, and, of course, ourselves. He was a man who held in himself the absolute certainty of failure and yet who still retained the power to make one last gesture of rebellion in the name of his beliefs. I remember that we read the closing lines of his story with a mixture of grave reverence and a sense of excited, almost eager, loss and sadness. "On John Andrews's writing table the brisk wind rustled among the broad sheets of paper. First one sheet, then another, blew off the table, until the floor was littered with them." * Ah yes, we breathed, reading the passage over and over, Ah yes.

The lyricism we felt in *Three Soldiers* was very much like that of *A Farewell to Arms*. It was a lyricism born out of the conflict between the delicacy of a romantic emotion that could not possibly triumph and the brutality of a destructive force that could not help but triumph, that must inevitably win out over the very good, the very gentle, and the very brave—as the war won out in the end over Frederick and Catherine. It was also, although we could not have seen it at the time, the product of a very real and finally fatal disillusion in Dos Passos. John Andrews was the most appealing but he was also the last of Dos Passos' Harvard aesthetes to fight back against the system. As such, he was the embodiment of the last of Dos Passos' illusions and of the last of Dos Passos' power to protest through the single, suffering sensibility. His strength as a lyrical abstraction derived from the subtle balance between the protest against war and the sense of the futility of protest that existed for a moment in Dos Passos' mind; but his

* From *Three Soldiers* by John Dos Passos, published and copyright, 1921, John Dos Passos and Doubleday & Company, Inc. (Doran), New York.

weakness as a character derived from that balance too; for it gave to everything he did a certain stubborn relentlessness that could not always be justified by the facts as they appeared.

Andrews was the symbol through which Dos Passos chose to project his hatred of the war. But at almost no time in the novel was Dos Passos able to discover the elements in Andrews's war experiences that fully accounted for his feelings or his final actions. Again and again we are convinced of the truth of Andrews's suffering; but we are just as often at a loss to know how to explain it. The early instances of army fascism and brutality are typical enough; but they are not powerful enough to justify Andrews's reactions to them. The battle scenes, during one of which he is wounded, are curiously remote from him: he moves through them as if he were a puppet being drawn by invisible wires across a painted backdrop depicting an imaginary war. Later on, after he has gone to Paris, been arrested by the merest chance, and driven to desert, he is still behaving like a puppet. He knows that he can return to his unit and that his friends will arrange it so that he will not be punished; but he insists on carrying his rebellion through to the end. After a while we begin to realize that, however admirable Andrews may seem as a romantic figure fighting nobly against overwhelming odds, he is not acting under his own power: he is the instrument entirely of the man manipulating the wires. Dos Passos has been using him all along to make a point. He has known from the beginning what Andrews's fate must be; and he has been so convinced of the inevitability of that fate that he has been indifferent to, or incapable of, the task of making its causes convincing. Andrews has to be destroyed whatever the causes; for Dos Passos must express his hatred however clearly he recognizes its futility.

With the disappearance of the aesthete from the center of Dos Passos' work, will power also disappeared. Andrews had been able to take action against the system because Dos Passos still felt the necessity to make a protest against the system. But now that his sense of futility had begun to dominate his hatred of the system, Dos Passos could do no more than create in his work abstractions of the futility he felt. His people became completely what Andrews was, by comparison, only partially—lifeless puppets manufactured for the sole purpose of being destroyed. His power, on the other hand, to reproduce in dramatic terms the circumstances of their destruction increased. No longer could there be any doubt about the credibility of the horror he described. He was capable now of evoking an entire world and of breaking it down into a thousand compartments of evil. He seemed suddenly to be gifted with an instinctual understanding of every subtle and tenuous influence that went into the making of a character from birth to death. He began suddenly to write novels about the American scene that were unparalleled in the savage accuracy of their violence. But in the process he seemed to have lost touch with the souls of his people and to have turned against his own.

Of all the men and women whose lives are so painstakingly recorded in *Manhattan Transfer* only Jimmy Herf, the weak-spirited mama's boy, is able to take action to save himself from the destiny which Dos Passos has prepared for him. Herf is a pallid ghost, the last expiring remains of the Dos Passos aesthete. He is a John Andrews with his illusions, ambitions, and hatreds removed; and when we compare the action he is able to take with Andrews's passionate rebellion, we can see him as a remarkably clear symbol of the change that has occurred in Dos Passos since he created Andrews. For at the end of the novel, after he has spent years floating from one sterile attachment to another, finding neither meaning nor promise of meaning in his life, Herf aimlessly and hopelessly walks out: " 'Say will you give me a lift?' he asks the redhaired man at the wheel. 'How fur ye goin?'

'I dunno. . . . Pretty far.'" * There is now no suggestion of an ambitious dream cut short, no tragic hint of loss in the quiet slipping of papers to the floor. There is only the dead and empty silence of a life that has been doomed to silence from the start.

But this new futility in Dos Passos is peculiarly unfocused in *Manhattan Transfer*. We feel it everywhere in the countless fragmentary case histories of which the novel is composed, but it does not mount in us to a climax of distinct emotional meaning. What is missing, perhaps, is a counteremotion on which we can project it and with which we can contrast it. We take note of the many separate instances of casual defeat as if we were glimpsing a series of bloody traffic accidents flashed on a screen by a speeded-up movie camera. We see them and they startle us; but the pace is so fast that we have no time to react to them fully or to fit them into an intelligible pattern. Besides, they are so much of a kind that after a while we forget the ordinary uneventful condition of safe driving, which, after all, is really the thing which gives them their horror.

Yet the shadowy image of a brilliant purpose shows through in *Manhattan Transfer*. It can be seen in the complex panorama of many-sided life which gives the novel the look of having been photographed rather than written; it can be sensed in the quick, raw-nerved violence of the prose which, although it is not yet a "style," seems to have been compounded out of the same dirty concrete as that of the city it describes. It is present, particularly, in the truly remarkable energy and daring of Dos Passos' conception. But it is, as yet, blurred and undirected. The energy and the violence lead to nothing because they have no object. There is no frame in which they can be concentrated and no purpose which they can be used to serve.

For Dos Passos, at the time he wrote *Manhattan Transfer,*

* From *Manhattan Transfer* by John Dos Passos, published and copyright, 1925, John Dos Passos and Houghton Mifflin Company, Boston.

there seems to have been no cause great enough to impel him toward a supreme integration of his powers. He had all the vitality and insight he needed to produce a major work of art; and he certainly had all the idiosyncrasy and passion he needed. But he had to believe once more in the necessity of taking a stand, of affirming a principle, before he could display his powers in a way that would be more meaningful than a mere cataloguing of disgust.

It is generally believed that the bitterness engendered in Dos Passos by the injustice done to Sacco and Vanzetti provided him with the focus and purpose he needed to write his immense trilogy *U.S.A.* However true this may be, one can just as easily explain his achievement in that work in terms of natural creative evolution. As we have already seen, there were two distinct forces developing in Dos Passos' work up to the time of *U.S.A. One Man's Initiation* was primarily a record of his early disenchantment with the ideals of war and his emerging sympathy with the victims of war. *Three Soldiers* was an open protest against the evils of war at the same time that it indicated the futility of the individual's revolt against the system responsible for the making of wars. In *Manhattan Transfer* Dos Passos' social sympathies had broadened to such an extent that he was able to depict the futility he felt in terms of a dozen lives; but his disenchantment rendered those lives meaningless. They did not add up to a powerful denunciation of the system—because Dos Passos had still not found a way of centering his sympathies on an object more precise than that of the undifferentiated human mass. But as the result of the experiments he made in *Manhattan Transfer*, Dos Passos was able to return to the material he had begun to explore in that book and see in it implications which had previously escaped him. He sensed now that the real victims of the system were the working classes and that the real evils of the system stemmed from wealth and power. He was thus able to focus his sympathies upon a specific social group and set them against his hatred of another social group, just as in his earlier work he had focused his sympathies upon the individual aesthete and set them against his hatred of war. He was able to write now within the frame of two distinct and separate worlds, two nations, and to bring to his writing the full power of his protest (for he believed in the cause of the working classes as he had formerly believed in the cause of the aesthete) as well as the full power of his futility (for he knew, in spite of his belief in their cause, that the working classes under capitalism must always be defeated.)

The dramatic intensity of *U.S.A.* derives from the perfect balance of these conflicting forces within Dos Passos. There is, on one side, the gradual corruption and defeat of the characters whose lives are depicted in the straight-narrative sections. There is, on the other, the implicit indignation of the harsh, cutting style, which runs persistently counter to the drift of the narrative and comments upon it. Then, in the "Camera Eye" and "Biographies" sections the style picks up additional counterforce. The lyric meditations of the "Camera Eye" recast in poetic terms the negation expressed in the narrative and serve as a sort of moral center for the book. Through them the author periodically reenters the book and reminisces on moments out of the past when men fought, and were punished for fighting, for the cause of labor. During these moments, he seems to be saying, occurred the real tragedy of which the characters are now victims. The "Biographies" comment on the narrative in still other terms. This time the portraits are of real men who have been instrumental in shaping the system, either by rebelling against it or by trying to dominate it. Those who have rebelled are, for the most part, martyrs to the cause—Debs, Veblen, Big Bill Haywood, Randolph Bourne, Sacco and Vanzetti. Those who have sought power are, for the most part, tycoons like Hearst, Carnegie, and J. P. Morgan. But, however much their aims may have differed, the destiny of both groups is the same: the rebels are defeated by the system and the tycoons are corrupted by it.

This hypothesis of universal ruin, introduced lyrically through the "Camera Eye" and historically through the "Biographies," is given dramatic proof in the narrative proper. Here all the social classes of *U.S.A.* are represented. There are J. Ward Moorehouse, Charley Anderson, Richard Ellsworth Savage, Eveline Hutchins, Eleanor Stoddard, the prototypes of privilege; and Joe Williams, Ben Compton, Mary French, the prototypes of unprivilege. Each has a different story, but all come to the same end.

The career of J. Ward Moorehouse, the central symbol of Dos Passos' American-dream-become-nightmare, links the three volumes of the trilogy together into one continuous narrative. Born near the turn of the century, Moorehouse is the typical product of the new industrial Success Myth. Like Fitzgerald's Gatsby, he begins early in youth to build his life around the simple pioneer virtues of Horatio Alger: early rising, hard work, thrift, honesty, self-confidence—"By gum, I can do it." His story, beginning in *The 42nd Parallel,* is a perfect leitmotiv for the naïve new century; and it is presented, fittingly enough, against a background of jubilantly patriotic headlines, "Biographies" of the new wonder men of science (Edison, Burbank, Steinmetz) and the new political rebels (Bryan, LaFollette, Debs, Big Bill Haywood), and lyric reveries of the "Camera Eye" narrator, who is still a child. But out of this background the stories of other youths also emerge. Mac, the boy who never had a chance, begins as a seller of pornographic books, drifts aimlessly over the country looking for work, gets a girl in trouble, leaves her to become a revolutionary comrade in Mexico; Janey Williams goes to work, gets lost in the gray office routine that is to be her life; Eleanor Stoddard, thin, sterile, hater of everything and everyone, struggles to get ahead as an interior decorator. And finally we see that the sickness which has begun to destroy these people almost from the moment of their

birth has infected Moorehouse also. Now no longer the innocent
trusting child of the new century, he has become a perversion of
its ideals and a burlesque of his own earlier hopes. After divorcing
his socially prominent wife because she is a whore, he begins to
perfect his talent for exploiting the talents of others. Janey Williams as his secretary, Eleanor Stoddard as his platonic mistress,
and Eveline Hutchins as Eleanor's best friend all come under his
influence and are carried forward by him toward a success that
is to be their common grave.

As Moorehouse's ambition characterizes *The 42nd Parallel,* so
the aimless drifting of Joe Williams, Janey's brother, sets the
pattern for *1919,* the year that marked the beginning of the end
of the Great American Dream for Dos Passos. As Joe wanders
from continent to continent, getting drunk, whoring, fighting,
hating, the generation he symbolizes plunges headlong into the
violence of the Boom years. The "Biographies" now are studies
in horror and destruction (Jack Reed, dead of typhus in Moscow;
the ghost of Randolph Bourne "crying out in a shrill soundless
giggle/ *War is the health of the state";* Woodrow Wilson, idealist
and dreamer, broken on the cause of Peace; J. P. Morgan—"Wars
and panics on the stock exchange,/ machinegunfire and arson,/
bankruptcies, warloans,/ starvation, lice, cholera, and typhus:/
good growing weather for the House of Morgan"; ° Joe Hill executed). The "Camera Eye" narrator is no longer a child but a disillusioned ex-soldier "walking the streets rolling on your bed eyes
sting from peeling the speculative onion of doubt if somebody
in your head topdog? underdog? didn't (and on Union
Square) say liar to you." Richard Ellsworth Savage, one-time
idealist and poet, becomes a Moorehouse underling; Eveline
Hutchins and Eleanor Stoddard fight for their share of the Moore-

° From *U.S.A.* by John Dos Passos, published and copyright, 1930, 1932,
1933, 1934, 1935, 1936, 1937, John Dos Passos and Houghton Mifflin Company, Boston.

house patronage; "Daughter," the reforming young Texas girl whom Savage has ruined, is killed in a plane crash; Ben Compton, the hard-working radical, is jailed. The forming patterns of *The 42nd Parallel* have now hardened into a mold; the pace has become faster and more frantic; and the hunger for success has become a mad lust for pleasure and power.

The corruption, greed, and spiritual torment of the years after the war shroud *The Big Money* in an atmosphere of chilly death. For nearly all the characters the American Dream has found a monstrous apotheosis in material triumph. Charley Anderson makes money, more money than he ever imagined existed in the world, but finds no happiness. Margo Dowling, after a life of incredible sordidness culminating in high-class prostitution, rises to spectacular success in Hollywood; J. Ward Moorehouse, grown old and empty, finally perceives his failure, collapses, and dies; Savage, realizing too late that he has sold out his ideals, sinks into homosexual corruption. The "Biographies" too have become portraits of waste and misused success (Frederick Winslow Taylor, the efficiency expert, who "never saw the working of the American plan" and who died with his watch in his hand; Hearst, "a spent Caesar grown old with spending/ never man enough to cross the Rubicon"; Henry Ford, the mechanical wizard, living a frightened old age surrounded by "thousands of millionaire acres, protected by an army of servicemen, secretaries, secret agents, dicks under orders of an English exprizefighter . . . ," attempting to "put back the old bad road, so that everything might be the way it used to be, in the days of horses and buggies"; Veblen, dying unrecognized, deliberately obliterating the last traces of his own memory—"It is also my wish . . . that no tombstone, slab, epitaph, effigy, tablet, inscription or monument be set up to my memory or name in any place or at any time; that no obituary, memorial, portrait, or biography of me . . . be printed or published"). Finally, at the end, in Charley Anderson's crack-up, the destruction is made pathetically complete and the last ideals of a great age are brought to ruin. There is only "Vag" now, the hopeless, embittered wanderer, hitchhiking, like Jimmy Herf, to nowhere on the big concrete highway; while overhead an air liner passes filled with transcontinental passengers thinking "contracts, profits, vacation-trips, mighty continent between Atlantic and Pacific, power, wires humming dollars, cities jammed, hills empty, the indian-trail leading into the wagonroad, the macadamed pike, the concrete skyway, trains, planes: history the billiondollar speedup. . . . *All right we are two nations.*"

The U.S.A. which Dos Passos describes is thus more than simply a country or a way of life. It is a condition of death, a wasteland of futility and emptiness. In it, the best and the worst must be defeated; for defeat can be the only answer for the inhabitants of a world in which all goals are unattainable and the most powerful gods are corrupt. Yet, although the thing he describes is death, Dos Passos brings to his description a savage kind of power which saves it from becoming dead too. Through it all, he has consistently hated and condemned; and he has expressed his hatred with great strength and purpose. This has given meaning to the meaninglessness of his characters, value to their valuelessness. His style has been the perfect instrument of that meaning, protesting at every step in its development against the horror of the thing it was disclosing. His "Camera Eye" and biographical devices have extended that meaning to the outermost limits of suggestion and elevated it to the stature of pure insight into the dilemma of our time. What was shadowy and unfocused in *Manhattan Transfer* is now brilliantly clear; the protest has broken free of the mere mass and become concentrated in a specific social phenomenon; and as this has occurred, Dos Passos has also been freed, to create the world of powerful despair which is his best and truest world.

The three-volume history of the Spotswood family which Dos Passos began in 1938 with the publication of *Adventures of a Young Man* represents a new evaluation, in the light of subsequent history, of most of the issues that concerned him in *U.S.A.* The first volume covers the early days of the labor movement in this country and ends with the Spanish Civil War. The second volume, *Number One*, explores the career of a Southern demagogue and a would-be dictator some time between the Wall Street crash and the inauguration of Franklin D. Roosevelt. The third volume, *The Grand Design*, mainly concerns the years of the Depression and New Deal and ends with the outbreak of World War II. In reexamining his old concerns, Dos Passos has disengaged them from the great mass of *U.S.A.* and presented each of them separately. Thus, *Adventures of a Young Man* has to do merely with the labor movement; *Number One*, with the possibility of a government of the common man; *The Grand Design*, with the struggle for survival of the democratic ideal in a bureaucracy. And in each of them, significantly enough, the story is one of failure and corruption, a far more final kind of failure and corruption than the kind depicted in *U.S.A.* For now it is not merely that the characters come to nothing but that, by coming to nothing, they have at last convinced Dos Passos that his hopes for a better world based on his old social principles must come to nothing too.

The Spotswood men, when we first encounter them in *Adventures of a Young Man*, are all high-principled and honest, as Dos Passos' men almost always are in the beginning. Herbert, the father, is a devout pacifist lately fired from a university teaching job because of his convictions. Glenn, his younger son, is fearless, stubborn, and incorruptible, and Tyler, his older son, is much the same, although he is considerably less disciplined than Glenn. Throughout the early part of the novel Glenn devotes himself religiously to the cause of labor. He organizes strikes in the face of overwhelming opposition from mine owners; he endures a severe beating at the hands of a gang of reactionary workers; he makes speeches at union meetings all over the country and even lives for a time under an assumed name so that he can better serve the cause. As a result of his activities and the suffering he has undergone, he becomes a Party hero and begins to take on duties of national importance to the labor movement. But because of his unwillingness to adhere strictly to the principles of Communism he is later expelled from the Party. In Spain, where he has gone to fight for the Loyalists, Glenn learns that what he thought was a war against fascist tyranny is actually a war to save the world for Communism. His irregular political background renders him suspect to the zealous Communists in his group; and before long he is thrown into prison on the charge of being a spy. When, a short time later, he is freed because of a sudden enemy attack and sent out to die on an utterly futile mission, the making of his martyrdom is complete and with it Dos Passos' disillusionment with the cause of the working class under Communism.

The evil which Glenn discovers behind the ideals of a revolutionary working class is balanced, in *Number One*, by the evil which Tyler discovers behind the ideals of a government of the common man. Tyler is initially drawn to a backwoods presidential candidate, who calls himself Number One, because he mistakes him for those ideals. But after several years of service as Number One's political flunky and personal secretary, during which he endures every imaginable kind of moral humiliation, Tyler begins to see the truth. He realizes that Number One represents a perversion of democratic values and that his finest ambitions for social improvement are really masks to hide an immense urge for personal power. By then, however, it is too late for Tyler to break free. During the course of his service, he has become involved in some questionable business dealings with Number One;

and when a Federal Grand Jury opens an investigation, he finds that he has been deserted by his employer and left to face trial alone. His failure of nerve at the end of the novel is a perfect corollary of Dos Passos' disillusionment with the idea of a people's government and a direct result of his earlier disillusionment with Communism.

We learn in *The Grand Design* that Tyler's experience has made him an habitual drunkard and a complete mental and physical wreck. But the bulk of the novel is devoted to the career of his father Herbert, who has risen to a position of influence as a Washington news commentator, and to the careers of various important government people with whom he comes into contact. Of these, two in particular, Paul Graves and Millard Carroll, bear the main burden of Dos Passos' message. Graves is an agricultural expert and a New Deal zealot. In the beginning he makes an heroic effort to carry out the government's agricultural reforms in the field. He sees, as does Carroll, the enormous possibilities for social betterment in the New Deal program. But both men are thwarted in their aims by political favoritism and the bureaucratic machinery of the war effort. By the end of the novel Carroll has resigned from the government a defeated man; and Graves is bitterly considering a commission in the Navy. Herbert Spotswood, meanwhile, has been publicly humiliated by the audience at a Communist rally to which he has gone to give a talk on the background of the war in Europe. He learns, as did his son Glenn, that the war, as far as the Communists are concerned, is a war for Soviet imperialism being fought under the guise of a war against fascist imperialism.

This disillusionment with the idea of social and political reform which the Spotswood books reflect has left its mark on their quality as novels. With the last of Dos Passos' hopes destroyed, there is nothing left standing between him and the blank futility of his world. He can no longer protest with the great power and conviction of *U.S.A.*, for his protest depended on the existence of those hopes. The best he can do is expose with a kind of listless irritation the evils he is now able to see but helpless to attack.

The change in Dos Passos can perhaps best be understood if we recall his state of mind at the time he wrote *Manhattan Transfer*. Then, as now, he had been disillusioned with an old ideal, the ideal of individual revolt against the system. Because of this, he was unable to focus his hatred of the system upon any specific social cause. His people were lifeless puppets, for he no longer believed in their power to help themselves. But the milieu which he created for them, that crowded, nightmarish New York world, was not lifeless: it was charged with all the violence of his hatred; and that violence gave the book what quality it had. We have already seen what a superb work of art Dos Passos was able to produce when he finally focused his hatred upon the conflict between the two worlds of *U.S.A.* There his hatred became an instrument of protest that played continually on the negation of his characters and charged them with meaning. But in the Spotswood novels Dos Passos has lost not merely his belief in the power of his characters to help themselves but his hatred of the system which has rendered them powerless. As a result not only are his characters puppets but the milieu in which he places them is never brought to life.

Adventures of a Young Man is little more than a case history of one man's experiences in the labor movement. Its style is flat and toneless; its material is dull political shoptalk interspersed with stereotyped events in the development of Glenn's career as an organizer. *Number One* deals with political corruption and the ruin of Tyler; but neither the corruption nor the ruin is convincingly dramatized. The whole novel is pervaded with the dead futility of Tyler's defeat and is finally canceled out by it. *The Grand Design* is perhaps the most successful novel of the three;

but its best effects are journalistic, and it has the same flatness of tone that debilitated the others.

Dos Passos' career has been a long process of running through and destroying the ideals which have seemed to him worthy of belief. Now, at the end, he has run through them all and been left with nothing. In *U.S.A.* he achieved a perfect blend of protest and negation which gave the book and its characters their power and value. Now it is clear that protest and negation constitute a formula without which he can barely function as a writer. Like Hemingway's code of loss and Fitzgerald's vision of Paradise, that formula is Dos Passos' means of ordering and making presentable in art the great social issues of his time, of which he is, at his best, more sensitively aware than any other writer of his generation.

Part II

THE NEW WRITERS OF THE FORTIES

CHAPTER VI

The Search for Values

THE QUALITY AND INTENSITY of a literary work will depend, to a very large extent, upon the success with which the writer can find and communicate his private truth in the public truth of his age. If we take the subject of a work to be the writer himself and his subject matter to be the fund of values, attitudes, customs, and beliefs which he shares with his audience and in terms of which he discovers what he has to say—his private truth—then it becomes clear that the events of the last fifty years, particularly the breakdown by science of public truth into countless isolated individual truths, have dangerously narrowed the area of subject matter available to writers and, consequently, crippled their means of discovering themselves and their age.

In their attempts to compensate for this, modern writers have been forced generally into one of two avenues of escape. Either they have tried to exploit their isolation from the life of their time and to buttress their paralysis before the failure of public truth with a private symbolism based on a concern for themselves alone, or they have turned away from the reality of the present and sought to find, in the worship of old gods or a simple primitivism, some substitute for all that they have lost. A third course not involving escape depends for its success on the marriage of talent and a propitious moment of history. In the modern age it has been possible for a short time under peculiarly fortunate circumstances for writers to discover dramatic material in the process and residue of the value breakdown itself; and it is this possibility which a few of them have until recently exploited admirably.

Most of the writers who came to maturity in the Twenties found relief in all three courses at various stages of their careers. Stein and Joyce developed a private language and to a large extent avoided the problem of direct communication. Their preoccupation with pure technique was a substitute for the community of values to which their writings might otherwise have referred. The later Joyce, however, went back to classical literature—as the later Eliot went back to ancient myth and finally to religious orthodoxy—in his search for a structure that would give his symbols meaningful reference outside themselves. The cult of the primitive obsessed Hemingway, Fitzgerald, and Dos Passos from time to time—as it did Lawrence, Conrad, and Huxley as well as Eliot and Stein—but it is as followers of the third course that they are important here.

All three of these writers—Hemingway, Dos Passos, and Fitzgerald—were able to turn the failure of traditional values into a value of art and to exploit a subject matter which was discoverable for the first time in the midst of that failure. Hemingway's code—that cloak of chivalric morality and nerve with which his characters covered their inner nakedness—is a concrete, dramatic expression of the distrust of all values outside those which the individual invents for his own survival. In his first novels and stories, it served him as a frame of artistic comprehension. Violence set against the code of loss was his formula, his instrument for discovering the truth of his age. Within that formula, he was able to function as the superb writer he is. But the moment he tried to transcend it, to affirm rather than deny, he gave way to those curious excesses which made partial failures of his last two novels. His major themes, furthermore, derive much of their power from their great capacity to shock: the importance of sex, violence, war, and death in his work is indistinguishable from their importance in an age just emerging from the dogmatic position of refusing to recognize their existence. In Dos Passos an almost identical pattern can be traced. The order of his art is formed directly out of the chaos of the society which it depicts, and its success, when it does succeed, is founded on the ironic spectacle of the individual going down under the shocking injustices of his time. Fitzgerald, the barometer of his generation's extremes, cannot be separated in either his life or his work from the time which formed him—its magic glamour, its poverty of faith, and, at the end, its sickness and ruin. In his vision of Paradise he too found a correlative of art. It was a dramatic symbol for a belief which was being destroyed—the belief, that is, in the possibility of happiness through material success—and it was effective not only as Fitzgerald's means of entry into the life of his time but as the means by which his time discovered him. What is important about Fitzgerald's Paradise is that both he and his generation sought it and that the failure to find it led to an identical disintegration in both. There was also on Fitzgerald's side, as on Hemingway's, the freshness and shock value of his material. When one considers how many of his early books were interesting almost solely as records of the rebellion of the young against the old and of the postwar moral decline, one realizes that he could not have been the writer he was in any other time.

But in the years since Hemingway, Dos Passos, and Fitzgerald began to write, the forces that gave impetus to their development —particularly the forces of disillusionment and denial released by the broken promises of the first war—have declined. The young novelists of the present generation are consequently deprived of that impetus at the same time that their own age and experience offer them nothing comparable. They have come through a war even more profoundly disturbing than the first; but the illusions and causes of war, having once been lost, cannot be relost. Their world, ironically enough, is almost the same world their predecessors discovered; but the fundamental discoveries of modern life can be made but once. America is more than ever a machine-dominated, gadget-minded country. There are more Babbitts now than when Sinclair Lewis invented the term and the expatriates shouted it in their battle cry for freedom, art, and exile. But who cares today to take up that cry, to denounce again with the same fury, or to escape forever into artistic exile?

One aspect of the problem is reflected in the technical differences between the writings of the two wars. Where Hemingway, Dos Passos, and E. E. Cummings (in *The Enormous Room*) were from the beginning innovators of new methods—even of a whole new literary language—with which to present the new experience of war, the new war novelists seem, for the most part, incapable of technical discoveries and resigned to working within the tradition handed down to them from the Twenties. One explanation is that the experience of war is no longer new and, consequently, does not require a new method of presentation. Another is that the Lost Generation writers were engaged in a revolution designed to purge language of the old restraints of the previous century and to fit it to the demands of a younger, more realistic time. Idiosyncrasy and defiance were part of their work because the things that had happened to them had happened to no generation before them, and because they were aware of their uniqueness and determined to communicate it to the world.

Today that revolution is over. The innovations of Hemingway, as he himself remarked, were "a certain clarification of the language" and are now "in the public domain." The unique has become the ordinary; young writers using the effects of their predecessors are often not even aware that those effects did not belong to our literature until years after many of them were born. The assimilation into the public domain has, in fact, been so complete that what we have now seems a technical conservatism. Certainly the styles of Vance Bourjaily, Norman Mailer, John Horne Burns, Irwin Shaw, Robert Lowry, Alfred Hayes, Merle

Miller, Gore Vidal, Truman Capote, Paul Bowles, and Frederick Buechner—while they contain overtones of practically everyone from Dos Passos and Hemingway to James T. Farrell and Henry James—show little evidence of new developments and, with the exception of Capote's, Burns's, and Buechner's, do little to flavor the material they present.

But there has been this change: the single perspective and narrow scope of the World War I novels have given way to huge comprehensiveness in which whole armies and social masses are encompassed. From the individual, neoromantic hero we have progressed to the multiple-hero or, more correctly, to the subordination of all heroes to the group. Mailer carries an entire army division—from general down to private—through a complex military engagement and then goes back to the beginnings of his characters and sketches them against the background of peace. Burns and Shaw take even more characters through action on three or four continents and months of closely packed experience; and all three manage to pay careful attention to detail and to give the actual texture of the background or event described.

This would be achievement indeed if it did not come so often at the expense of insight, form, and power. Taken as a group or singly, the novels of this war simply do not have the impact that those of the first war had—nor, for that matter, do the novels that have been written so far about the aftermath. They are incomparably better written, to be sure. Almost any one of them will show fewer lapses and roughnesses than can be found in the best of the earlier group—*A Farewell to Arms, Three Soldiers, The Enormous Room*. But it is as if they had been written too easily and their authors had had too painless an apprenticeship. Their finish is more often that of a machine-made, prefabricated product than of a finely wrought piece of craftsmanship, the sort that can be obtained if more problems are avoided than are met and overcome.

But it is in the material itself with which their novels must be concerned that the new writers face their greatest difficulty. Although they have arrived at the end of the tradition of loss, negation, and revolt, and have known none of its benefits, they have inherited the conditions out of which that tradition emerged. They are finding that modern life is still basically purposeless, that the typical condition of modern man is still doubt, confusion, and fear. But because they have never known life otherwise and were not exposed, as their predecessors were, to the process by which it became as it now is, they can write of it from neither the perspective of protest nor that of disillusionment and loss. They are faced with the same material from which Hemingway and Fitzgerald drew their artistic impetus, but they are denied the dramatic values which those men found in it. Loss is no longer the spiritual climate of the age, but the chaos of loss is still its typical material.

To compensate for the lack of that climate and the symbols which made it demonstrable in art as well as for the failure of a new climate and new symbols to appear, these writers have up to now shown signs of developing in at least four directions, all of them overlapping and interwoven. If, first of all, they have insight into values that seem worthy of affirmation and point the way out of the chaos of loss, they can superimpose them upon the old material which is still available. They can, in other words, assert the need for belief even though it is upon a background in which belief is impossible and in which the symbols are lacking for a genuine affirmation in dramatic terms. Second, they can escape into journalism, exploit facts and events for their own sake, and thus conceal for the moment their lack of an attitude toward their material. Third, they can seek new subject matter in what little material remains which has not been fully exploited in the past and which, therefore, still has emotive power. They have so far made two important discoveries in this area—homosexuality and racial conflict. Fourth, they can conceal their failure to find something significant to say by elaborating their manner of saying. Pure technique—technique, that is, which has been detached from its proper base in subject matter—has become for some of them not a means of expressing new material or insights but of revitalizing old and worn-out material and insights; and it has helped to give their writing a veneer of idiosyncrasy and life. Nearly all the novels the new writers have produced show one or more of these tendencies; but none, unfortunately, has offered more than temporary relief from the dilemma which made it necessary.

The false note of courage in literature, like the uneasy grin on the face of a boy lost at midnight, is a compensation for the lack of a suitable attitude toward feelings of confusion and fear. It most often takes the form, in the new novels, of an insipid reminder made by the author to his characters that all will at last be well, that even as they are engaged in futile and mechanical love-making, compulsive drinking, and considerations of suicide, he has great plans for them and they should not despair. The empty young man without talent will nonetheless write his novel and be very famous; the Jew beset on every side by prejudice will none-theless escape and find peace and understanding among his own people; the career girl with the uncontrollable passion for taking strange young men into her bed will nonetheless make the happiest of marriages. By the end of the novel only the suicide who did not wait to consult the author will miss the delights that are in store for him.

The defect of such writing is that the solutions or conclusions presented are incompatible with the presented material: the young men act and speak in a milieu of futility and grow daily more morose, the young women are motivated by a lust which can arise only from a sense of the utter hopelessness of all higher action. Yet even as the narrative sets the scene for suicide, nervous collapse, and the triumph of that lust, the author is preparing a destiny which is affirmative and, therefore, contrary to the facts as they appear.

One explanation is that the author is trying to squeeze fresh meaning out of old material. If he remains true to his insight, he cannot avoid describing the situations of his time as they predominantly are, that is, as meaningless, valueless, and futile. His world is crowded with young men and women who do not know what they are or were meant to be and who express, or escape, their confusion in incessant drinking and automatic sex. But at the same time that he perceives this world and is bound by his perception to portray it as it is, the author is also aware of the need to discover some hope and value for it, some assurance that all is not as bad as it seems. His attempt to dramatize this need, however, usually requires him to invent some other outcome for his characters than their situations make logically possible, and he is at once committed to forcing them against their natures in the direction he wishes them to go. The result, of course, is that instead of dramatizing the need, making it grow organically out of the substance of the novel, he has succeeded merely in converting it to an empty optimism which has about the same relation to the plight of his characters as a patriotic speech to a demoralized army.

The young writer is faced, from the moment he begins his first novel, with the unavoidable fact that the only hope for a successful dramatic effect lies today in the depiction of the grotesque and abnormal; for it is there and there only that the tragic situation of modern life exists. The mediocre and the undaring, the businessman who goes unswervingly to business, the family man who lives out his days in domestic mediocrity, are unpresentable in dramatic terms. Their adjustment to life is made at the expense of no conflict. Their happiness has no consequences. The most that can be said for them is that they have managed to arrive at a state of life in which nothing of importance is ever likely to happen. If the writer sets out to depict them, he finds himself poverty-stricken in events and symbols. They may represent a *condition* of positive value, of hope and virtue, but they take no *action* in the name of virtue, and it is upon action that literary art depends.

Suppose, however, that the businessman can be made to throw up his business or the family man to desert his family, crises so admirably described in the books (and the life) of Sherwood Anderson. At once the situation becomes dramatic and suited to the writer's purpose. But it has ceased to be the typical situation. The typical has been sacrificed to the more desirable intrusion of the spectacular, the chance deviation from the dull, and with it are sacrificed the affirmative values which existed only in the typical or inactive state and which cannot exist, as long as the mass of society is what it is, outside that state. If at some future time it should become necessary for people to exert a little daring to become good citizens or to fight as hard to achieve virtue as they do now to avoid thinking about it, our writers might be able to produce a literature of goodness equal in quality to a literature of evil. But as long as goodness is synonymous with conventionality and conventionality with inaction, they never will.

A careful distinction should at once be made, however, between the writers who are sincere and the writers who are palpably fake, between those who are trying to find an honest basis in experience for the values they wish to affirm and those who are willing at every moment to serve up synthetic values drawn from synthetic experience. The second- and third-rate writers of any time will endeavor to write not as they must but as their public wishes them to write. In a time like the present, they will attempt to allay the prevailing confusion and fear by offering clichés in place of truth, a prefabricated Heaven for every natural Hell. They will gain entrance into the minds of the uncritical by appealing to their little wishful dreams and the myths which they currently hold sacred.

The great danger of such writers is the danger of any charlatan in any profession; and it is proportionate to the extent to which their work is not literature but a willful misrepresentation of the facts. If we think of literature as the meaningful arrangement of truth, then we can have no patience with an attempt made under the masquerade of literature to falsify or distort the truth. If we think of the effect of literature as a heightening of awareness, then we cannot accept an effect which involves a decrease of awareness and a substitution of baseless fantasy for thought. The picture of American life which some of these writers give in their novels has no more relation to American life than the fairy-tale America manufactured in Hollywood. It is founded not on things as they are but on things as the writers and their readers wish them to be; and things as they are wished to be are almost never in this country either attainable or worthy of being attained.

It is true that today people everywhere are asking to be reassured and comforted. It is also true that in the last several years no work of fiction of genuine quality has been able to do either. That fact may indicate not only that a successful affirmative writing cannot be produced without affirmative experience but that the values which most people wish to see affirmed are really false and unworthy. It seems to me that the best literature in America will continue to be negative so long as the country's values are such that no writer of honesty or insight can possibly take them seriously.

Reading through some of the new novels is rather like going through a well-furnished house in which every chair, table, and picture has been arranged with the skill of a professional decorator but which manages, nevertheless, to give an effect of utter lifelessness and sterility. Their perfection of style seems to have been achieved, in far too many cases, at the expense of subtlety and symbolic richness. The very ease with which they are executed seems to indicate that the basic problems of art have been avoided rather than solved and that genuine insight has found too convenient a substitute in mere facility. Many of them are not novels at all but pseudo novels, works of skilled journalism contrived to pass as fiction but lacking the one ingredient which all good fiction must possess—the power to make meaningful and orderly the chaotic processes of life.

Journalism is a helpful crutch for a writer of slight or immature talent in a time of doubt and confusion. Through journalism he is able to present material without taking an attitude toward it or judging its significance. As long as he concentrates on facts, the way things *seem*, and on events, the things that happen, he is relieved of the task of determining what things *are* and what happenings *mean*. He is, of course, desperately dependent on the strength of his facts and events to stand by themselves without support from him, and his entire success will depend on the power they have of evoking a strong emotion in the reader. If for one moment the events chosen cease to be important or the reader, having been exposed to too many events, ceases to react to them, then the writer is thrown into a dilemma from which only greater talent than he possesses can possibly free him.

There is reason to believe that that moment is now at hand. For years writers have exploited the devices of journalism to keep alive in a period during which events have occurred so rapidly that all but their surface implications have been lost and they themselves have been in great doubt as to what to say and how to say it. But the ironic dilemma of journalism has at last begun to claim them: just as they have been unable to judge the significance of events, so events are losing their significance to the public. The sex incident, the brutality of war, the grotesque contents of the insane mind are ceasing to be satisfactory substitutes for artistic talent and insight.

It might be said that journalism was the special province of the writers of the Twenties. It was usable to them because the events they exploited were still sensational and could still be counted on to arouse in the reader the kind of response which, if he did not discriminate too finely, could be taken for the sort traditionally aroused by the great literature of the past. The intrusion of sex into a novel, if it was intruded skillfully enough, could be made to seem as important as, if not identical with, a portrayal of complete love. Sex was still a function startling enough in itself to need no support beyond itself. The depiction of the violence of war was effective so long as violence and war were new and the emotion aroused by them could still obscure the writer's failure to show in precisely what way they were meaningful or dramatic within the terms of his work. Sensationalism thus became in much of the writing of the Twenties a substitute for insight; journalism was able to appropriate some of the effects of literary art; and the mere event was made to stand for the meaningful interpretation of event.

But as literature has evolved beyond sensationalism to a point where its most standard materials are no longer shocking by themselves, it has become clear that journalism is a decadent form and that the new writers have already carried it beyond the limits of exhaustion. That they have not been motivated by any intent to compromise is obvious when one realizes that they have had no other means of presenting the chaotic experience of recent years and no such convenient attitude toward that experience as their predecessors had toward theirs. If the age of transition and loss is past, its passing has shown how dependent upon the sensational values of transition and loss its writers were; and it has left the new writers without those values at a time when they have been unable to find new ones.

One of the last successful uses of journalism can be found in some of the novels that have come out of the second war; and it is a reinforcement of the argument to observe that now that the events of the war have begun to fade in memory the dramatic value of most of these novels has faded with them. But at the time of their appearance such novels as *The Naked and the Dead* and *The Young Lions* were greatly enhanced by the sheer power of the events they described and almost entirely because those events were at once too immediate in time to be overly familiar and too involved in the destinies of all of us to be unexciting. The achievement of Mailer and Shaw, as of most of the other war novelists, consisted mainly of an exceedingly workmanlike job of recording in minute detail the progression of event after event, violence after violence, in a war situation which was by itself perfectly suited to their purposes. Wars have a beginning, a middle, and an end and are, therefore, vastly more adaptable to fiction than the normal human situation which, lacking innate form, must be artificially arranged. Events occur in wars with such intensity that they need not signify or connote. Characters may react to them in any way they will. They may collapse inwardly, be destroyed outwardly, or they may feel nothing. In any case, the events and the reactions do not need to be meaningfully related to one another. The events are significant enough simply because they have happened. The reactions can take care of themselves because they will be inconsequential next to the impact of the events.

A young writer who has produced one war novel has thus actually revealed relatively little about his true or potential stature as a writer. The war relieves him of the necessity to invent a dramatic situation and to discover a precise motivation for the feelings and actions of his characters. He is able merely to present the war, and his presentation will be effective if it is true to the facts and for as long as the facts retain their freshness. To prove himself as a writer he must, therefore, write a second novel outside the frame of the war and take up characters and situations that will demand some imaginative support from him. That many of the novelists of both wars have failed to fulfill the promise of their early war writing is an indication of the extent to which their best achievements have depended on the ready-made dramatic structure which only war provides.

It is in some of the second novels which the new writers have produced that the weaknesses of journalism show through most clearly. Merle Miller's *That Winter,* for example, represents an attempt to vitalize a thin substance through the devices of journalism, and it is a failure to the extent that those devices are no longer capable of arousing the intended emotion or of replacing invention and insight. Sex in *That Winter* is the nearest any of the characters come to dramatic action, but it shows itself to be mere shadow action as soon as one perceives that it is a disguise to cover the lack of all real motivation within them. When Miller can think of nothing else for his people to do, he puts them to bed together or he gets them drunk or he has them commit suicide. At any other time, these incidents might have passed for drama; but they have been so thoroughly exploited and we have become so thoroughly weary of them that they seem merely pointless and dull.

The fault of such books is that as soon as these incidents cease to be exciting or pseudodramatic and the facts they report cease to be topical the basic failure of the writer to find something important to say and to say it significantly begins to show through. Deprived of sex, drinking, and suicide, *That Winter* is deprived not only of the elements which might have allowed it to pass as a novel but of the elements which might have made it good journalism. A novel expands symbolically the world it presents; good journalism makes good copy of the world it presents. *That Winter* does neither: its characters and situations have not been expanded beyond themselves and they have not been made interesting enough for even cursory mention in tomorrow's headlines.

Homosexuality and racial conflict seem to be the only discoveries which the new writers have been able to make so far in the area of unexploited subject matter; and they are promising discoveries to the extent that they have served to replace the old subjects as sources of potential melodrama. If the vein of public response to novels of ordinary lust and violence has about run dry, it has been possible for the novels of homosexuality and racial conflict to set it coursing again, this time on a slightly different level and through different channels.

Both subjects are excellently suited to a time when writers have lost almost all contact with their audiences and been unable to find dramatic material in the normal situations of life. Homosexuality, like ordinary sex in the Twenties, carries with it such vast potentialities for shock, strikes so deeply into the obscure hatreds and secret yearnings of the human mind, that the writer is assured that at least on that level he will be able to reach an audience. Besides, his subject is likely to be dramatic in itself. The homosexual, like the Negro and the Jew to a lesser degree, is a man in conflict with his environment, a tragic figure fighting for life against overwhelming odds. As an outcast, he affords the writer a perspective from which the evils of society can be observed and condemned. He is thus an ideal subject, one that is practically guaranteed not only to reach an audience but to attain the widest possible significance as a symbol.

Unfortunately, most of the novels of homosexuality have not been successful as novels. Too many of them come through simply as social tracts, and their authors have been too content to let the sensational values of their material replace the literary values which, under other circumstances, they might have struggled to achieve. Gore Vidal's *The City and the Pillar,* for example, was purely a social document that was read because it had all the qualities of lurid journalism and not because it showed the craft and insight of an artist. Ward Thomas's *Stranger in the Land,* a very similar book, had almost nothing to recommend it except the homosexuality with which it dealt. Yet up until recently it too was being read, and Thomas may well achieve a stature in the popular mind that will be wholly incommensurate with his talents as he has so far demonstrated them.

The main defect of both these novels, as of most of the others of their kind, is that their characters quickly recede into types rather than expand into symbols. The young homosexual is always and only the homosexual: the other qualities which he might be expected to have and which might have made him human have been sacrificed to the one quality which the author wishes him to represent. In the case of Vidal's Jim Willard in *The City and the Pillar* we know only one real fact about him, and he is presented as having only one real motive—the desire to renew an adolescent homosexual love affair. He is forced into such an infernal consistency that from the first chapter of his story to the last we are aware, in every detail of the narrative, of the exact outcome. Nothing can possibly change that outcome, for Willard is a static figure, a lifeless puppet manipulated by Vidal only at such times and in such ways as will best emphasize the product he has been created to sell.

A strong preoccupation with homosexuality as a literary theme runs through nearly all the novels the young writers have produced, and it has become one of their most distinguishing characteristics as well as the most curious. When it is not part of the central theme of their books—as it is in *The City and the Pillar, Stranger in the Land, A Long Day's Dying,* and *Other Voices, Other Rooms*—a novel of pure homosexual fantasy—it appears as a subsidiary theme. *The End of My Life* contains one character who is destroyed by homosexual tendencies. A distinct but submerged homosexual tension exists between Lieutenant Hearn and General Cummings in *The Naked and the Dead;* and both of John Horne Burns's novels, *The Gallery* and *Lucifer with a Book,* are often obsessively concerned with homosexual types and situations. When one considers that the authors of these books make up almost the entire younger literary group, such a preoccupation becomes interesting indeed.

One explanation is, as I have already shown, that the homosexual is one of the last remaining tragic types. His dilemma, like that of the Negro and the Jew, provides a conflict which is easily presentable in fiction and which can be made to symbolize the larger conflicts of modern man. But this hardly seems adequate to explain the recurrence of the theme in the novels of Gore Vidal, the intense narcissism and sexual symbolism in all of Truman Capote's work, or the coy posturing and giggliness just behind so much of what John Horne Burns writes. Their preoccupation with the theme is such that it seems to preclude their coming to grips with whole areas of normal emotion. Vidal has not yet created a single convincing female character. His women are either mother types, sister types, or men dressed up as women. Capote's Idabel is more grotesquely masculine than she is feminine. Burns's women are often feminine enough, but they are usually simply lust objects for men, and they are seldom introduced at all unless they are intended to fulfill some sexual function.

The importance of homosexuality in the development of a writer is always difficult to determine. At its best it is probably no more crippling than a strong taste for women or dry martinis. It may even be beneficial in so far as it frees the writer from the dangers of premature domesticity and enables him to go on having fresh emotional experience long after his more normal contemporaries have settled into a comfortable emotional fog. But the homosexual experience is of one special kind, it can develop in only one direction, and it can never take the place of the whole range of human experience which the writer must know intimately if he is to be great. Sooner or later it forces him away from the center to the outer edges of the common life of his society where he is almost sure to become a mere grotesque, a parasite, or a clown. The homosexual talent is nearly always a precocious talent, but it must necessarily be a narrow one, subject to all the ills of chronic excitation and threatened always with an end too often bitter and tragic.

Since the end of the war there has been scarcely a serious novel produced which has not at least touched on the dilemma of the Negro or the Jew in modern society, whether in the fascist circumstances of war or the mistrustful atmosphere of dubious peace. Yet of all the novels that have attempted to deal with the problem of race not one has been completely successful as dramatic literature nor fully escaped the weaknesses which have inhered in the novel of homosexuality.

Like all special social problems, the Negro and the Jew will be plausible in fiction only so long as they are conceived and portrayed within the limits of their specialness. They may have great capacity to symbolize the entire human dilemma, but they cannot be effective if, in terms of action, they are made to usurp or replace that dilemma. Within a novel their problem must occupy the subsidiary position it occupies in life, and it must not be detached from the other problems with which the novelist must be concerned if he wishes to give a balanced interpretation of life. This is another way of saying that the Negro or the Jew, like the homosexual, is usable to the novelist in so far as he is allowed to preserve his humanity: his uniqueness as an individual must not be sacrificed to his universality as a type.

Yet the Jewish character in three of the new novels of the war and the aftermath—*The Naked and the Dead, The Young Lions,* and *That Winter*—is distinguished by his Jewishness only; and in the last two novels, that one quality so distorts the authors' perspective that it forces the character to act in a way that is inconsistent with reality and with human nature.

Snaw in *The Young Lions* was apparently able to see Noah Ackerman as simply a symbol of Jewish fortitude and loyalty. He was required, therefore, to endow him with only those virtues and to place him in only such situations as would demonstrate them effectively. But after surviving the first of his ordeals—a series of brutal beatings given him by the most powerful members of his army unit—Ackerman emerges as a creature of such incredible fortitude that one can no longer believe him possible. He has, in fact, ceased to exist as human in the midst of that ordeal and become the godlike champion of his race. And when, toward the end of the book, he is made to act at considerable personal risk out of great loyalty to a friend, and the friendship, as it has been portrayed, does not warrant such action, one is finally convinced that Shaw's Ackerman, like Vidal's Jim Willard, is simply a puppet figure designed to function solely as an allegorical device.

Lew in *That Winter* is seen entirely in terms of his conflict with the forces of racial prejudice. He is rushed on the stage only when those forces are in play, and he is rushed off into the wings the moment the scene shifts. His sole purpose is to belabor the point that racial discrimination is a bad thing, a point Miller might have made more convincingly if he had written an essay about it. But the real trouble with Lew is that in making his point he makes no other. The man he might possibly be is perpetually obscured by the type he is. His quarrel with his fiancée, his attempt to change his name, his final decision to face his problem and return to his father's business are all stereotypes in the history of the cardboard Jew. And as he struggles through them, as an actor struggles through a part he hates, it is as if he were growing increasingly bored with his own triteness.

It is probable that racial conflict and homosexuality will be imperfectly presented in fiction so long as writers go on attempting, through journalistic rather than symbolic means, to make them something more than they are. The truth is that at the moment and on the purely factual level they remain simply minor issues. They cannot, therefore, be other than minor subjects for a kind of writing which operates only on that level; and they will cease to be usable altogether as soon as the public tires of them or ceases to find them shocking. The new writers have not yet discovered subjects which are as central to the meaning of this age as despair and the sense of loss were to the Twenties. Until they do, it cannot be said that they have really discovered this age at all.

By technique we ordinarily mean the writer's instrument for discovering his subject matter. The best technique will be the one which discovers a given subject matter the most thoroughly, which illuminates and makes meaningful the greatest area of raw material through which the writer moves in his search for meaning. Raw material cannot be subject matter until it is illuminated by technique, just as crude ore is not gold until it is illuminated by the miner's lamp. But it is possible for writers gifted with an acute sense of language to exploit the devices of technique without illumination or discovery and to make technique serve as a compensation for the lack of subject matter at a time when they are in doubt as to what their true subject matter is.

At least three of the new writers—Truman Capote, John Horne Burns, and Frederick Buechner—have elaborated their techniques to a degree that is in excess of the demands of their raw material. It is as if, in their confusion before the exact implications of that material, they had tried to create a false reality of words alone that would give it an appearance of life and truth which it did not by itself possess. They have dealt with a thin substance and managed to make it rich by perfecting their manner of presenting it; and in the process they have made the obvious obscure and the familiar overly strange.

The real world behind the nightmare which Capote gives us has been refined almost completely out of existence. Where in suc-

cessful ironic fiction—such as Kafka's—and in successful caricature—such as Abner Dean's—the real qualities of the thing
commented upon are constantly heightened and enriched by the
outlandish manner in which the artist presents them, in Capote
the outlandish and grotesque stand alone. They do not refer back
to models in the reality we know, nor does their validity depend
upon an innate satiric or ironic comment. Joel, the central figure
in *Other Voices, Other Rooms,* is neither a boy nor a caricature
of a boy. He is a creation entirely of Capote's talent for the
grotesque, and is what he is entirely because Capote invented him
in a burst of pure technique and not because Capote perceived
his original in life and evolved the technique that would best
express him. Cousin Randolph, Joel's father, Idabel, and Miss
Wisteria are similarly creatures who have meaning only within the
context which Capote invented for them. They die the moment the
eye is lifted from the page. They haunt some secret horror chamber
of Capote's mind where their distortion is sufficient unto itself
but not to us.

In John Horne Burns's second novel, *Lucifer with a Book,* pure
technique is made to cover the vacancy left by the disappearance of the kind of subject matter which Burns discovered through
The Gallery. In that book he evolved a technique suitable
to the immense store of material at his command, but in the
second the technique alone has been inherited, and one can watch
it being cast frantically about in search for something important
enough for it to say.

The result of the failure of this search is that the world of
Lucifer with a Book is a world of invented significance. It is puffed
up to size by the strength of Burns's passion and anger and not
by the strength of the conditions it presents to evoke passion and
anger. We are faced throughout with the brilliant spectacle of
Burns in the act of being bitter, but it is part of the failure that we
are not sufficiently aroused to join him. This is mostly because his
characters have been exaggerated to a point where their humanity

becomes grotesqueness and their every act an hallucination and
not a burlesque of life.

Mr. Pilkey, his son Herman, the son's wife—Nydia, Philbrick
Grimes, Guy Madison, Betty Blanchard, and Mrs. Launcelot
Miller, the woman with the corncob pipe, are all monstrous abstractions who have lost their real-life counterparts. What they
say and do is justified only because Burns tells us it is. Herman
openly fondles Nydia's breasts at a public gathering, and the act,
instead of illuminating Herman's character, merely impresses us
with his implausibility. Mrs. Launcelot Miller's pipe is significant
only because she smokes it. What Mrs. Miller is to the pipe or the
pipe to Mrs. Miller we do not know, any more than we know
what Guy Madison and Betty Blanchard are to each other.
Ostensibly they enjoy being together in bed, but the situation is
at once complicated by the fact that up to the introduction of
Betty we have been subjected to a number of Hudson's reminis-
cences on past love partners whose sex is left in considerable
doubt.

The work of both Capote and Burns suffers from their effort
to give it freshness through idiosyncrasy and from their tendency
to confuse idiosyncrasy and life. They have strained every nerve
to keep from being trite and, in the process, they have committed
the opposite crime of excessive uniqueness. With a suitable and
discoverable subject matter, a set of values which they could make
the basis of their work, they would not need to strain so hard.
But it is part of their dilemma that, lacking those values, they
must continually seek a substitute in sheer technical display. The
way of attempted affirmation, the way of journalism, and the way
of homosexuality and race are also part of that dilemma. They
are ways of compensation and not of solution. They serve for a
little while as frames through which the chaos may be ordered,
and, as such, they afford the new writers one last chance to have
their say in a time when all writers, both young and old, are working under an immense compulsion to be silent.

CHAPTER VII

The Neo-Hemingways

And the Failure of Protest

THE ABSENCE of genuine technical innovation in the majority of the novels of the second war is the direct result of a difference in the responses which the two generations were able to make to war. Where Hemingway, Dos Passos, and Cummings, facing for the first time in history the special experience of modern war, were impelled to discover a new technique with which to present it, the writers of the second war, facing that experience for the second time in history, were denied the means of technical discovery. Advances in technique occur in moments of profound social dislocation when suddenly all the old forms and manners of writing, fashioned on some reality of the past, come to seem ineffectual under the impact of a new reality. Technique, in other words, is as much the product of fresh experience as fresh subject matter is the product of a successful technique. But the aborting truth of the second war was that its experience was no longer new and that the basic emotions it aroused were the old ones and could be expressed in the old ways.

The Hemingway influence is an example of the extent to which a set of literary mannerisms, formed out of the fresh experience of the first war, has been carried over and adapted to almost identical experience in the second. The Hemingway influence has survived into the work of the new novelists because it is uniquely the language of war. The tensely modulated tone, suggesting as

107

it does the whole history of human suffering and an intimately personal awareness of death, has become inseparably attached to certain fixed war responses, with the result that once a writer attempts to deal with those responses he is almost invariably committed to presenting them in Hemingway's terms.

It might thus be said that the writer who allows himself to be influenced stylistically by Hemingway is also allowing himself to be influenced in his selection of material and, therefore, in his attitude toward his material. Not only is the style attached to certain emotions but the emotions are attached to certain situations, and it is out of his selection of these that a writer's attitude emerges. If the events of the second war were too vast and complex to be captured whole, they could be captured at least partially through the use of a technique which reduces to simplicity everything it touches and which excludes everything that cannot be so reduced. The writer using the terse, staccato style of Hemingway is at once forced to deal with only such emotions as can be expressed in a terse, staccato style and with only those characters and situations which can sensibly give rise to such emotions. Whole areas of experience, almost all subtleties of feeling and thought, are, of course, automatically placed beyond his reach. But this is really an advantage; for the less experience his technique will encompass, the less the writer will be obliged to understand. If love can be reduced to a single act of bedroom violence, if honor and fortitude can be suggested through mere taciturnity (that capacity for witless silence under stress with which the Neo-Hemingways endow their heroes to cover their ignorance of how men really act under stress), then the writer will be able to pursue his craft indefinitely with no more talent or insight than one might expect to find in a reasonably sensitive child.

The Neo-Hemingways of this war have been remarkable for the extent to which they have been infected with the superficialities of Hemingway and the success with which they have resisted his profundities. They have generally lacked his poetic power, his sure command of the idiom, and his gift for ironic understatement, but they have borrowed his constructions and some of his sillier idiosyncrasies. The essences—the delicacy and tenderness that lie behind his every word, the immense unspoken meanings that play beneath his themes like a counterpoint of ruin—have eluded them. They have ridden into the literary profession on the back of his pony, but they have not come by the way he has come or seen what he has seen. They have not been able to reproduce in themselves the shock with which he first encountered war; but they have made use of the words he put down to record that shock, and in the process they have had to pare down, rearrange, and in some cases falsify their own perceptions.

The result is that the novels written in the Hemingway manner have been, for the most part, flat, mechanical, and contrived. What emotion is in them seems irrelevant to the experience presented, as if it were, as, indeed, it often is, an emotion designed for another context in another age. One feels that the sensibility of the author has been warped to accommodate material which he has not truly seen but has merely borrowed, and that if he alone, without the presence of Hemingway's constant ghost, were perceiving and recording, he would do so in other terms and another language more nearly his own.

The fault of all imitative work is that it has not been achieved by the single mind working out its own consciousness in its own terms. It has not been shaped out of a living response of the whole being to life. It has not, in other words, endured the destructive process of creation. It has merely been lifted ready-made from the work of another, from a different order and relation of part to part. As a counterfeit of the original, it relates to the original as a quick sketch on paper relates to a living tree. There is a similarity, but the substance of the one is paper and ink while the substance of the other is growing tissue.

The war novels of Alfred Hayes and Robert Lowry, like the postwar novels of Merle Miller, illustrate most clearly the defects of the kind of imitation Hemingway seems to inspire in his followers. All three writers, having committed themselves to recreating Hemingway's world, are already bound firmly to locales and situations in which such re-creation is possible—Hayes and Lowry to wartime and postwar Italy (the world, roughly, of *A Farewell to Arms*) and Miller to a tiny group of numb souls in postwar Manhattan and Washington (the world, at least spiritually, of *The Sun Also Rises*). Hayes shows almost no sign of being able to write at all outside the frame of Italy, and even though Lowry attempted it, he only succeeded in transferring the war emotion intact to another setting. His women act the same whether they are Italian or American, in Italy or America, and his ex-soldiers in New York are identical with his infantrymen on leave in Rome. Italy has provided them both with a dramatic setting; the dilemma of the soldier, lost and drunken in the streets of Rome or Naples, who futilely pursues some sentimental vision of a "clean, well-lighted place" and some sad lonely girl to share it with him, affords them an excellent excuse to write novels like Hemingway's.

It is interesting to notice how close the parallel really is. "The wind blew through Europe," begins Hayes's *The Girl on the Via Flaminia*. "It was a cold wind, and there were no lights in the city. It was said the cabinet was about to fall. Nobody knew for sure whether the cabinet which was in power at this time would fall and another coalition government would be formed. There was nothing that was very sure, and all one knew was that, if the cabinet did fall, the government which would be formed from the ruins would be another coalition one, and that the wind was cold. It did not look at this time as though the war would end, although actually the war was coming to an end. Nobody knew at this time that the war would end in a few months." * Here one is struck by nearly all the old formula tricks: the careful, dead-pan repetitions; the air of opium sleep in which all things take on an equal unimportance; the use of the elegiac tone on commonplace material, echoing the opening paragraphs of *A Farewell to Arms;* the official vocabulary that, in juxtaposition with simple concrete words, gives to the idea of cabinets, governments, and coalitions a certain futility and impermanence; the avoidance throughout of the indefinite article. Another typical effect may be found in this paragraph from Hayes's *All Thy Conquests:* "There are Latin inscriptions on the Palace and there are many famous statues of many famous lawgivers in the courtyard. If we had a priest here he could read the inscriptions. The inscriptions probably say many wise things about justice. But what do the inscriptions say about corrupt judges and false courts? If we had a priest here we could ask the priest if the inscriptions say anything about corrupt judges and false courts." † This is straight Hemingway of the "irony and pity" period. Notice the famous repetitive last sentence, the doped preoccupation with key nouns, the air of faked innocence and illiteracy, and beneath it all, the old sly nudge, snicker, and wink.

Of the two, Hayes has a much better ear for Hemingway's effects than Lowry. At his best, he is more like the young Hemingway than the old Hemingway can hope to be. Lowry, on the other hand, shows signs of developing a distinctly personal idiom at the same time that he remains limited by the Hemingway tone and approach. His dramatic formula (so much like Hayes's that some parts of their books may be interchanged at will) depends upon the reduction of all things to the simplest terms. Throughout his work there are two emotions: brutality and a kind of tender lust

* From *The Girl on the Via Flaminia* by Alfred Hayes, published and copyright, 1949, Harper & Brothers, New York.

† From *All Thy Conquests* by Alfred Hayes, published and copyright, 1946, Howell, Soskin, and used by permission of Crown Publishers, New York.

that is meant to pass for love; and it is out of a very few combinations of the two that whatever power his writing possesses is drawn. As in Hemingway, there is in Lowry first and always the violence and suffering of war, not the war of Anzio, Sicily, or even Caporetto, but the occupation war of Rome and Naples with its bearded GI's on five-day pass and its young Italian girls in search of food and love. Set against the war, in typical Hemingway fashion and on the lowest level, is the blind urge of the men and the hunger of the girls. Set against both the war and this simple lust on the next higher level, still in typical Hemingway fashion, is the more complicated feeling of characters like Joe Hammond in *The Wolf That Fed Us*. What he does to the various girls he takes to bed is distinguished from the rapelike couplings of the other men with prostitutes only in being slightly less rapelike. But there is in Hammond, as in Frederick Henry of *A Farewell to Arms*, an element of pity, and it is this which, in the general context of pitilessness, gives him a certain humanity. The weakness, of course, is that Hammond's pity is nothing outside that context. Like Henry's feeling for Catherine Barkley, it depends on a background of unrelenting opposites: in the midst of death, any hint of life becomes all life; in the midst of unfeeling, the barest feeling becomes complex and sublime. But where the emotion of Frederick and Catherine was made nearly convincing as love by virtue of these opposites, Hammond's emotion is revealed, in spite of their help, as only a momentary twinge of conscience.

The difference between the two emotions may be ascribed to the failure of what might be called the lyric response to war. Although the Neo-Hemingways in books like *Casualty, The Wolf That Fed Us, All Thy Conquests,* and *The Girl on the Via Flaminia* have duplicated Hemingway's technical effects and typical situations and have even drawn on elements of his dramatic formula, they have not been able to reproduce in themselves his intense reaction to the experience of war nor, particularly, his tenderness and compassion for those who are caught up helplessly in it. The dignity and life which Hemingway was able to give to Frederick and Catherine derived, to a very large extent, from the deeply poetic, almost religious feeling he had for the material of their story—the same feeling which, when directed upon language, led him to develop a new technique that would express such material more truly than it had been expressed in the past. But his imitators, even though they are writing with much the same material, have failed to infuse it with his lyricism, depth, and conviction. They have merely carved out of wood small-scale models of his books. The surface resemblance is there, but the life is not. The life can belong only to Hemingway; for it is part of a world he created out of experience which he saw for the first time when it was fresh and new and which he endowed with a meaning that was true for him alone.

It is highly significant that just as the new war writing carries forward rather than radically alters the stylistic stream of the old war writing, so it deepens and enlarges the stream of protest which the earlier writers set in motion. It is one thing, however, to say that the protest has been deepened and quite another to say that it has been more effectively presented. The truth seems to be that even though the insights of the earlier writers into the evils of war seem limited and often naïve in comparison with those of the new writers, they were, nonetheless, treated far more powerfully in fiction.

The main reason for this is that the subjects which Hemingway, Dos Passos, and Cummings chose for their books were ones about which they felt intensely as individuals. Hemingway wrote about the brave going down under the physical violence of war, Dos Passos about the sensitive young man facing the loss of his personal freedom under the regimentation of war, and Cummings about the moral degradation of the individual in the midst of the sickness, filth, and privation of war. In each case, the emphasis was on the individual rather than the mass, the simple and concrete rather than the complex and ideological. The evil of war was a personal affront; it could be concretely blamed and specifically attacked.

Equally important is the fact that all three of these writers brought to the first war the fresh perspective of another time, a time of security, idealism, and peace, having been raised, as Dos Passos said, in "the quiet afterglow of the nineteenth century." As a result, they awoke to the truth of war abruptly and responded as only young men can respond at the moment of shocking first encounter. They may have lacked the detachment they needed for a full understanding of the thing that had happened to them. But they were able to draw out of their assaulted sensibilities a vigorous record of their loss of faith and to put down at least a rough outline of the evil which had caused it.

To the young writers of the second war that evil was clearer, but the passage of time had made it infinitely more complex. In the years between wars the age of idealism had receded still further, and the disillusion of the older generation had become the spiritual trauma of the younger. They could no more recapture the state of mind of their predecessors than a middle-aged man can recapture the impressions of his childhood. They were aware now that the evils against which the older generation had rebelled were merely symptoms of a larger and more terrible disease. But they were perhaps unaware that even as they gained in understanding of the complex issues raised by war, they would be more and more deeply affected by the futility of what they saw, and their work would suffer a corresponding loss of power.

An acute realization of these issues and a sense of the utter hopelessness of any attempt to resolve them exist side by side in the war novels of Hayes and Lowry and of Burns, Mailer, Shaw, and Bourjaily. In them, as in no novel of the first war, one finds an elaborate documentation of wartime misery, ranging from the suffering of the common soldier under the fascist hierarchy of the American Army to the suffering of civilians in countries dominated by a corrupt American occupation force. Mailer and Shaw explore the dilemma of the soldier as only Dos Passos attempted to explore it before them. But what Dos Passos saw in terms of the experience of three men, these writers see in terms of whole armies, whole societies, and complex philosophical systems. Hayes, Lowry, Burns, and Bourjaily stress the cruel disparity between our ideals and our practices, the ideals which won us the war and the practices which lost us the peace.

These books are full of bitter contempt for the conduct of the American Army in Africa and Italy, the ruthless exploitation of the women, the thousand criminal acts of inhumanity committed against the innocence and faith of the conquered. *The Gallery, All Thy Conquests, The Girl on the Via Flaminia, The Wolf That Fed Us, The Young Lions, The Naked and the Dead,* and *The End of My Life* all have to do with the failure of Americanism abroad. They are all indignant novels, and they have buried in them a surgical, despairing hatred that, if successfully presented, would make the bitter irritations of Dos Passos, Cummings, and Hemingway seem ineffectual and naïve. But the protest implicit in them is almost always merely implicit. It exists amid a detailed exposition of the evils which caused it, and those evils are so complex and overpowering, so much more conducive to paralyzing despair than to active hope, that they seem to cancel out all possibility of change—a possibility which must underlie all truly effective novels of protest.

One feels that the writers of these novels have seen, felt, and understood so much that they have been stultified and frozen in a helpless attitude of horror. There is no longer for them the clear assurance of a single, tangible enemy, the enemy that overcame the simple young heroes of their predecessors and drove them to picturesque ruin. The troubled, Proustian speculations of Mailer, the confused, panoramic searchings of Burns and Shaw, and the numb disgust of Bourjaily, Hayes, and Lowry are all symptoms of minds that have been wounded by the shock of too much reality and of talents that have exceeded their capacity to express the full meaning of that shock.

The retreat from Caporetto and the death of Catherine Barkley brought to an end far more than simply an army and a war romance. They marked the finish as well of a whole way of thinking, feeling, and writing about war. Hemingway was fortunate enough to be on hand to record that finish, to give it meaning and a kind of tragic grandeur. But since his time there have been too many wars, too many deaths, until now the grandeur has faded and the meaning has been lost. The sad but intensely excited young men who came to modern war for the first time and found in it a frame for the magnificent tragedy of their youth have given way to the tired young men who lived through it all a second time and who write of it now with a deepening futility and a muffled anger. The distance between their war world and Hemingway's is the distance between the tenderness Frederick Henry felt for Catherine and the fleeting pity of Lowry's Joe Hammond as he set about his systematic rape of Rome.

It would be a mistake to assume, however, that this distance can be measured solely in terms of war emotion and experience. Actually, the war served merely to crystallize in the new writers attitudes which had from the beginning set them apart from the world of Hemingway and his generation—attitudes that stretched back into their childhoods to the times into which they were born and which had already formed them when the war began.

CHAPTER VIII

Vance Bourjaily

The Two Worlds of Skinner Galt

In comparison with the innocent boys who set out, more than twenty years earlier, to save the world for democracy, the young men who went into the second war seemed terribly aware. The illusions they might have had about war—the patriotic illusions of courage and noble sacrifice—had all been lost for them that first time and long since replaced by cynicism and a conviction of the international double cross which was sending them out to be killed. Unlike their predecessors, they had no need for adventure or relief from boredom. Their lives, as far back as they could remember, had been spent in a world continually at war with itself, in an economic order that fluctuated from dizzy prosperity to the most abject depression. They could remember nothing but domestic unrest, fumblings at peace conferences, Asiatic invasions, and South American revolutions. They came to consciousness in the midst of breadlines, strikes, and milk riots.

There was for them no warm world of childhood to which they could return when things went badly. Childhood was no longer the simple memory of trout flashing in a sunlit stream up in Michigan or the clean smell of hay in a red barn where you shot sparrows with an air rifle and lost all the years in between. Childhood now was other memories: the failure of a business, a bank door locked shut with the family savings inside, a milk truck overturned on a Nebraska highway by farmers carrying clubs, and long lines of men waiting in front of courthouses through Arkansas and Tennessee. The generation of the Twenties had found themselves

117

lost in a world they had never made. The generation of the Forties could never be lost because the safe and ordered world had never been theirs.*

In college during the first years of the war there was no leisurely exchange of native values for the values of international learning. The bright young men who grew up through the Depression had no native values to exchange. They had been homeless from the moment they were born, and their lives, if they were typical, had been one long process of moving on. The transition from high school to college was simply a continuation of this process, involving further retreat from ideals which they had never had and a final rejection of the mass superstitions to which their parents had exposed them but in which neither they nor their parents had ever really believed. By the end of the second or third college year most of them had taken refuge in a philosophy of unbelief so pronounced that it seemed to strip away even their sense of individual identity and to render them eternally aloof from the complex problems of their time. The events leading up to the war had made more demands on the imagination than the imagination could bear. There had been too many vast issues, too many dislocations of whole societies. Quite suddenly there had been the explosion of a world into nothingness.

Because they had no illusions, this generation found themselves

* It might be pointed out at this juncture that this profound dislocation, this disappearance of values, was as apparent to the writers growing up in the Thirties as it was to the particular group, the writers of the Forties, with which I am specifically dealing. The writers of the Thirties—Steinbeck, Saroyan, and their contemporaries—were made to pound the pavement hunting work when jobs were scarcest and the country's economic outlook bleakest. They watched the slow and inexorable approach of World War II, from the Japanese invasion of Manchuria in 1933 to Pearl Harbor in 1941, with a completer understanding of the magnitude of the impending tragedy than had the writers of the Forties. In this analysis, I am excluding the writers of the Thirties not because they did not share this same chaotic and uprooting experience but because I feel they had less effect and influence upon, and are more distantly related to, the writing of today.

beyond the possibility of disillusion and denied even the impetus of revolt. Sex and liquor were no longer good for brave gestures in defiance of convention. There was no fixed standard to rebel against. The result was that youth had greater freedom than ever before and almost no interest in exploiting it. In fact, it seemed at times as if the movement toward revolt, having been carried to its logical end in the Twenties, had reversed itself and become a movement back to respectability. Many girls who a decade earlier would have been intent on losing their morals were entrenching themselves behind a fatigued virginity, apparently with the thought that by sealing off their sexual compartments they could conserve what little energy they had left for the greater struggle of war. Others, following a more complex logic, lost their virginity because they felt there were no morals left to lose and then discovered, with small triumph, that they were just as respectable as they had been before. Young men managed to get very drunk over the purposelessness of life and then gradually slid into a purposeless sobriety. Parties still consisted of many people talking at once, but it was beginning to be evident that parties were an empty gesture made to an outmoded exuberance and that the people who came to them had their minds on something else altogether.

Wherever people gathered in the early 1940's, one could detect a subtle desperation, a nervous overplaying of parts which everyone knew had long ago lost their power to hold an audience. The laughter and talk in a room would be pitched too high and loud, as if there were a general conspiracy against some obscure and terrifying silence. Couples who had scarcely met would make frantic and impossible promises to each other without the slightest intention of keeping them. Everywhere men were disappearing into uniform, and hardly anyone knew when they left. There were no military parades, no triumphant marches to the station. It was typical of the times that when the war came to the young men it should come quietly and mysteriously, as if it had nothing to do with them personally, as if they were simply numbers that someone very far away had drawn from a fish bowl.

Those who were sent to Europe found exactly what they expected to find. The travel folders had been outdated before they finished high school. The novels they had read concerned a Europe that might as well have never been. They found themselves in a place stripped of gaiety and romance. The picturesque little villages were in ruins; the girls were no longer lovely nor very eager; the good wine was gone. Whatever hopes some of them might have had of seeing the country, mixing with the civilian population, browsing in libraries and art galleries, were stifled in a tightly organized military system where no allowances were made for individual preferences and no one was treated as a gentleman. The Cook's tour was clearly over; the ambulances all seemed to be driven by someone else.

Most of the young men saw Paris the way they saw the rest of France—from the back of a truck or the top of a tank; and they remember it as a momentary relief from the stiff enemy resistance they had been encountering, perhaps as a dejected and threadbare city where they stopped just long enough for a shot of cognac. After the years of German occupation, the life seemed to have gone out of Paris; the glamour and charm had been corroded away by fear; and it was hard to realize that American artists had come there not so long before to escape the raw frontier of home.

The rest of the time—for those in combat—it was cold and miserable. That winter along the Moselle and at Bastogne the roads were crisp and dry underfoot or deeply rutted and soft with mud. The snow when it came lay everywhere—on the roofs of farmhouses, in yards, on the sagging surfaces of tents, in the holes where the young men slept. It covered the dead cattle lying in the fields, the broken tank treads that were like the uncoiled springs of smashed pocket watches, the blackened tree stalks, the lines of abandoned, burned-out vehicles. There was the snow, and there was the war. Beyond these there was nothing. The spectacle of death was neither touchingly poignant nor exciting. The trucks going by that were loaded with so many dead that arms and legs hung out over the tail gates might have been carrying ammunition or firewood. For the second time in a century, a generation of Americans were close to the truth of war; but this time they saw it nakedly, without illusions or romance. The numbing process which had begun in childhood and continued through college had insulated their minds against analysis. Still, truth came too often at the expense of hope, in the midst of futility, like the last chapter of a book without meaning.

The process by which the young men discovered the truth of war in the midst of war has been suggested in a dozen good novels over the last few years, but the full history of the process, from its beginning in the era between World Wars I and II to its climax in the futility of the period between World Wars II and III, can be traced in only one of them, Vance Bourjaily's *The End of My Life*, the most neglected but, in many ways, the most promising of them all.

To the generation who entered college in the first year or two of World War II, left college for the war in the third or fourth year, and came out of the war in the fifth or six, *The End of My Life*, in spite of its occasional callowness and crudity, will always have a special charm; for it is uniquely their story. No book since *This Side of Paradise* has caught so well the flavor of youth in wartime, and no book since *A Farewell to Arms* has contained so complete a record of the loss of that youth in war. Actually, Bourjaily has written the one-volume, contemporary equivalent of both. His Skinner Galt is at first a wiser and far more self-destructive Amory Blaine, and later a counterpart of the Frederick Henry who left everything behind and walked through the rain into nothingness after the death of Catherine; and his Cindy is a younger and much more innocent Catherine—strong, courageous, devoutly in love, and also fated to die, as all the truly living and loving, the very good, the very gentle, and the very brave, are fated to die in a futile and loveless world. But this is not to say that Bourjaily has attempted to reconstruct the world of either Fitzgerald or Hemingway. Rather, he has recaptured the flavor of a world that existed twenty years after Fitzgerald wrote *This Side of Paradise* but that Fitzgerald would, nevertheless, have understood; and he has written of a war experience that Hemingway never knew but that Frederick Henry's loss foreshadows. If much of his novel seems to fit more into their tradition than into the tradition of his contemporaries, it is perhaps because it has its roots in a time that was very much like theirs, a time that ended with the war and that remained outside the range of the other war novels. But *The End of My Life* is the last of that tradition. The lyric emotion and romantic irony of its early sections quickly give way to the black horror with which it ends and which is one of the distinctive trademarks of the literature of this war.

The long flash back to Skinner Galt's college life and his love affair with Cindy, which is introduced midway through the novel, belongs to the prewar time and the old tradition. It is dominated by a Fitzgeraldian fever-glow and a muted frenzy not unlike that of *The Sun Also Rises*. The time is roughly 1942, and even though the war has already begun for Americans in Africa and the Pacific, it has not yet really touched the college campuses. Its immanence, however, is everywhere. At fraternity houseparties young men get drunk with the recklessness of the doomed and pass out on the living-room sofa with somebody else's girl. In the dormitories young men gather in intense groups and discuss the fate of civilization until dawn. Benny Goodman's "I Got It Bad and That Ain't Good" and T. S. Eliot's *The Hollow Men* form the incongruous lament of the generation that could never be lost because it had somehow never been found.

Skinner Galt is an extreme symbol of its neurosis. Born in the

Twenties, he is the product of denial even though he has never known the values that were denied. Brought up in the Thirties, he remembers the tragedy of the Depression but not the prosperity which preceded it. Faced with war in the Forties, he knows only that he was taught to be cynical about war and that the books he has read have given a bitter picture of war. If Skinner were a writer he would write like Hemingway. If he wants to make a point in conversation he is likely to quote Eliot. But he has absorbed what Hemingway and Eliot have had to say without having had their experience. He has never known the innocence which made Hemingway bitter; and if he had ever felt the indignation which is behind *The Hollow Men,* he would have been afraid to admit it even to himself. The last refuge for him and those who are like him is casual indifference. "We've figured that as soon as we replaced all the illusions with defenses we'd be mature." * But the defenses are effective only so long as there is something to defend; and in a generation without values, without hope of values, the defenses are likely to conceal only emptiness.

Yet there is something about Skinner's cynicism in these early stages of his story which neither he nor Bourjaily seems to understand but which has great bearing on his whole development. To Skinner cynicism is, as he later says of suicide, "an intellectual position." It is an attitude toward life, a philosophical compromise with the problem of belief, and as long as he holds to it, it keeps him from being hurt—"You've got to tear things down . . . before they get a chance to fall on you, and you don't get hurt." It is the philosophy of a disillusioned absolutist, one who will believe nothing if he cannot believe wholly; and it is the product of an age which has wrecked more than it has built. But for Skinner denial is itself an absolute; without it, he could not possibly survive. This, then, is the significant fact. As an intellectual position, cynicism

* From *The End of My Life* by Vance Bourjaily, published and copyright, 1947, Charles Scribner's Sons, New York.

for Skinner amounts to an act of faith. Like the Lost Generation's belief in *nada*, it has nothing to do with his emotions except to free them, and like Frederick Henry's early belief in the war, it gives him the sense of security he needs to live fully and exuberantly.

The tense excitement, daring, and essential confidence of that first year or two of the war have never been more clearly illustrated than they are in Skinner, and they are perhaps the most significant qualities of his story; for they show, if Skinner is typical, that for a brief moment before they were all caught up in the war this generation was secure. Their deep concern over the prospect of war was rationalized by their belief in the meaninglessness of the war. Their very uncertainty, along with the sense they had of coming to the end of something, became, in a way, a certainty which released their minds from all further concern and left them free to live intensely in the time they had left. Although they had arrived by a different road, they were as near to the Lost Generation at this point as they would ever be. The war had not yet turned their cynicism to horror, transformed their intellectual position into paralyzing emotionality.

This atmosphere of certitude-amid-chaos can be felt throughout the flash-back sections of *The End of My Life*. It is present in the frenzied college parties, the drinking, and the love-making, and it is very much present in the bacchanalian revels, the wild orgies of negation, of Skinner and Cindy in New York. These scenes make it vividly clear that at least at the beginning the cynicism could be an exhilarating game and part of a restless search for thrills.

A few days before Skinner is to leave for the war, he, Cindy, and their friend Benny Berg fall into a discussion of belief. Benny is a Communist and has, so Cindy thinks, "a nice, reassuringly affirmative answer to this question of whether life is . . . worthwhile."

"Most of the people who say 'Yes,'" Benny says, ". . . base it on one central belief. There are even some people who think the whole thing through, and can't find a central belief, who say yes anyway, just for the joy of saying it. They do all right."

"But what are the other things you can base it on?" Cindy asks.

"Oh, religion. Art. Belief in mankind. Lots of things. If your belief is political, it probably boils down to belief in mankind."

"But why don't any of these things work for Skinner?" she wants to know.

"Well," Benny replies. "You can take the simple explanation and say he's a masochist, and doesn't want any of them to work. But that's too easy. I figure with those guys, it's a case of there being two ways of believing. If you're an objective believer, if you have to be sure something is true first, before you believe it, you'll never find anything that will satisfy you for long. You have to believe subjectively, believe because you find it satisfying, believe by faith without requiring proof. A cause or principle is just as true as the amount of devotion you give it. If you wait for it to become true because it's undeniable, you wait forever."

The outcome of this discussion is a chart which the three of them gleefully draw up, showing how the great writers and thinkers of the past and present would look as two rival football teams representing the affirmative and negative views of life. Lincoln, Lenin, Cindy, Twain, Franklin D. Roosevelt, Falstaff, Christ, D. H. Lawrence, Marx, Wolfe, and Heywood Broun make up the "Yes" team, and Andreyev, Swift, Hemingway, the early Huxley, Freud, Voltaire, Waugh, Henry Miller, Hart Crane, Fitzgerald, and the early Eliot, the "No" team. Skinner is the ball, Johnny Walker the referee, and the timekeeper is Death.*

But this does not satisfy Cindy. She has already learned from

---

* *The End of My Life*, incidentally, is the only new novel which gives to books their true importance as source material for this generation's ideas and attitudes. It will probably never be known how deeply our responses to the second war were affected by the novels of the first war or how differently we might have thought, felt, and written if we had never read Hemingway, Fitzgerald, Eliot, and Wolfe.

observing the progress of Skinner's denial of life that "there is one final and unavoidable conclusion at which those who hold that life is basically intolerable must arrive to be consistent," so she asks Benny for another kind of answer.

"He," Benny replies, pointing at Skinner, "is a pre-war neurotic. Same symptoms, world-weariness, enlarged death-wish, tendency towards self-pity. . . . You see, we've all been involved in this war unconsciously, ever since we were old enough to know what the word inevitable meant. It was so clear that it was coming. All of us are pre-war neurotics to some extent—Skinner almost a perfect one. The pressure was terrific, Cindy. Every time we read a book about the last war, we were fighting this one."

At this point Skinner, who has been trying throughout the scene to turn the conversation away from the tender subject of himself, solemnly dumps the contents of his liquor glass over the top of his head. Benny's mouth drops open and he begins to laugh; Cindy, half shrieking, half whooping, springs out of her chair and throws her arms around Skinner's neck; and the whole affair dissolves into a fantastic, drunken dance of death. Benny has just finished saying that "the pattern of reaction was taking chances, being amoral, doing anything for a laugh," and now the situation becomes an outlandish parody of his words. Cindy begins to choke Skinner and he sinks, crucified, to the floor. "Again we kill Christ," Benny cries, pounding at Skinner's hand with his empty glass. A red vase is hurled through the window, then a cushion, a phonograph record, a salt shaker, an ash tray—everything red in the room. They squirt ink on one another's wrists to simulate cocaine injections. Benny climbs to the top of the piano and prepares to jump. "Don't forget to count ten before you pull the ripcord," says Skinner. "I'm in it for thrills," Benny replies. "I'm only going to count five." Newspapers are lighted and dropped flaming out of the window. They run the mile, the half mile, and the quarter mile, and the twenty-ninth of a mile around the tiny apartment. Finally they collapse, exhausted and purged, having courted death and found her willing. The "pattern of reaction" has been asserted, but asserted with action and an exuberant willingness to live.

Skinner's war service is, in most respects, ideal. Unlike the vast majority of his contemporaries, who either entered one of the college training programs or were drafted directly out of college into the Army and Navy, he leaves college and joins the British Field Service. As an ambulance driver serving with a foreign army, he is one of the very few American gentleman volunteers of this war. Even his attitudes toward the war assert his kinship to the old privileged tradition of Hemingway's Frederick Henry and Dos Passos' Grenadine Guards and set him apart from his contemporaries. "I promised myself," he says at one point, "that, whatever happened, . . . I'd never take this war seriously. And I never will. It's just a big joke." And Frederick Henry had said twenty-five years before: "This war . . . did not have anything to do with me. It seemed no more dangerous to me . . . than war in the movies." Skinner is still "in it for the laughs," still living out "the pattern of reaction." But the years separating him from Frederick Henry also separate him from the old kind of war. Skinner had said in the beginning that he wanted "a nice, small war . . . with clearcut issues. There should be more than just a villain you can hate. There should be a side you can love too." But the nice, small wars belong to the past, the issues that were once simple are now complex, and this time there are villains to hate on both sides.

The fact is made clear to Skinner in the sudden desertion of his friend Rod Lujack, an incident which divides *The End of My Life* into two distinct parts, almost exactly as the retreat from Caporetto divides *A Farewell to Arms*, and which prepares the way for Skinner's destruction. The material dealing with the early phases of his war service and leading up to Rod's desertion really belongs with the flash-back material dealing with his prewar

experience. Not only is it dominated by the same lyric emotion—
so much like that of Hemingway and Fitzgerald—but it shows
Skinner as still essentially unaffected by the war. There has, of
course, been the brutal episode at the "Glass House," that chamber
of military horrors to which men are confined for obscure dis-
ciplinary reasons and which they will do anything to escape. But
even that has been largely canceled out by the exuberant non-
sense of those nights in Beirut, particularly the one when Skinner
disturbs the careful propriety of a British Army brothel with a
cleverly faked sadistic orgy. He and his friends are not yet working in a combat area. Their ambulance runs are short, pleasant,
and widely spaced, and they have plenty of time to drink, make
love, and explore the city.

But Rod's desertion introduces a new element. Rod, the frus-
trated musical genius, had been, before the war, a piano player in
nightclubs and bars. Between engagements, when short on funds,
he had been the paid lover of countless rich and unattractive
women whose vulgarity had disgusted him. As a result, he had
turned to part-time homosexuality and had an affair with one of
the men in the ambulance unit. Now he sees no alternative but to
desert. Skinner tries to persuade him to ask for a transfer to another
unit, but Rod realizes that he will always be a "pushover for any
fairy, anyplace." If, before, the war had been "a big joke" to Skinner, it now begins to be "a bad joke," part of a vast and impersonal
system of evil which is capable of striking down one's self and one's
friends at any moment. The effect on Skinner is to bring back his
old sense of helplessness, his deepening remorse.

The trouble, he thought, was the old business of having no one to
blame. . . . What were you going to blame? Society for being anti-
social? Humanity for being anti-human? You can never blame. You can
only mourn.

By now, Skinner's position closely parallels Frederick Henry's
immediately after Caporetto. Through Rod, the war has hurt him

personally, threatened his detachment, and turned his self-possession to self-doubt. By touching him directly, it has made him aware, for perhaps the first time in his life, of human values. But cynicism has become so advanced in Skinner, so much a part of his being, that a violation of those values, instead of rousing him to indignation and protest, merely confirms in him his old conviction that life is indecent and that "war is the most grossly indecent thing of all."

This is revealed in the next episode of his story. As a result of Rod's desertion, the ambulance unit is broken up and Skinner is sent to an isolated camp where he serves with a regiment of African Bechuanamen and their British officers. His hatred of the cruel treatment the men receive soon makes him an outcast in the camp and turns him in on himself; and his resentment becomes a weapon of spite which he uses against Cindy in his letters to her.

There existed a compulsion he did not try to understand, which made him inspect all the bright things they had had together for signs of tarnish. It almost seemed that he could not go to sleep easily at night until he had picked a favorite incident and turned it over and over until he found the weak spot that allowed him to see it as sordid.

First, there had been the war, then Rod, and now Cindy. And when Cindy could no longer be made to take the blame, there was himself. The "one final and unavoidable conclusion" which Cindy had feared had at last been reached.

For me suicide is an intellectual position, the inevitable result of thinking things through to the end. It is the final stink, in a way, the only way of finally proving to myself that I don't actually care.

But like all Skinner's intellectual positions, suicide fails in the execution. As he walks through the camp gate with an automatic hidden in his shirt, he does not respond to the sentry's command to halt and narrowly misses being bayoneted before he is recognized.

He had been guilty of gross self-deception, had figured something so thoroughly wrong that it was no longer permissible to act on it. He had not tried to avoid the sentry's charge with the bayonet. So suicide was not an intellectual position. It was pure emotionality, after all.

While Skinner's failure to avoid the charge is probably not the best way to describe the thing that is happening inside him, it is apparently intended to illustrate his loss of conscious control (therefore suicide is *not* an intellectual position) and to lead him to the conclusion that he has been guilty of "gross self-deception." But we feel, in spite of the imperfection, that the changes which have been occurring within him throughout his war experience are, at this moment, fully climaxed. The paralyzing events of the last few months—the horror of the "Glass House," the injustice of Rod's desertion, the brutality of the camp—have finally broken through the walls of his detachment, undermined his confident cynicism, and brought him into naked and uneasy contact with life. The "intellectual position" has become "pure emotionality," and the change has reminded him of his basic humanity. But it has also swept away the last of his props and prepared him for the final emergence of the destructive impulse which has been driving him steadily toward ruin.

Not long after this, Skinner's unit is sent to Italy. There are months of combat duty and finally a short leave during which he meets Johnny, an American Army nurse, who persuades him to take her on a tour of the front.

It was screwy, he thought, but why not? He could drive past Capua, around the artillery position he had passed two days before, and they could hear the guns go off in comparative safety.

But it is not to be that easy. They reach the artillery position safely, but on the return trip, their ambulance is strafed by a German plane and Johnny is killed. Skinner's urge toward negation is thus ironically realized; the bad joke is on him.

In prison after he has been court-martialed, he receives word that Cindy is in Italy with the USO and wants to see him. She arrives a few days later with one of Skinner's friends; but he refuses to let himself show any sign of his old love for her. "Cindy," he said flatly. "You shouldn't have come." "I came because I loved you," she replies. But his friend Freak knows better. "That's not true, Skinner. She didn't want to come. She came because I asked her to."

That was it then. Even as he had lost Rod . . . he had lost Freak. Even as he had lost Cindy, he had lost his friends. And that was it.

But dying, now that it was all but done, came hard, and Skinner made a last effort to defend himself from Cindy's grief and Freak's accusation. And in so doing, put into words what Benny had known, what Rod had felt, what Freak had learned, and what Cindy could not admit. "We were war-born," he said. "Listen, the war made us. Let the bad joke of the past die decently, along with the clowns who tried to make it funny."

The story of Skinner Galt, then, is the story of the "war-born," the generation that grew up without a childhood, without values, and with only an inherited disbelief between themselves and ruin. In many ways, it is like a postscript to the story of the Lost Generation. Skinner's arrival at that final state of negation, which is as near to death as the living can come, is the furthermost evolution of the process which Frederick Henry and John Andrews began. But Skinner carries their loss beyond loss, to the utmost meaninglessness and futility, and the final cancellation of self.

In literary terms, *The End of My Life* stands as a transitional novel squarely between the two generations. Its early lyricism that is so much in the spirit of the old war writing gives way to the dead futility at its end that anticipates the spirit of the new war writing. The development of Skinner through the novel, from the confident cynicism of his prewar attitude to the self-destructive horror induced in him by the reality of war, sets the pattern of the new writing as surely as if he had written it himself. It shows how the discovery of war's truth carried this generation beyond the narrow but highly effective literary frame of simple disillusion and left them with an acute but essentially inexpressible awareness of the complex ills of their time. They witnessed the defeat of human values in the midst of war and were sickened. But they were able only to present the gigantic zero of what they saw, for they never had the hope and the essential faith they needed to make an effective protest. The greatest failure this generation has suffered, the thing that has left its stamp upon the weaknesses of all their novels, has been the failure in their time of a basic belief in the dignity and goodness of man. The sense of his tragic yearnings, his endless struggle to attain the perfection of a god, has been bred, analyzed, or frozen out of them and been replaced by a dazed contempt for his corruption and folly. In this respect, Skinner Galt is their first and best ambassador; for he represents their experience and contains in himself the seeds and the justification of their failure.

CHAPTER IX

Mailer, Burns, and Shaw

The Naked Zero

PEOPLE FIRST BECAME conscious of the new war novelists with the publication, in 1946, of Alfred Hayes's *All Thy Conquests,* the first important novel of World War II and a disturbing one to older readers whose picture of the war had been formed on the hygienic productions of Marion Hargrove and Ernie Pyle. At about the same time Gore Vidal and Robert Lowry appeared with their terse little books, *Williwaw* and *Casualty,* which, along with Hayes's novel, helped to carry the tradition of Hemingway into our own decade. Then, in 1947, John Horne Burns published *The Gallery,* a fine book which almost everybody read, and Vance Bourjaily made his all-too-brief appearance with *The End of My Life,* which was an equally fine book in its way but which, for some reason, almost nobody read. It was not until 1948, however, when Norman Mailer's encyclopedic *The Naked and the Dead* appeared that the general public fully accepted the new war literature.

To account for the remarkable success of a book as full of bitterness and horror as this one is, it is necessary to remember that up to the time of its appearance there had been no book like it and that when it appeared the public was ready for it. *All Thy Conquests, Casualty, Williwaw,* and the others had all told the truth of war as their authors had seen it, but the vision that had gone into them had been limited and, for the most part, confined to one or two special areas of the war experience. None of them had been truly conclusive or able to crystallize the evil

133

of war within a philosophical framework. There was, further-more, for the first year or two after the war, a period of general reaction and apathy when the public was emotionally incapable of responding fully to the issues raised by any serious war novel. But by 1948, the war was far enough away for people to remember it with some detachment and to begin to speculate on its larger meanings. They had long been vaguely aware of the existence of a complex moral and philosophical design that lay behind the surface reality of campaigns fought and men killed and wounded; and Mailer was the first writer to attempt to make its implications clear to them.

This design arising out of a narrative of intense dramatic action makes *The Naked and the Dead* something more than simply a journalistic catalogue of war; while the dramatic element playing constantly beneath the design keeps it from becoming simply a philosophical discourse on war. No novel since *The Red Badge of Courage* and *War and Peace* has contained a more vivid or terrifyingly accurate picture of the conditions of actual war-fare, and certainly no novel of our time since *U.S.A.* has projected its theme on a more variegated background of human experience. On page after page and in episode after episode, it is Mailer's magnificent reportorial sense, his gift for evoking the tactile essence of a scene, that sustains the book and that will keep it alive at least as long as the events it describes live in the memory.

Curiously, the great dramatic power generated through the novel does not arise from any superlative quality of the language in which it is written. Mailer's style is actually one of his major weaknesses. It varies from a purely functional baldness in the straight narrative sections to an inflated, and often embarrassingly inept, rhetoricalness in some of the descriptive sections. But the sure instinct, the master reporter's instinct, is always there in the best scenes to save them from bathos and mere sensationalism. And that instinct is fortified in these scenes by the absolute integrity of Mailer's emotion, which, at its most intense, endows the suffering of the men, the brutal punishment of their bodies and minds, the debilitating terrors of incessant combat, with a nightmare outrage that lifts them to the heights of drama.

The philosophical burden of the novel is given emphasis in these scenes of physical action and suffering, but it is revealed most explicitly in the relations of the characters with one another. When the purely narrative material—the sections devoted to accounts of battle and descriptions of the jungle—is set aside, it becomes clear that at its core *The Naked and the Dead* is primarily a novel of character. It is around character that the entire action revolves, and it is through character that Mailer finds his central theme in the moral dilemma of men at war.

As the outline of this dilemma grows more and more distinct in the course of the novel, one gradually becomes aware of a crucial problem. It is imperative to Mailer's purpose that the men of *The Naked and the Dead* be destroyed by the military ideology of war and that their destruction arise directly out of the action in which they are engaged. Unlike *U.S.A.*, which in some other respects it closely resembles, *The Naked and the Dead* consists of a single frame of reference—the war. Consequently, it is in proportion as the characters refer back to the war rather than to circumstances prior to or outside the war that they are successful and the theme they are intended to develop is evoked. But where Dos Passos was able to introduce character into the mass experience of *U.S.A.* through the use of a natural deterministic method—since the backgrounds of his people were also part of the mass experience—Mailer is forced to introduce character through the flash-back method and is up against the immediate difficulty that the backgrounds of the men do not refer to the war at all and cannot, by themselves, justify the destruction which he intends the impact of the war to cause. His "Time Machine" portraits show us merely that the lives of the men were more purposeless and futile before the war than they can possibly be made as a result of the war. Poverty and ignorance have been the real instruments of their defeat; the jungle, the weather, and the enemy are, by comparison, incidental. The men, in other words, have no dignity, no hope of life. They cannot, therefore, be represented as losing either.

"Red" Valsen, the enlisted counterpart of Lieutenant Hearn, is typical. Like most of the other men, Valsen is clearly intended to function as a symbol of the destructive effect of war-induced fear on the courage and integrity of the human spirit. In the beginning, free of fear, he is able to hold himself aloof from the war, and to preserve his detachment. But as the campaign progresses, his health begins to weaken, and through his conflict with Sergeant Croft, he learns to be afraid. During the climb up Mount Anaka, he turns on Croft and demands that the patrol go back. The men are frightened and exhausted, and they have begun to realize that they are being exploited to satisfy Croft's insane urge for domination. But when Croft threatens to kill Valsen if he does not continue the climb, they do not dare to interfere, and Valsen's resistance along with his self-control is broken.

The difficulty here is that Valsen's self-control has been based all along on negation. Like Skinner Galt, he has held himself together and been able to function by believing in nothing. His life before the war has been one long process of escape from attachment, and his life in the war has been made bearable by his faculty for escaping the war. His defeat, therefore, instead of being the tragic moral breakdown obviously intended, is merely a meaningless exchange of one negative position for another.

The same can be said for Lieutenant Hearn, the most important character in the book. Hearn is ostensibly broken by General Cummings, the embodiment of military fascism, but he is represented from the beginning as something of an empty shell and therefore lacking all the potentialities of destruction. His problem all along has been one of belief. Like Valsen, but even more like Skinner Galt, he has spent his life drifting from one intellectual position to another, remaining in each just long enough to discover the "shoddy motive" which will allow him to abandon it. His class reservations prevent him from becoming a good Communist; his Communist reservations prevent him from becoming a useful member of his class. In the Army he is torn between his obligations to the military hierarchy to which, as an officer, he automatically belongs and his obligations to the men under him. His initial fascination with Cummings is the result of his inability to resolve these differences; and his conflict with Cummings is the result of Cummings's insistence that he stand on one or the other. It cannot be said, however, that Hearn is compromised by Cummings. If he is compromised at all, it is by his own lack of integrity. The evil of the system which Mailer sets out to attack is demonstrated in its power to break the will of a strong man. But Hearn is not a strong man and cannot, therefore, demonstrate that evil effectively.

To be sure, there is a moment in Hearn's story when he seems on the edge of integrity and nearly capable of moral choice. As the patrol advances, he gradually puts aside his self-analysis and begins to lose himself in the joy of positive action. But even as he does so, he realizes the "shoddy motive" behind the action, and then, by extension, behind his whole life.

> . . . All his life he had flirted with situations, jobs, where he could move men, and always, as if he had sensed the extent of the impulse within himself, he had moved away, dropped things when they were about to develop, cast off women because deep within him he needed control and not mating. . . .*

This moment of awareness is the first suggestion we have of a possible change in Hearn. In the midst of the only genuine act

* From *The Naked and the Dead* by Norman Mailer, published and copyright, 1948, Rinehart & Company, New York.

of his life, he learns that basically he is motivated by a lust for power, that, unknowingly, he has always belonged emotionally to the class which intellectually he has despised, the class of his father, Cummings, and Croft. His impulse now is to turn back with the platoon, acknowledge to himself and to the world that he is unfit to command, and give up his commission. But before he is able to act, he is tricked by Croft into resuming the mission and a short time later is killed.

Hearn's death and the slip of command which gives the incompetent Major Dalleson, in the absence of Cummings, the tactical initiative to wipe out the Japanese forces on the island and conclude the campaign form the double climax of the novel. Both are intended to be ironical, but in practice they only serve to weaken the structure of protest on which the point of the novel, to be effective, must rest. Our respect for Cummings—and thus our respect for the danger he represents—is immediately collapsed when we learn that a man like Dalleson can do by chance in a day what a man like Cummings, for all his tactical genius, could not do in many months. Once we have lost respect for Cummings, Hearn seems even more purposeless because there is now no real justification for the control Cummings had over him. Hearn's death is brought about through the treachery of Sergeant Croft, the enlisted counterpart of Cummings; and if Mailer had left it at that the ironic impact of the situation might still have been saved. But Croft is made ridiculous when, by a highly improbable fluke, he fails to lead the patrol over Mount Anaka. All possibilities for a single dramatic effect are reduced to zero when the men of the patrol find themselves incapable even of despair over the news that the mission on which they have risked their lives has contributed nothing to the success of the campaign.

It is interesting to see how this reduction is made inevitable in the relations of the characters. Valsen and Hearn are set against Croft and Cummings. Valsen loses his self-control and is made afraid when Croft forces him at gun point to continue the climb up the mountain. Hearn loses his self-control and is made afraid in an exactly parallel situation when Cummings forces him, under threat of court-martial, to pick up a cigarette butt from the floor. Hearn brings into single focus the complementary powers of Cummings and Croft, first, when he is sent on the mission and, finally, when he is killed through Croft's deception. But Cummings and Croft have also been made afraid. It is Cummings's basic insecurity and fear for his command that cause him to humiliate Hearn and to send him on the mission; and it is Croft's fear that Hearn will usurp his command that causes him to bring about Hearn's death. At this point, with both Valsen and Hearn defeated, the machinery of protest is set in motion and the way is prepared for the final triumph of evil (Cummings and Croft) over good (Hearn and Valsen), which is the typical climax of the "protest" or "exposure" novel and directly in the tradition of the older war fiction, particularly Dos Passos' *Three Soldiers*. But Cummings's power is canceled out in the triumph of Dalleson, and Croft's power is canceled out in his failure on the mountain. The good are humiliated or suffer a fatal deception; the evil are made ridiculous; and the mediocre ride to victory on an accident. Instead of rising through successive stages to a supreme indignity, the novel descends through a series of reductions to an absolute zero.

It is as if Mailer had carefully constructed a framework of protest and then, as each step in the labor was completed, had just as carefully cut away the ground beneath. Or it may be that at some time near the end he saw through to the real implications of his material (that there was no vestige of hope on which to base protest) and abandoned the framework of protest in favor of the inevitable direction in which his material was taking him. In any case, the parts remain; the scaffolding and the stacked timbers testify to his uncompleted purpose; and the resulting half triumph, half failure is the more regrettable for having been reached through a resolute determination to risk all those parts rather than falsify the whole.

What Mailer felt, and felt powerfully, he put into his descriptions of the concrete horrors of war. These scenes of nightmare combat and tormenting hardship form by themselves a potent condemnation of the fascistic military system which the novel as a whole attempts to attack. But the moral implications of that system were another matter. They demanded a set of values, a hierarchy of law in terms of which evil and good, futility and hope, could be meaningfully opposed; and this neither Mailer nor his material possessed. He was sure of his emotions, and he was able to express them dramatically as long as he could find their object in single events. But the abstract truth of the master design he could neither comprehend intellectually nor present significantly.

At first glance, *The Gallery* seems a much more successful book than *The Naked and the Dead;* and then one realizes that it seems so merely because it is a less disturbing book. What was in Mailer a bitter, unrelieved anger that could find no outlet in literary protest is in Burns a quiet indignation relieved by a human and, therefore, a more compelling sympathy, one that surrounds his book with a friendlier air and gives it the appearance of greater depth and emotional range. There is also on Burns's side the richness and vitality of his style which, in direct contrast to Mailer's, flashes constantly through his material and supercharges it with vivid metaphorical suggestiveness. It is full of strikingly brilliant figures; it is always alive with emotion; yet it is never ornate, because the varied and intense experience on which it operates rises at every point to meet and justify it.

But perhaps the main difference between the two books is one of scope and structure. Mailer attempted to encompass not only the vast physical but the vast philosophical design of war, and he failed. His book expanded horizontally over the great world of war and then collapsed from sheer size and overextension of its moral resources. Burns sets out consciously to do less and, therefore, does it more completely. He avoids the panoramic view of the whole and focuses all his attention on the scattered details which contain the significance of the whole. Like Mailer, he is primarily interested in character, but, unlike Mailer, he cares less for the reactions of character in the mass than he does for the inner reactions of character in isolated individuals. One always saw Mailer's people as representatives of their class. They were affected in a particular way by the war because their social positions had already prepared them to be affected in that way. One sees Burns's people as special cases. They are affected in a particular way because the war has uprooted them from their class and thrown them back on themselves.

This probably explains why *The Naked and the Dead* is a novel and *The Gallery* is a collection of character sketches and travelogues. Mailer was able to create a single social milieu and fit most of his characters into it. They could be shown reacting as a group to the common experience of war because their reactions were nearly all the same. But Burns is faced with the task of creating a separate milieu for each of his characters because each of them reacts differently, is, in fact, experiencing a different war. There is, however, one point of contact for them all. In the Galleria Umberto in Naples during August, 1944, they experience the moment of revelation by which we discover them and they discover themselves.

There's an arcade in Naples that they call the Galleria Umberto. It's in the center of the city. In August, 1944, everyone in Naples sooner or later found his way into this place and became like a picture on the wall of a museum. . . . The Americans came there to get drunk or to pick up something or to wrestle with the riddle. Everyone was aware of this riddle. It was the riddle of war, of human dignity, of love, of life itself. Some came closer than others to solving it. But all the people in the Galleria were human beings in the middle of a war. . . . They were all in Naples where something in them got shaken up. They'd never be the same again—either dead or changed somehow. And these people who became living portraits in this Gallery were synecdoches for most of the people anywhere in the world.[*]

Alternating with these "Portraits" are the "Promenades"—first-person meditations on the cities of Africa and Italy and on the larger moral issues of war. It was presumably Burns's intention or his hope that the "Promenades" would knit the "Portraits" together in a unified whole with a single impact. Actually they serve no such purpose, for there is no fundamental relationship between the pieces in the two series. Hemingway, in his first book, *In Our Time*, was trying for the same effect when he set his brief sketches of war violence against the longer stories dealing with Nick Adams's boyhood in Michigan. He succeeded because the overt violence of the sketches served as counterpoint to the implicit violence of Nick's life; the one intensified the meaning of the other; and the two series were bound together by the same emotion. But Burns uses the "Promenades" as the medium for a kind of material and a kind of emotion which cannot be found in the majority of the "Portraits." As he muses on the war in the "Promenades," he repeatedly expresses his faith in the power of human dignity and love to triumph even in the midst of war. The cities of Africa and Italy have awakened in him a sense of the true values, values that America has lost. He has been charmed and transformed by the simple goodness and deep wisdom of the people; their suffering has taught him compassion and tolerance. Ideally, then, if·the book is to have a single effect, this overt affirmation of values should lead directly to a demonstrated affir-

[*] From *The Gallery* by John Horne Burns, published and copyright, 1947, Harper & Brothers, New York.

mation of values in the "Portraits." But this never happens. The "Portraits" nearly all end in defeat. Most of the characters in them arrive too late at the realization that, like Major Motes, they are out of their time, have been destroyed by a reality which nothing in their lives has prepared them to face and endure. The fact that Burns felt compelled to use the "Promenades" at all would indicate that he himself saw that the "Portraits" alone were not affirmative enough to make his point and that they needed to be reinforced with additional evidence superimposed from the outside.

The portrait of Hal, the neurotic lieutenant, may not only exemplify the problem facing Burns but be analogous to the dilemma which the entire book represents. Hal seeks values in a world in which all values have been stripped away. Like Burns he desires them to be implicit; he wants to "seek God directly." But being himself a product of that world, Hal has lacked values all his life, lacked even a sense of his own identity. Before the war he had many friends who loved him for "the reflection he gave them back of themselves." People to Hal were all little pieces of himself that he gave away; and it was in Naples in August, 1944, that he, like Fitzgerald's charming Dick Diver twenty years before, discovered he had nothing left to give. In him, the necessity to affirm becomes stronger as the possibilities of affirmation recede, and he requires an understanding of the war that he never required of the less chaotic world of peace. The result is that he soon crosses over the line separating illusion from delusion and begins to think of himself as a kind of Christ bringing the light of salvation to lost souls. His position is thus the exact reverse of Skinner Galt's and Lieutenant Hearn's—the alternative reaction to an identical experience. Hal could possibly be cured by learning to accept futility, which is the only answer to the equation of his life; but as his refusal to accept that answer forces him to superimpose an irrational answer, so the same refusal forces Burns to superimpose values that are in excess of the equation of his material.

Moe Shulman, the infantry platoon leader, learns to accept futility. As he goes out to die, he sees no meaning in his life or death, and the perception gives him a comfortable sense of the irresistible logic which is carrying him to extinction. "It doesn't matter what the war means or who wins it," he says. "But I'm tied up in a set of circumstances I've got to follow through. . . . I don't have any ideas that the world will be any better for me living or dying. . . . It's just the way things have panned out for me. There's been a logic in my life. A crazy logic. And this is part of the logic." To be sure, there is a kind of victory in Moe's acceptance, but it is a passive thing, a victory in defeat. Like Skinner Galt, he gives in to the immense zero of life and war and lets it take him. There is one brief moment when the real truth of it all, the sadness, the suffering, the eternal emptiness, comes clear to him. But that, like the rest of him, is lost as he completes the pattern of his life by dying.

It is because of this acceptance that Moe's characterization is effective; but it does not complete or justify the affirmativeness of the "Promenades." Nor do most of the others. Major Motes, the typical old-school disciplinarian, perceives, during his moment of revelation in the Galleria, that he is out of his time. "I'm a gentleman from Virginia," he decides. "Such must suffer in Naples of August, 1944." Louella, the Red Cross worker with a mission in life, is also outmoded. Her conception of the needs of the men she serves contrasts ironically with their true needs; her usefulness is canceled altogether because her ideals do not provide her with the strength to face the realities of war. Momma, the Neopolitan barkeep, loves the homosexuals who come to her bar; they are more sensitive and alive than other men. But, like Louella, Momma cannot see the torment and suffering that lie beneath the surface; and when the accumulated tensions in her bar suddenly explode at once, she collapses in comic helplessness. Father Donovan and Chaplain Bascom manage to settle the differences of faith that separate them, only to be destroyed in the faithless world of Naples in August, 1944. All Burns's characters either cling to identities that are no longer equal to their experience or lose themselves entirely. Only Giulia, the pretty Italian girl, may be said to have found a way out, but the only assurance she has that the American she loves will come back to her is a wartime promise.

Taken separately, these "Portraits" carry immense conviction and dramatic power. They are full of accurately observed, deeply felt life; they go to the bottom of the moral and psychological dilemma of human beings lost in the middle of war; and they all testify to the remarkable range and intensity of Burns's talent as a writer. But they do not constitute the whole of *The Gallery* nor contain the full meaning Burns intended it to have. They tell the story of the war as he saw it, but they do not tell the story of the war as he wished it to be. For that, he had to fall back on the "Promenades."

The result is that *The Gallery* is a hybrid book, made up of two kinds of material set in two different literary devices that are never fused. The affirmation of values in the "Promenades" is constantly thwarted by the negation of values in the "Portraits"; and the nondramatic treatment of the one is in the end completely overcome by the tensely dramatic treatment of the other. There is one step Burns might have taken to ensure his point. He might have disregarded altogether the innate potentialities of the material he put into the "Portraits" and twisted the action in such a way that the book would have been forced to end on an affirmative note. He *could* have allowed Hal his moment of triumph, Moe his meaningful, perhaps heroic, death, Louella the satisfaction of a mission performed, Major Motes his victory of command;

but it would have meant a deliberate falsification of the truth as he saw it, and Burns was too scrupulous an artist for that. Like Mailer, he had no choice but to let the real meaning of his material carry him where it would even if it meant a serious and inevitable weakening of his total achievement.

The influence of *The New Yorker* magazine on the values and attitudes of this generation of writers will probably never be accurately estimated. Influences are usually clear only in their primary stages. As they are absorbed they tend to merge with originality, so that after a while it becomes impossible to tell whether a writer is seeing life in a particular way because his temperament requires him to see it that way or because outside influences have taught him to see it that way. But the *New Yorker* influence is a special thing, and when it is very strongly present in a writer's work, it has a way of taking over the work, cheating the writer out of his rightful ownership, and stamping it with that anonymous but universally familiar *New Yorker* label.

The code which *The New Yorker* teaches its writers is evident in everything they write—from the delicately thin little fantasies of Shirley Jackson that trail wispy spider webs of horror across the mind to the robustly thin little anecdotes of John O'Hara that echo farther and farther down the corridors of manful understatement until they refine themselves out of earshot. It is a code based on a fear of all emotion that cannot be expressed in the whisper of a nuance. It depends for its existence upon a view of the world as a vast cocktail party where the very best people say the most frightening things about themselves and one another in a language which the servants are not expected to understand, where the most tragic confession of personal ruin is at once diluted by the ironic titter in the speaker's voice. It is a world kept faintly amused by perpetual gossip about the cannibalism of sweet little girls in white, the madness of little boys beating dead dogs in vacant lots, the neurosis of lonely shop girls who fancy themselves pursued by daemon lovers or trapped in crumbling skyscrapers. It is a world where the most monstrous infidelities can be arranged and dismissed with the bored flicker of an eyelash and where all the impoverishment of modern man can be expressed in a single turn of phrase.

The writing that comes out of this world is distinguished by its overwhelming accuracy, its painful attention to detail. Produced out of a morbid fear of emotion, it loses itself in trivia so that it will not have to express emotion. It derives its power from a skillful arrangement of the endless unimportances which make up its parts—scraps of brittle dialogue, bits of carefully contrived scene and setting, little stifled orgasms of dramatic climax. But more than anything else, it is assured writing, rich with the wisdom of sour experience in the countless minor bars of many continents. Never is there a mischosen word, an inept phrase, a misplaced emphasis. It all has the slick perfection of freshly laid concrete, as if it had all been produced at the same moment by the same machine.

Irwin Shaw's *The Young Lions* might conceivably have appeared in a special issue of *The New Yorker* given over entirely to war fiction. Like John Hersey's *Hiroshima,* which it in no other way resembles, it has that special look of having been tailored to *New Yorker* specifications. Even the experience with which it deals appears to have been carefully arranged to happen by some *New Yorker* stooge who, one imagines, stood obligingly by ticking off climaxes with a stop watch while Shaw noted them down in his neat, bloodless prose. Everything about the book has an air of prefabrication and contrivance, of editorial rooms, expensive secretaries, and lunchtime martinis; and one finds it difficult to believe that Shaw went any farther for his material than the Algonquin and the *Times* morgue.

But the style is only the vehicle of other qualities that link the novel even more firmly to the *New Yorker* world. The dramatic value of many of the most important scenes is repeatedly crippled by that curious pulled punch which is the approved *New Yorker* method of dealing with emotion that might, if left alone, become strongly and genuinely serious. Where *The Naked and the Dead* at least had the strength of its emotional, if not its philosophical, conviction and managed to lift itself above failure by means of that strength, *The Young Lions* is as blandly and calculatedly subdued as Eustace Tilley himself.

This is most evident in the scenes devoted to New York life during the early years of the war. Like the people for whom *The New Yorker* seems to be specifically written, the people in these scenes have carefully cultivated the art of living perpetually with their spiritual guards up. They have developed a technique for dealing relaxedly with the constant tensions of their existence, for turning the world's irony upon themselves and defeating it with innuendo. On the most crucial occasions, they are never at a loss for the right word, the sleek phrase which will reduce the moment to manageable terms. Their conversation, whether it has to do with suicide, divorce, professional failure, or the advisability of having another drink, is all conducted in the same key, as if all subjects had an equal value and deserved an equal indifference.

There is no suggestion here, as there is in the best of Hemingway's stories, of violently controlled passions: the language does not draw vitality from the implication that there is a hidden truth, immense and terrible, lying like a smoldering explosive just beneath the surface of the taut nerves and the monosyllables. These people are not members of a secret society, living by an unwritten code which preserves them from destruction. If they were, they would have a complexity worthy of our interest. They are simply sterile, meaningless shadows, talking mannequins, acting out the slick pantomime of life which Shaw has manufactured for them.

They might be suitable as devices for satire, but there is no evidence that they are meant to be taken as satire. Shaw's method proclaims on every page his absolute commitment to their world. Its atmosphere seeps through the whole of his book until the method and the created world merge and become inseparable.

The contrivance that is clearly visible behind the architectural design of the novel is also part of this world. Like *Three Soldiers, The Young Lions* is built around the experience of three men, each of whom belongs to a different level of society and all of whom react in widely different ways to the impact of the war. But to compare the two books would be to give the genuine and the false an equal value; for Dos Passos' men, whatever else they may have been, at least had the breath of life in them, while Shaw's men, after they are through being all that Shaw wants them to be, have the breath of life crushed out of them. His Michael Whitacre, Noah Ackerman, and Christian Diestl, who epitomize, respectively, the quasi-liberal New York intellectual, the simple, persecuted, but ultimately valorous American Jew, and the bravely dedicated but ultimately defeated German soldier, are merely stereotypes. Their humanity is smothered again and again in the tight confinement of the roles they are intended to play, until, by the end of the novel, they are lost in a confusion of message and cheap rhetoric.

Shaw attempts to inject meaning into the vast panorama of experience which the novel encompasses through a system of carefully contrived parallels, near-parallels, and pseudo parallels which are apparently intended to flow back and forth through one another and give an effect of dramatic irony. Without them the novel would be, at best, merely three separate accounts of miscellaneous incidents occurring in several different countries over a number of years and variously affecting the lives of the three principal characters. At worst, it would simply be a chain of faintly related anecdotes or a series of second-rate short stories.

Through the parallels Shaw manages to give the novel at least an appearance of unity, but when we look closely we discover that it is merely a unity of structure and not a unity of dramatic or symbolic meaning.

The parallels may be divided into two types, the primary and the secondary. The big primary parallel which brings together the main events of the novel and fixes them in an over-all design rests on what may only be described as the most improbable of coincidences. In the first chapter, Margaret Freemantle, an American girl on vacation in Austria in 1938, meets Christian Diestl, a young Austrian ski instructor who, although a Nazi, is still decent and humane. Later in the book, Margaret meets Michael Whitacre, a young and attractive Broadway director, and has a serious and extended affair with him. Still later, Whitacre, now in the Army, meets Noah Ackerman, whose story has been developed through the novel concurrently with Whitacre's and Diestl's. Then, in the closing chapter, Ackerman and Whitacre, having been separated, reunited, and brought through the last phases of the war together, are fired upon from ambush by Diestl, now a defeated and corrupt Nazi soldier with just enough strength left for one last act of resistance. His shot, of course, kills Ackerman, and it is left to Whitacre to bring the novel to a righteous end by tracking down Diestl and putting a bullet in his head. The horror which Margaret Freemantle glimpsed in Austria before the war and which Diestl then defended and later epitomized is thus loosed upon Ackerman (martyr to Nazi hate) and then revenged by Margaret's lover, Whitacre. All the principals are brought together on the stage in time for the grand finale.

The secondary parallels are even more interesting. It is particularly clever of Shaw to open the novel with three chapters devoted to the activities of the three main characters on the same day, New Year's Eve, 1937–38, in their widely separated worlds—Diestl in the Austrian Tyrol with Margaret Freemantle, Whitacre in New York, and Ackerman in California. It is also clever of Shaw to have Diestl, Margaret, and Whitacre attending New Year's parties while Ackerman sits in a cheap hotel room waiting for his father to die. But the cleverest stroke of all is Shaw's manipulation of the events which climax the two parties. While Margaret is fighting off a drunken Nazi who is attempting to rape her, a has-been playwright at Whitacre's party almost succeeds in committing suicide. Both incidents are apparently intended to illustrate the basic corruption and sickness which underlie the German and American cultures and to stand in ironic contrast to the drab but innately pure suffering of Ackerman as he waits by his father's bedside.

As the novel progresses, the three men are repeatedly set against one another, and each time the parallel is effected through a set of carefully planted and painfully obvious clues. Whitacre and Diestl are both prevented from rising to officer rank in their respective armies because of their prewar Communist affiliations. Ackerman cannot hope to be accepted even by the men in the enlisted ranks because he is a Jew. In the fourth chapter Diestl suffers a slight wound in the face while leading an armored unit triumphantly into Paris. In the fifth chapter, on the same day back in America, Whitacre suffers a similar wound when his enraged wife hurls a badminton racquet at him. But where Diestl's wound was a mark of the victory of his army, Whitacre's is a humiliating reminder of the defeat of his marriage. Immediately after each incident both men fall into a nostalgic conversation with a friend who has lived in Paris before the war, and both have direct contact with the French. But again Whitacre is the loser; for Diestl and his friend are enthusiastically welcomed by the prostitutes in a Paris brothel, while Whitacre and his friend are curtly dismissed by the two elderly French women who are present at the badminton party. In the seventh chapter Diestl, on a two-week leave in Berlin, enjoys a drunken orgy with his lieutenant's wife and her roommate. In the thirteenth chapter Ackerman and his wife enjoy an idyllic two-week honeymoon on Cape Cod. In the sixteenth chapter Diestl and Lieutenant Hardenburg leave their men to die defending an impossible position and retreat to fight again in another part of the front. In the eighteenth chapter Ackerman, after surviving a series of fist fights with the most powerful men in his company, deserts from the army and goes to New York to puzzle out his relations with the war. In the twenty-second chapter Whitacre, in London after a particularly severe German air raid, muses on the element of chance which makes the difference between life and death in war a matter of the slightest miscalculation of range in a frightened bombardier. In the twenty-fifth chapter Diestl, lying wounded on the coast of France after a British strafing attack, ponders the same idea. In the twenty-sixth chapter Diestl, cut off from his unit during the Allied Invasion, bolsters the courage of his men with brandy. In the twenty-seventh chapter Whitacre, assigned to temporary duty in an army replacement camp, bolsters his own courage with gin.

The list could be infinitely extended—but to little purpose. It is true that the parallels bring certain minor ironies and paradoxes out into the open. They emphasize, for example, the familiar truth that corruption and fascism exist in all armies, that because of their common suffering, men fighting on opposite sides in a war often feel a closer kinship to one another, and often bear a closer resemblance to one another, than they do to their respective superiors. But the more thoroughly one examines them, the more one is convinced that the parallels do not yield up a significance that justifies the pains Shaw took with them; and one is forced to conclude that they are pointless embroidery intended either to give the novel an appearance of meaning which it does not in fact possess or to satisfy the reader's demand for complexity so well that he will be led to overlook the even more dubious devices Shaw uses to hammer his real message home. For there can certainly be no doubt that when we have been made aware of the parallels we are still no nearer to the sources of what the novel seems really to be saying.

To make his real point, then, Shaw resorts to other means; and foremost among these is distortion of the action itself in such a way that all the major events in the story are warped to fit the argument with which he wishes to convince us. His primary aim is to make a dramatic affirmation of faith in the struggle of the Jew for equality in the modern world. He wants to expose the corruptive evils of modern fascism in both America and Europe, and he wants particularly to show how the Jewish fight against fascism can end not only in Jewish victory but in victory for others who are inspired by the example of the Jew. Ackerman, Whitacre, and Diestl are the appointed instruments of his purpose, but, unfortunately, in acting out that purpose both Ackerman and Whitacre are reduced to implausibility as characters and, through a perverse irony, only Diestl manages to be convincing.

The single unavoidable truth of the events with which the novel is concerned is that war is a brutalizing and destructive experience. It is a truth that rises so inevitably out of the events—from those which transform the victorious German Army into an amorphous mass of frightened fugitives to those which turn the war careers of Ackerman and Whitacre into a nightmare struggle for survival—that the only possible consequence of them is disaster. Diestl is successful as a character because his development through the novel is the logical outcome of the events. As the events of the war turn the German advances into a series of accelerating retreats, he is changed into a defeated personality. He is brutalized and corrupted in strict accordance with the brutal and corrupt picture of war which Shaw presents.

But Ackerman and Whitacre, as the bearers of Shaw's affirmative message, pose an altogether different problem. Logically, they too should be defeated. They are victims of the same war, and Ackerman particularly is subjected to an incredible amount of punishment. But to have allowed them to be defeated, Shaw would have had to allow his point to be defeated. He was required, therefore, to twist them so that, logically or not, they would emerge from the war victorious. To do this, he had to treat the two men in such a way that they would take on character and meaning as the war destroyed character and meaning in the world around them. He had somehow to show them as changing from bad to good as the circumstances of their existence increasingly demanded a change from good to bad. Thus Ackerman is made to develop from the condition of meaninglessness and futility in which we find him at the death of his father through a series of triumphs to a condition of positive strength: he overcomes the deep racial prejudice of a Vermont farmer in order to marry his daughter; he fights the most powerful men in his company to assert his right to be treated in the army as a human being; he performs a magnificent act of heroism in battle out of sheer determination to prove himself; he becomes, in short, a living dynamo of Jewish fortitude. Whitacre is transformed from a soft, overcivilized intellectual, who has all the proper, liberal sentiments but who has never really believed in the war, into a serious and devoted soldier who ultimately takes positive action in the name of the war. These changes are effected through such a complete reversal of the impression the two men have previously made as characters that, by the end of the novel, they have left their humanity far behind and taken on the attributes of beatific emissaries.

The charge that Shaw had to go against the inner logic of his material in order to make his point is even more justified when we notice how forced and one-dimensional the concluding section of the novel seems. By now Shaw has put aside all pretense of credibility and concentrated his full energies on the final sermon which ties the novel into a nice neat package. The unit to which

Ackerman and Whitacre belong arrives at a Nazi concentration camp a moment after the prisoners have rebelled against their guards and overthrown them. As order is being restored in the camp, one of the prisoners, a Jewish rabbi, approaches the American commander, Captain Green, and asks permission to conduct a Jewish religious service in the camp yard. Over the objections of an Albanian fascist who is conveniently present, Captain Green, who like Whitacre has up to now shown little sign of moral courage, replies as follows:

"I am going to guarantee that you will hold your services in one hour in the square down there. I am also going to guarantee that there will be machine guns set on the roof of this building. And I will further guarantee that anybody who attempts to interfere with your services will be fired on by those machine guns." He turned to the Albanian. "And, finally, I guarantee," he said, "that if you ever try to come into this room again you will be locked up. That is all." *

At this point it would seem that there could be nothing further left to do but bring up the music and flash on the coming attractions. But a few moments later, as Ackerman and Whitacre are walking on the road outside the camp, Ackerman strikes the final resounding chord. "The human beings are going to run the world!" he shouts. "The human beings! There's a lot of Captain Greens! He's not extraordinary! There're millions of them!" And it is of course at this instant, with the words still echoing in the sun-tipped treetops, that Diestl's shots ring out with a truly fiendish irony and Ackerman falls mortally wounded to the ground.

The indictment to which the *New Yorker* overtones and the manufactured parallels gave condemning testimony comes completely clear in these closing pages. What Mailer and Burns could not honestly affirm without distorting the inner truth of their material and, therefore, did not affirm, Shaw affirms through de-

* From *The Young Lions* by Irwin Shaw, published and copyright, 1948, Random House, New York.

liberate distortion and contrivance. The result is not a novel in the true sense but a piece of propaganda designed to give us not a man but a social problem, not an action drawn from life but a pseudo action drawn from Shaw's vast concern for the suffering of the Jewish race. The honesty and intensity of his concern is not our concern, nor is the social importance of the problem with which his book attempts to deal. Our concern must be with the honesty and intensity of his work in so far as it represents a literary achievement, and it is on these terms that his book is a failure.

It is to be hoped that the problems of race will eventually be treated successfully in a literary work of the first rank. If they are, they will be treated as human problems, and the dramatic situation through which they will be discovered will be a natural outgrowth of human emotions and not of forced polemics journalistically presented.*

---

* Joyce's treatment of Leopold Bloom in *Ulysses* and Hemingway's treatment of Robert Cohn in *The Sun Also Rises* are, in my opinion, the most successful portraits of the Jew to be found in modern literature. Bloom and Cohn are convincing precisely because they are presented as human beings caught up in a concrete human dilemma and not merely as Jews reacting only when the forces of discrimination are in play.

CHAPTER X

Merle Miller

Journalist of Sham

THE PARALLEL BETWEEN Skinner Galt and Peter, the narrator-protagonist of Merle Miller's *That Winter*, is strikingly close. Both should have been killed in the war but perversely were not. Both were indirectly responsible for the death of a friend who obviously deserved to live more than either of them; and both are burdened with a sense of guilt. But where Skinner was sentenced to a term in prison, during which, presumably, he was able to complete the process of becoming dead and thus expiate his crime, Peter is restored to civilian life and sentenced to his own remorse, a fate considerably more unnerving than Skinner's. Peter's remorse, unfortunately, is the sort that gains rapidly in volume, if not in conviction, as the martinis are downed and the party grows more maudlin and the other guests begin to unlock their own secret hearts. Like most sentimentalists who have gone sour, Peter is at his best when he is being laconic and hurt and is parading his pathos before an audience of those who love him enough to be able to endure him. He plays at being the very, very sad young man with great skill; and no one anticipates his effects more closely than he.

Perhaps this is why Peter is a fool and *That Winter* is, in most respects, a foolish book. The author plays Peter's role a bit too cleverly; he anticipates his effects like a carpenter fitting together a prefabricated house; and he writes too glibly to be altogether on the level. Ordinarily, we do not take a novel more seriously than the author appears to take it. In this case we must assume that the author is laughing with us. It would be uncharitable to think otherwise.

The dominant tone of the novel is one of contrived indifference. It is not merely that the characters and the life they represent are contrived and indifferent, but that the manner in which Miller describes them is so patently false that we must conclude that he saw them in those terms. If indeed he took his people at all seriously, he seems to have been uncertain just how much importance he should assign them at the same time that he was fairly convinced that they were really quite trivial. Throughout the novel, consequently, there is evidence of the split in motive which must have troubled his mind. There is evidence also of a deeper confusion. The story must obviously center around the dilemma of the characters and derive its significance from the significance of that dilemma. Yet Miller manages to write with his tongue so far around in his cheek that we are disposed to sneer at most of the important questions he raises. As if this were not enough, he then proceeds to falsify them so fraudulently in context that the last of whatever value they might have had for him or for us is drained away into absurdity.

We are introduced, at the outset, to a variety of persons of whom the principals are veterans and nearly all of whom have ostensibly been scarred or numbed by the war. The men are Peter, a young writer employed by a weekly news magazine; Ted, a rich young alcoholic who has lost an arm in combat; Lew, a Jewish youth with the problem of racial discrimination very much on his mind; and Dick Westing, a once-sincere novelist who has compromised his principles for money. The women are Martha Westing, Dick's somewhat martyred wife; Katherine Hutton, Peter's ex-girl-friend back in Iowa; and a couple of New York career girls named Joan and Gloria, whom Peter phones periodically during the course of the narrative but without conspicuous success. We look on while these people drink and make love and have fights, and we are properly impressed when they mention real places—Louis and Armand's, the Stork Club, and "21"—and then go to drink and have lunch in them. Touches like these add the right amount of verisimilitude to a tale that is about as natural as a plastic dish.

It is surprising how little of importance happens to these people and how little we really know about them. They are all terribly sophisticated of course. They have all the proper enthusiasms and prejudices that life in New York can give them; and they are as free of rough edges and character as their creator's prose. Like Miller, they love to be laconic and hard-bitten; but in comparison with Hemingway's people, they are as soft and innocent as lambs. They dote on all the best plays—and even on some of the bad ones just to be different. They admire the correct actors but not always for the correct reasons. They are absolutely certain of their tastes and have a kind of instinct for slick analysis which tells them what it is fashionable to discuss in a bar, how it is fashionable to drink, where it is fashionable to be seen dining, and how long after two people have been introduced it is fashionable for them to go to bed together. An example is Peter's description of Joan:

. . . she had an interesting figure, nice legs and good breasts, blue eyes and dark hair. I've always liked the combination of blue eyes and dark hair. Joan had read most of the books I'd read and usually liked the same ones. She enjoyed French movies but didn't make much of a point of it, and she didn't like modern ballet and did like the theater, and she thought Elizabeth Bergner was a bore and Ethel Merman wonderful; she cried at Bette Davis movies, thought Tallulah Bankhead was one of the greatest comediennes now living; and she didn't apologize for laughing at Fred Allen, Jack Benny, and, especially, Henry Morgan, or liking popular songs, modern jazz, and even Tchaikovsky. . . .*

* From *That Winter* by Merle Miller, published and copyright, 1948, William Sloane Associates, Inc., New York.

The really interesting thing about this description is not what it reveals about Joan but what it reveals about Peter. Notice the sham and sophisticated hatred of sham and sophistication— "didn't make much of a point of it," "didn't apologize for laughing," "even Tchaikovsky"—the faked air of easy carelessness, the cheap cosmopolitanism, the smartly terse language, the slickly knowing manner.

It is difficult to imagine any of the larger issues arising out of this milieu and, as a matter of fact, none does. What happens is that Miller superimposes his issues after they have been cut down to size and had their subtler implications planed off. Near the beginning of the novel we are confronted with the problem of Ted. Ted, if we do not delve too deeply, is a conventional product of the war. He found a purpose in the Army which he cannot find in his overrich civilian life; and the resulting despair has him well on the road to a Park Avenue alcoholic ward. Later on we take up the problem of Lew and finally of Peter. The Jewish boy, Lew, came out of the Army only to face a life of suppression as a civilian. Peter finds himself in a compromising position on the news magazine and struggles rather feebly until he decides to make good his debt of honor to the wife of the man for whose death he was responsible. As soon as Miller tries to resolve the difficulties of his cast, he begins to reveal his weaknesses.

If the detailed attention he gives to the war in his innumerable flash backs is to be justified, he must show that the war was really the factor which precipitated his characters' dilemmas. Either that, or he must give more attention to characterization. But since he fails to do the latter, we are left with a vast motivating experience which has almost nothing to do with the characters as they are described to us. Ted's problem actually has no bearing on the war but upon the life of the very rich. Before the war, Ted was just as purposeless. He always had too much money. His suicide, especially as it follows upon the doubtful climax of the fight with

Westing is, consequently, in excess of the motive we are asked to accept for it. Lew had learned long before the war the difficulty of being Jewish in this society. After the war it was neither better nor worse. His decision to change his name, his argument with his fiancée Jane Walker, and his final decision to return West to his father's business, are, therefore, crises he would have had to meet and overcome at any point in his life, war or no war. For Peter there would always have been compromise, although if it had not been for the war he would not have known Gene Wenisloski nor decided to go to Mississippi and write his novel. But consider once again the evidence we are given for Peter's decision. The story of Wenisloski is revealed only near the end of the novel. Before then, Peter is confronted with more immediate factors than his remorse. There is Ted's suicide; Westing's degeneration; the trip back to Iowa; his father's funeral; and the encounter with Katherine Hutton; and apparently what is more important than any of these to Peter, the departure of Lew and the marriage of Joan, in whom Peter is more interested than he is willing to admit. The war and the death of Wenisloski are incidental. They are significant only as they are reinforced by these other occurrences.

Miller might still have made a convincing novel without the war if he had been able to endow his people with individual convictions which would have grown in credible fashion out of their backgrounds. But this he failed to do. We do not believe in Ted, Lew, Peter, Westing, or especially Peter's friend Harry Myers, the ex-Communist, because they are never realized as characters. Ted and Lew are social problems, case histories rather than human beings. They are inconsequential next to the theme they are intended to carry. Westing cannot be distinguished from his type nor can Peter be distinguished from the hundreds of bright young men who are supposedly selling their souls daily to editors precisely like the ones described. Myers is the biggest fraud of all because he is as coincidentally encountered in the narrative as he is by Peter during his short stopover in Chicago between trains. Besides, Myers is, like the others, so obviously contrived, so clearly the sum of the author's pseudo social notions rather than of human parts, that he fails utterly to make his point.

The war should have served Miller better than it does. It *ought* to be a satisfactory explanation for what is wrong with his young men. But it is precisely because this war had, in comparison with the first war, relatively little effect upon those who fought in it that Miller was forced to delve back before the war for the sources of his characterizations. He still believed, nonetheless, that the war ought to be significant. Without the war, he was deprived of a precipitating factor. The issues of racial discrimination and spiritual compromise he also felt to be important; but he was unable to reconcile them with the view of life which his own perceptions required him to present. The truth was that in saying what they had to say and in believing what they had to believe or in failing altogether to believe his people were futile and purposeless. It was his attempt to make them otherwise that caused them to seem false and contrived.

Miller's tone and manner stand against him in this regard. Where Hemingway's style set the key and served as a reinforcement of his attitude, Miller's—so much like Hemingway's in its superficial effects—directly contradicts the ideas he presents. The resemblance is itself to blame; for we are given a style which has come to be the common denominator of futility and asked to accept an affirmative attitude couched in the terms of that style. It is not merely that Miller could not disengage his ideas from his mode but that he could not bring to bear on his ideas a mode which would display them most effectively. This seems to me to account for the sense one has of artificiality if not of actual falsification. The novel is really composed of two directly opposite views—one, perhaps most genuinely the author's, which is based upon his awareness of the inherent meaning of his material, and another based upon his notion of the meaning that ought to arise out of his material. Like Shaw, Miller could not bear to let his insight take him where it would.

I am not one of those who feel that Miller's third novel, *The Sure Thing*, is an improvement over *That Winter*. A great many of the reviewers were persuaded by the timeliness and complete justice of its theme to think it was. They took it, as they took Gore Vidal's *The City and the Pillar*, on its extraliterary merits and they found it a sincere and passionate book. I can, of course, sympathize with any reviewer who is able to approach literature in such a way that he need make no distinction between a competently written piece of journalism and a work of serious creative art. I can, in fact, even envy him; for there are so many problems which simply must not exist for him. But for those reviewers to whom such a distinction is crucial, I feel it should be pointed out that *The Sure Thing*, for all its sincerity and passion, which I am by no means sure it has, is not a work of serious creative art but a competently written piece of journalism.

As such, it is in many ways a less satisfactory book than *That Winter*. Setting aside for a moment the special question of its theme, one can see in it, in greatly expanded form and without benefit of the old excuses, nearly all the tricks, affectations, and transparencies which cheapened the earlier novel. The flash backs, which were formerly acceptable if one could accept the war as a convincing motivating force, have now greatly multiplied and lengthened and become, for the most part, nothing more than fill-ins. The endless descriptions of the personal habits of the characters, the lists of the contents of their handbags and suitcases, the names of living celebrities and existing bars, which, in *That Winter*, had a certain charm and novelty, borrowed, perhaps, from the charm and novelty of one or two of the characters, have also become, now that the charm has faded, merely space fillers. Even the style has changed for the worse: the old irony and pity, which had, at its best, some of the qualities of a counterfeit Hemingway, has now become frank and open glibness; the terseness has relaxed into mere monotone; and the excitement that Miller was able to generate out of experience which one knew he had felt intensely is now gone.

There is also in *The Sure Thing* an annoying reappearance of certain situations and character types that were made stock by their appearance in the earlier book. Not only do we find ourselves back in the same old bars and restaurants, renamed, of course, and shipped from New York to Washington, but we are called upon to endure another suicide, another ex-boy-genius who has sold out, regretfully, to the system, another nice young man (this time a liberal instead of a Jew) who is persecuted by the system, another rich boy who made good in the Army and never made good again, another encounter with a homosexual, another collection of fascist windbags (this time politicians instead of magazine editors), and another assortment of women who are always sitting in bars and talking in that clamp-jawed, Navy Yard manner which seems destined to remain Miller's approximation of the way women who are habitually sitting in bars always talk.

But even more annoying is the reappearance of some of the same attitudes that were expressed in *That Winter* and that were just beginning to seem phony when that book ended. Foremost among these is Miller's militant veteranism which gave us some rough moments before and which gives us several more now. In *That Winter* the veteranism of Peter, the narrator, functioned as a distinct moral code, the only one the novel could possibly have supported. It was the principle that divided the characters into opposing camps and endowed them with the qualities that made it possible to tell them apart. The "good guys" were those who had served overseas in combat, preferably with a rank below that of staff sergeant, and who, because of such service, had developed a deep respect for the simple virtues—honor, courage, honesty, loyalty, and that cardinal distinction of the fighting man, "grace under pressure." The "good guy" could always be counted on to sense immediately whether a girl was a "lay," a "broad," or a "nice girl," and to act accordingly. He always knew just how much liquor he could take and still retain the ability to talk out of the corner of his mouth. He was always unfailingly tolerant, belligerently liberal; he was, in fact, so belligerently liberal that he was always ready to take a swing at anybody who was *not* a Negro, Communist, or Jew. He loved his friends with the kind of passion that is sometimes suspected in boys' camps and boarding schools. But he had a deathly fear of homosexuals. They were always coming up to him in bars and parks and making suggestive comments; and he would always turn quietly away after manfully suppressing an urge to take a swing at them.

Peter, Ted, and Lew were all "good guys" in *That Winter*. So were Harry Myers and Gene Wenisloski. But Dick Westing and Joe Davidson were "bad guys." According to Peter's code, all non-veterans and nine-tenths of all veterans who held a rank above that of staff sergeant were "bad guys." Westing was one, first, because he was a nonveteran and, second, because he had "sold out" in direct violation of the simple virtue of honor. Davidson was one, first, because he had held the rank of Captain and, second, because, in spite of his service, he had not learned the simple virtue of humility. He had been overbearing and arrogant during the war and had made the grave error of treating Peter, on one occasion, as an enlisted man. When, after the war, he appeared as a candidate for a job on the news magazine, Peter was afforded the rare opportunity to pay him back. The scene in which Peter has his revenge on Davidson is one of the high moments in the chronicle of Miller's militant veteranism.

In *The Sure Thing* the protagonist Bradley Douglas, his friend

Jerry Milton, the rich boy who is the counterpart of Ted, and Edwin Emerson, the fatherly old gentleman who commits suicide because of Douglas's predicament, are all "good guys." Although Douglas shows, on at least two occasions, the sort of virtue necessary to admit him to the category, it is Jerry Milton who carries the main burden of good-guy-ness through the novel. Jerry is really perfect for the job because he is not only a combat veteran but an ex-prisoner of war. He is also rich without being vain or corrupt. His devotion to Douglas is pure and steadfast but carefully masculine. His devotion to women, liquor, and money is sincere but deliberately nonchalant. He knows and respects the value of sex and tries to take as many women to bed as he possibly can. Yet he loves and is loved by none. He has that easy, controlled elegance of manner which *Esquire* and Eastern prep schools bestowed upon the enlightened members of the younger generation. It is a manner that derives as well from the glib but highly selective congeniality of life at one of the better Ivy League colleges and that is ordinarily perfected after a few years of editorial experience on the staff of *Time* or *The New Republic*. Jerry acquired it in childhood when he found out that for the rest of his life he was to have a little too much money. He perfected it in college, and then made it a bit more perfect by adding to it just the right touch of detached longing and regret which he had learned in the Army and which he knew gave women the impression that he was perpetually reliving in his memory the horrors of the war and the dark tragedy of his fallen comrades.

With a few more characters like Jerry, each making his weary and sardonic way through the bars that are named after real bars and picking up the weary and sardonic women who are always waiting to be picked up in them, Miller might have made *The Sure Thing* into an amusing, second-rate comedy of manners; the title could then have referred to the ease of sexual conquest. But he had the urge to devote the bulk of the novel to something more serious, to a detailed exposé of the terrible consequences of the Washington witch hunt to the private life and professional career of Bradley Douglas; and it turned out to be as misguided an urge as the one that compelled him to find a meaning and a solution for the lives of the people in *That Winter*. The dilemma of Bradley Douglas is so thoroughly tainted with the phoniness of the milieu in which Miller places it, with the phoniness of characters like Jerry and of the attitude implicit in the writing itself, that we are urged, after a while, to conclude that this fundamental problem is phony too.

The nightmarish evil which Douglas's predicament represents is, in itself, as serious and true as any issue of our time. It is the terrifying evil of guilt by association, of accusation without specified charge, of punishment without trial. It is the kind of evil which makes it possible for one group of men arbitrarily to invent a crime and then to accuse other men, just as arbitrarily, of having committed it, even when many of those men have been guilty of nothing more than the exercise of their right to be skeptical and others had merely been intellectually associated with the crime years earlier when it had been fashionable for perceptive men to be intellectually associated with it and long before it had been made into a crime. Kafka, Orwell, Sinclair Lewis, and many others have written brilliantly about this kind of evil. But when Miller writes about it he manages to do what one would think would be nearly impossible: he manages to make it trivial and unworthy of the men who have been destroyed by it.

The first and most obvious weakness in Miller's treatment of Douglas is a tactical one. Instead of making Douglas a man victimized for a crime he did not commit or simply for his liberalism, his intelligence, or his association with guilty friends, he makes him a man victimized for a crime he did commit. Not only was Douglas a card-carrying Communist for a brief time during the Thirties but, what is most important, he was guilty of concealing the fact when he applied for a job with the State Department. The crime he is accused of committing need not, therefore, be merely Communism but deliberate falsification of government records. Thus, the sympathy we should feel for him, along with our respect for the danger his predicament represents, is seriously weakened; and we are forced to remind ourselves again and again that the real threat is not to men like Douglas who really were Communists but to all those others who never were. If, on the other hand, Miller definitely intended Douglas's guilt to show that society itself was responsible for the crime, that is, that Douglas was actually forced by society to lie about a youthful indiscretion in order to save his job, reputation, and future in this country, then Miller's was a concept well conceived but poorly executed.

Douglas's case is weakened further by Miller's failure to make him important as a character. As is always the case with Miller's people, we know almost nothing about him at the same time that we know almost everything about his life. We are introduced to him in the same way that the silent young men of the FBI are introduced to him—through the medium of biographical research and investigation into his private life. We know what he was like as a child, what books he read as a youth, what views he held in college, what kind of women he married, what kind of life he had with them, what kind of worker he is, what he eats for breakfast, what brand of cigarettes his ex-wife smokes (Pall Malls), even what his I.Q. is (128). We are given all the facts, but we are not given the man. We are never allowed a glimpse of his mental processes; we are never allowed to experience the subtle changes of his mood, the growing apprehension as he begins to feel himself drawn into the net of intrigue, the final terror and despair as he realizes he is trapped. All this we might well infer from the thick mesh of detail which surrounds him; but we are not shown it or made to feel it because it was never there to begin with.

The fault is traceable once more to the grave limitations of

Miller's method. In both his novels Miller has revealed his gift for highly skilled reportage. He is a master journalist and a sensitive observer. He can describe surface appearances and actions as well as any of his contemporaries. He can catch the precise feel of a situation and formulate a gesture or a characteristic phrase with swift, sure strokes. But his vision never extends beyond the range of a candid camera. It is a comprehensive vision; it takes in everything that can be seen, however important or trivial it may be; but it is unselective and essentially unimaginative. Another man with a modicum of insight and comparable skill could say more in a few pages than Miller can say in an entire novel.

But the thing which is by far Miller's gravest limitation is his lack of seriousness, his tone of mockery and simulation, which gives to everything he writes a touch of phoniness. It is as if he were perpetually belittling his function as a writer while performing the act of writing, perpetually struggling to hide his scorn for his characters at the very moment of creating them. Or perhaps it is simply that he is too completely committed to their world, to their slick-magazine values, their cocktail-lounge philosophy, and their tepid, passionless little intrigues, to be able to rise above them and give them a stature and a significance which they do not possess.

CHAPTER XI

Gore Vidal

The Search for a King

GORE VIDAL, at twenty-five, occupies an enviable position in American letters. Not only is he the youngest of the group of new writers whose first books began attracting attention right after the war, but he has already produced as large and varied a body of work as many of his contemporaries may be expected to produce comfortably in a lifetime. Since 1946, when his first novel, *Williwaw,* was published, Vidal has written a novel a year—*In a Yellow Wood* in 1947, *The City and the Pillar* in 1948, *The Season of Comfort* in 1949, and now, in 1950, *A Search for the King.* He has a sixth novel, *Dark Green, Bright Red* completed and awaiting publication and a seventh already in progress.*

Williwaw—written when Vidal was nineteen and still in the Army—was a slight and unpretentious book about the war. It was done in the clipped Hemingway manner; the sentences appeared to have been telegraphed and then pasted over the page. But there were no signs of Hemingway's purposeful understatement, his suggestion of hidden layers of immense unspoken meaning. The approach was literal and bald, the props had been carefully cut away rather than concealed, and the emotion was so rigidly controlled that one had the impression of reading a book which had only just managed to get written. Yet there was evidence of

* Since *Dark Green, Bright Red* was published some time after the manuscript of this book went to press, it could not be included in the discussion of Vidal's work to date. I might point out, however, that its appearance does nothing whatever to alter the pattern of Vidal's achievement or to justify a revision of the opinions I have expressed here.

170

real, if premature, mastery in the handling of the central situation—the struggle of the men to bring their ship through the williwaw—and more than an intimation of potential insight in the brief characterizations. Vidal seemed to have learned early the trick of the narrow scope, the tight portrait. Where most young writers try to grapple with an outsized situation and too many characters and succeed only in revealing their youth, he apparently saw the advantage of leaving certain material alone until he grew up to it. His characters, consequently, were purposely unrealized, made up simply of a very few deft touches that gave the illusion of a total, although shadowy, outline. By concentrating on a single trait of a man, Vidal implied others. By yielding even scant information with reluctance, he forced the reader into a contest in which the winning of a single clue became—since it was won with such difficulty—more satisfying than complete revelation.

But the real power of *Williwaw* lay in the faithfulness of its intention to its impact, its tone to its material. In the williwaw—a violent storm common in the Aleutians—Vidal found the perfect instrument for making dramatic the emotion around which the novel was constructed and for which his terse style set the key. The truth of the war for the men who lived in its boredom but were denied its dangers was purposelessness. The contrast between the excitement and terror of the storm and the utter indifference of their reaction to it was thus the supreme, ironic example of that purposelessness.

Up to the beginning of the storm the situation of the characters is the typical one of men who find themselves lost seemingly forever in the backwash of war. They have all been away from home too long; their assignment involves an endless series of dull runs in their ship between islands in the Aleutians. Their sanity depends on the extent to which they are able to lose themselves in the petty diversions available to them outside the routine of their jobs.

They get drunk and make love to prostitutes when they are in port; they get drunk and quarrel among themselves when they are at sea. Their trip to Arunga, on which the main action is based, is simply another dull and unimportant job. Only the storm has possibilities of making it otherwise.

But even at its height the storm fails to be an activating force. To be sure, coordinated effort is required to save the ship, and individual differences are submerged in the struggle; but the change is only temporary. As soon as the storm is over, the monotony resumes, and the conflict among the men moves toward its inevitable climax as if nothing whatever had happened. During a quarrel over the favors of a girl, one of them is half-accidentally, half-purposely killed. Nearly everyone on the ship suspects the man responsible, but none will accuse him. Even the officer who has evidence of his guilt decides to say nothing. A certain primitive loyalty arising out of their common danger during the storm has bound the men together after all. But it is a loyalty without a basis in moral action. It is simply a gesture of contempt for all authority and law, a sort of conspiracy into which they enter against those who have not shared their purposelessness and exhaustion.

The final effect is similar to that of *The Naked and the Dead*—utter futility. But where the parts of Mailer's story anticipated a protest in the conclusion, *Williwaw* moves logically through the futility of its parts to the climaxing futility at its end. The childishly simple plot, the elemental action with its emphasis on one or two concrete emotions, the absence of all ideas, and the carefully underdone prose are excellently suited to the type of world which the novel presents. They are also excellently suited to the talents of a very young man who has experienced a great deal and had the good sense to write only of what he knows, can clearly see, and unthinkingly understand.

The sure technical control and simple amorality of *Williwaw* is preserved through the first half of Vidal's second novel, *In a Yellow Wood*. The numb purposelessness of men at war is now transferred to the exhausted and uneasy world of the war's aftermath and centered in a young man who came out of the war drained of personality and interested only in losing himself in the business routine. Like the men of *Williwaw* he is doped·on a continual round of mechanical acts which serve to insulate him from the complexities of the life around him. He rises in the morning and dresses himself with great care. His breakfast is a solemn ritual performed cautiously with a doting waitress. He preoccupies himself with subway posters so that he will not have to talk about the war with the man sitting next to him. At the brokerage office where he works he is met with the usual greetings from the other employees; he is polite but reserved with the pretty secretary who finds him attractive; he does his job with the prim efficiency of an adding machine; he makes a methodical trip to the washroom. The story of Robert Holton's morning reads like the itinerary of a desensitized Leopold Bloom; and in the style in which it is described, Vidal once again finds the perfect medium for the utterly purposeless and banal.

But the sudden intrusion of Carla, Holton's wartime lover, midway in the novel sends deep tremors through his detachment; and as this occurs, the style is required to take on a burden that is beyond its powers. The technique that served so well as a journalistic device for reporting concrete simplicities and drugged actions of external people now begins to crack and loosen as the story demands a shift to the abstract ideas and emotional states of internal people. For Vidal, the entry of Carla obviously meant an opportunity to introduce a theme, make an ideological point, and to show a contrast between the dead world of Holton and the intensely alive and struggling world into which Carla attempts to entice him. But the two worlds really have nothing to do with one another. Not only are they basically incompatible but Vidal cannot manipulate his style into bridging the gap between them.

To reinforce the weak purchase he has on his theme, Vidal introduces a third character, George Robert Lewis. In sharp contrast to Holton, Lewis is an extremely sensitive homosexual who is profoundly aware of the human need to find spiritual fulfillment in something greater than the self. It is through Lewis that this need is finally developed into the central theme of the novel; and it is also through Lewis that Holton is afforded a glimpse of the peripheral nighttime world in which Lewis lives and fulfills himself in art and in which Carla and Holton must live if they are to fulfill themselves in love. But such a theme cannot be adequately objectified in the cold and mechanical style with which Vidal wrote the first half of the novel, just as the idea it signifies cannot be made meaningful to the cold and mechanical person Vidal has shown Holton to be. The result, therefore, is that the theme is superimposed on the style and the idea is superimposed on Holton's life. While the style toward the end of the novel maintains the monosyllabic pace which it set in the beginning, it is now reinforced with long passages of rhetoric inserted at intervals through it. These passages—such as those presented in the form of speeches made by Lewis to Holton and Carla in the nightclub and later recalled by Holton in a sort of dream-reverie as he falls asleep—carry the theme, but since they remain outside and above the action, they are merely undigested assertions. They never touch the dilemma of the characters, which has already been revealed on the active level, because Vidal cannot make them concrete in terms of the style in which he has previously described that dilemma.

The style is as clearly Holton's prison as his conventionality is supposed to be. If we assume that the Frost poem from which the novel's title is taken contains the key to his predicament as Vidal sees it, then we must assume that Vidal intends us to accept Holton as paralyzed in the act of choosing between two divergent

roads, a life of timid security as a businessman and a life of
Bohemian freedom and love with Carla. But from the picture
we are given of Holton in the first half of the novel we conclude
that he is firmly committed to conventionality long before Carla
arrives to give him the opportunity of choice. The style which is
so perfectly suited to his emptiness also prevents him from being
anything more than empty; and he must develop into something
more if we are to accept the idea that he was tempted, even momentarily, to choose Carla's way.

To do what he wanted to do in *In a Yellow Wood*, Vidal needed
a subtler and far more flexible technique, one that would serve
as the formula not only for Holton's sterile purposelessness but
for Carla's affirmative ideal. He also needed a point of view, a set
of values, through which he could make his theme dramatically
meaningful. But the emptiness that is behind these first two novels
makes it clear that he never had them, that, in fact, the search of
his characters for a spiritual center is really the shadow of his own
private search for an artistic center of meaning.

In *The City and the Pillar*, Vidal's third and best-known novel,
this search is still unrewarded, and the technique that proved
too weak to carry the ideological weight of *In a Yellow Wood* now
shows signs of being thoroughly flattened. The old terseness has
given way to hollowness; the old theme is felt everywhere in the
material but it is now, one feels, almost shamelessly planted. All
the effects in the novel come out a uniform shade of gray, and
every page bears testimony to exhaustion and haste.

Perhaps the most significant change in *The City and the Pillar*
is a structural one. Where in his first two books, at least up to the
beginning of the second half of *In a Yellow Wood*, Vidal was careful to focus his narrative on a single action and on one main
character through whom the material was seen as a whole, he
now begins to build outward toward a multiplicity of actions and
a number of characters, through whom the material is seen in

fragments. There is, of course, the one dominating problem of Jim Willard around which the other actions and characters are gathered; but the story of Willard's struggle to recapture the reality of a childhood homosexual experience neither centers the novel thematically nor orders it structurally.

Willard's problem is simply a larger difficulty set down in the midst of several smaller difficulties: it touches all of them but they would be as separately meaningful without it. The same can be said for the theme which his problem suggests. Like Willard, the other characters—Maria Verlaine, Ronald Shaw, and Paul Sullivan—are all searching for the perfect spiritual union in love; and all, with the possible exception of Maria, fail to find it. But each of their problems is a particle rather than an aspect of the central theme. Each remains separate from the others; each has its own motivation and, in the end, its own resolution.

This is another way of saying that there is no master design, no unifying philosophical principle behind *The City and the Pillar.* In building outward Vidal had to transcend his former limits and try to find the ingredients of his old theme in the variegated experience of many lives. He found them finally, but he found them everywhere—with the result that he put the ingredients alone into the novel; the theme, by then, had eluded him.

It is interesting to see that as he loses touch with the dramatic resources of his theme Vidal falls back on the same nondramatic device he used in the last part of *In a Yellow Wood.* As Jim Willard moves from one sterile homosexual relationship to another, each time coming a step closer to the perfect one he seeks, he encounters a variety of persons, both lovers and chance acquaintances, who philosophize on the need for fulfillment in love. Like Lewis's in *In a Yellow Wood,* their ideas take the form of speeches made during arguments at cocktail parties or in bars. The only difference in the usage of the device in the two books is that where Lewis spoke affirmatively and his words were set against Robert Holton's paralysis, the characters in *The City and the Pillar* speak of the impossibility of fulfillment and their words are set against Willard's hope. But the fact that Vidal has to resort to the device at all would indicate that he could not find in the hope alone a strong enough medium for his theme and was forced to editorialize upon it.

The journalistic atmosphere which such a device tends to generate is present throughout the novel. Jim Willard never seems to be living through the ordinary cycle of *human* experience; he is always meeting and overcoming a particular obstacle in the particular cycle of obstacles which Vidal has carefully contrived to make a sociological point. The characters are nothing more than allegorical shells designed to illustrate the plight of the sexually abnormal in modern society. As such, their absorbing interest is sex, but Vidal has managed to squeeze the life so thoroughly out of them that their sex is neither lusty nor passionate. It is as far removed from their bodies as they themselves are removed from flesh and blood.

We never really sympathize with Willard as he gropes pathetically through the novel for the one perfect love of his boyhood, and we have to sympathize with him if the novel is to have any excuse at all for being written. He is presented entirely from the outside; we are told that he moves from place to place (Hollywood, Texas, Guatemala, New York) and is involved in various occupations (tennis instructor, gentleman's companion, army private); but we see nothing inside him to justify his movements or to convince us that he feels anything whatever. And when finally his search is ended and his frustration becomes a murderous rage which he turns on the man who cannot love him, we are still unmoved, as if we were witnessing a dumb show of emotions that have no basis in truth and, therefore, no consequences.

But when we have explored all the flaws of the novel we have still not really arrived at the basis of its total failure, which is that it is at bottom a thoroughly amoral book—not *immoral* in the conventional sense, because it deals with homosexuality, but amoral in the purely ethical sense, because there is no vitality or significance in the view of life which has gone into it. It seems to have evolved out of an absolute spiritual nothingness in which all things suffer from the same poverty of content and in which the vitally important and the cheaply trivial are viewed alike. If Vidal showed signs in his previous work of a weakening of his technical and dramatic power, he here shows the far more disturbing signs of a spreading aridity of soul.

It is perhaps because Vidal began to sense these symptoms in himself that he sought in his next book to turn away from the world of his maturity and to find the sources of his problem in childhood. Certainly the attempt was sound enough; for the other novels were all immediate translations of present experience; the characters in each were at about the same stage of development that Vidal was when he conceived them; and he must have realized that at least part of his trouble lay in the fact that he had no perspective on the material with which he was working. But one is forced to conclude that the attempt was a failure. *The Season of Comfort* is an even emptier and more chaotic novel than *The City and the Pillar.* It is totally without form; its parts have almost no relation to the whole; and its characters are dead.

Vidal seems to have stood in utter confusion before the material he put into the novel. It is apparently autobiographical; for it has all the defects of personal experience partially digested and imperfectly recalled. The episodes that make up the individual parts seem to have been used simply because they have a basis in life and ought, therefore, to be important. They seldom have reference to the main point of the novel; and most of them do not even have the virtue of being interesting in themselves. They are simply unselected fragments which Vidal has put together to fill out a story he felt vaguely needed to be written, perhaps to solve a problem he knew he had but never fully understood.

The result is that the novel approaches its material with the same groping perplexity as that with which Vidal approached the experience he put into it. The first half is devoted to a detailed portrait of the Hawkins family from which, much later in the book, the figure of William Giraud, the main character, is finally disengaged. But long before this happens, we are subjected to countless irrelevant flash backs to the girlhood of William's mother, Charlotte. We learn that she had an incestuous relationship with her brother before he went off to die in World War I and that the experience affected her whole view of life in some mysterious way. We learn that she and her mother, Clara Hawkins, always hated each other, especially after she accused her mother of being drunk most of the time. We learn that, on the other hand, she greatly admired her father, Vice-President Hawkins, because he was a great man and a national figure. But none of this information is ever made meaningful in terms of the central action of the novel, and after a while it is quietly dropped. We may assume from the amount of space Vidal devotes to it that he thought it *ought* to be meaningful, but he seems to have been uncertain precisely in what way.

The same can be said for the information we are given about William. We watch him as he moves through a succession of preparatory schools, acquires a homosexual tenderness for his best friend, Jimmy Wesson, and gradually develops into a promising painter. In between, through many flash backs and other odd interspersions, we catch glimpses of him attending the funeral of his grandfather and then of his grandmother, having long discussions with a girl to whom he is distantly attracted, and finally developing a long-overdue awareness of the unhealthy emotional dependency which binds him to his mother.

But the difficulty is that this awareness dawns on William and the reader at the same time. There is nothing in the action leading up to it that would indicate that such a dependency exists. It is true that one is occasionally aware of a slight tension in the relationship, but it is so thoroughly smothered in the mass of irrelevant material intruded upon the story that it never becomes overt enough to be taken seriously. It is obvious, however, that Vidal meant it to be taken seriously because he suddenly builds a major climaxing scene around it. Through a device which he calls "parallel construction" he juxtaposes the thoughts of William and Charlotte (the two interior monologues occupying facing pages) as they take out their resentments on one another. After the rather pointless contents of their minds are thoroughly exposed, William manages to rouse himself to a supreme denunciation of his mother, and their relationship is ended, presumably for good.

It is interesting to see at the very end of the novel, after William has gone to war and been wounded, that the factor which finally releases him from the past and prepares him for a new life of freedom is neither the war nor his break with his mother. It is the death of Jimmy Wesson, with whom, earlier in the book, he had been in love. Once again, as in *In a Yellow Wood* and *The City and the Pillar,* the true emotional basis of the characters is homosexuality; and one suspects that the problem which Vidal thought was identified with William's feelings about his mother was more truly identified, perhaps on a less conscious level, with William's homosexual feelings for Wesson. Certainly, the awkward and unconvincing treatment of the mother-son conflict as well as the sudden and unexplained reference to Wesson at the end would suggest that such is the case. At any rate, *The Season of Comfort* is full of some stuff that Vidal could not bring to light and objectify. Its true significance is buried, while its apparent significance is so slight that the material that went into it remains inert and unused.

There is one important difference between *The Season of Comfort* and the two preceding novels. Where before Vidal super-

imposed his characters' search for fulfillment upon the action of the story, he attempts here to demonstrate that search in William's struggle to free himself from his mother. He also finds a concrete symbol to replace the hazy abstractions he previously used to present the need for a spiritual center. In the chapter entitled "The King" he writes: "Oh, it would be good to have the King in the house since the center of this house was dead. The two women needed it, mother and daughter, needed the central man. . . . The King was a man, of course, and, some said, a disagreeable one, but today he would not be accepted as human. Today he was to be their symbol, and they were no longer aimless fragments but, for a time, satellites, with a path to follow. . . ." *
The center is now the king, the great man in whom one can still have faith in spite of the world's chaos and futility. It is a symbol which is only briefly suggested in *The Season of Comfort;* it never becomes really meaningful and it does nothing whatever to reduce the technical confusion of the novel. But in Vidal's next novel *A Search for the King* it is expanded into a philosophical foundation on which the entire central action is based.

Toward the end of *The Season of Comfort* Vidal, like Henry Adams generations before, speaks of the twelfth century as "the age of faith." It is fitting, therefore, that he should find a frame of reference for his new novel in that age. If the novels after *Williwaw* were failures because he could discover nothing in modern life that would make faith tangible, he could at least go back into the past to a time when faith was still a living presence and the symbol of the king was part of the common experience of man.

The search of the legendary troubadour Blondel for the captured King Richard is an allegory designed to illustrate in dramatic terms the full implications of Vidal's theme. In the beginning Blondel thinks of Richard as simply a convenient means of self-

---

* From *The Season of Comfort* by Gore Vidal, published and copyright, 1949, E. P. Dutton & Co., Inc., New York.

preservation. Richard's power protects him from the hazards of ordinary minstrel life, and Richard's friendship protects him from loneliness. But as the search progresses, Richard loses his practical function and becomes, in Blondel's mind, the symbolic king who is the goal of all our searching. The giants, werewolves, and vampires whom Blondel meets in his journey through the medieval world represent obstacles which all men must overcome if they are to arrive at the spiritual center of life. "But the people who have no future and no history can go from place to place fearing nothing since they are protected by the present; they recognize none of the boundaries of time; they cross no frontiers; they move only in the present across the world and only a few, like Blondel, realize, if only vaguely, that they must find a king. . . ." *

But Richard's release from captivity brings Blondel's search to an end and ironically defeats it; for Richard's imprisonment was its sole justification. With Richard lost, Blondel was truly a man deprived of a center and forced to examine the deep spiritual premises of his life; but with Richard found, Blondel is restored to his former position as mere friend and entertainer moving "only in the present across the world." As a result, Blondel seeks a center in the boy Karl, in whose strength and innocence he sees a reflection of his own lost youth. But Karl is killed in the battle for Richard's throne, and Blondel's urge toward fulfillment, like that of his predecessors in the other novels, is pathetically thwarted. "It had ended; his own youth lay dead in the rain and he'd be old now, unprotected, centered in himself and never young again."

It would be gratifying to be able to say that in *A Search for the King* Vidal's own search for an artistic center of value comes to an end. But the novel can be taken only for what it is—a simple exercise in light historical fantasy. It does not solve the problem which all the other novels were unsuccessful attempts to solve; it is simply a momentary avoidance of the problem. In his next

* From *A Search for the King* by Gore Vidal, published and copyright, 1950, E. P. Dutton & Co., Inc., New York.

book, Vidal will have to pick up where he left off in *The Season of Comfort* and try once more to fit what he has to say into the experience of his own time.

Right now Vidal is acutely aware of the need for values in both life and art. He is himself one of the best illustrations of the need, and his frantic productivity as a writer testifies to its urgency. The work he has produced up to now clearly shows his sincerity and his restless determination to explore every possibility that might lead him to his goal. But it shows just as clearly the reason for his recurrent failure. The only order Vidal ever found he found in the war, in the terse emotions and simple negation of the men of *Williwaw*. The moment he tried to move into larger and more complex areas of experience he was lost. His writing after *Williwaw* is one long record of stylistic breakdown and spiritual exhaustion. It is confused and fragmentary, pulled in every direction by the shifting winds of impressionism. It is always reacting, always feeling and seeing; but it never signifies because it never believes.

In this sense, Vidal is typical of his generation. He has lived through some of the most crucial events of history. He has read all the books, listened to all the psychiatrists, and been thoroughly purged of dogma and prejudice. The experience has left him with the great virtue of an open mind. But it has taught him one thing which it is sheer suicide for a writer to learn too well—that all things are relative and that there are at least twenty sides to every question.

Vidal's dilemma is wholly inseparable from the dilemma of his characters. As they search for a center of life, so he searches for a center of art. If they move forward, so must he, and finally they must succeed or fail together. For the goal they seek can exist only if Vidal can make it exist by discovering a way of giving it the maximum significance in his art, and that depends, of course, on his discovering a value and a morality for them and for himself.

CHAPTER XII

Paul Bowles

The Canceled Sky

IF THE STRUGGLE of the new writers to make a dramatic affirmation of value could be plotted on a graph, the result would be a parabolic curve extending from the absolute zero of Vance Bourjaily to the absolute zero of Paul Bowles. In first position, at the point where the curve begins its ascent, would come Norman Mailer. Because the lives of the men he chose to portray in *The Naked and the Dead* did not contain positive values, Mailer was deprived of the means to make his protest against war dramatically convincing. He was obliged, therefore, to depend for his dramatic effect on the straight reporting of war violence. In violence he found a way to shock the reader into an acceptance of at least part of his total indignation. John Horne Burns, in the next higher position on the curve, set out to affirm the values of human dignity and love in a milieu of war. But like Mailer, he could not find those values in that milieu and was forced to get them into his book by describing them in the "Promenades." The "Portraits," meanwhile, flatly contradicted his point by demonstrating that the real values of his material were emptiness and futility. Irwin Shaw and Merle Miller would come at the top of the curve because they made the most overtly deliberate effort to affirm, Shaw by warping his material to fit his polemical purpose and Miller, at least in *That Winter,* by simply disregarding the logic of his material and imposing the affirmative destinies of his characters upon it. Vidal, coming at the declining end of the curve, disintegrated artistically because

184

of his failure to find a value for his characters that would make them dramatically meaningful.

To the extent that all these writers have avoided considerations of value and fallen back on a direct rendering of the more violent and sensational forms of experience, their work has achieved a measure of success. To the extent that they have tried to deal dramatically with those considerations, their work has been confused and imperfect. Violence and sensation carry with them their own dramatic value; they are both manifested in concrete action; and they do not depend for their significance upon a hierarchy of moral judgment or belief. An affirmation of value, to be dramatically significant, does, however, depend on such a hierarchy as well as on a kind of experience in which values have concrete reference; and neither of these exists today.

There is, however, another side to this proposition. If the work of these writers shows clearly that a successful dramatic affirmation is impossible today, the work of Paul Bowles shows just as clearly that a successful dramatic negation is equally impossible. To be dramatically successful, negation must have behind it a strong compelling force; it must be angry and rebellious and dogmatic; and in the end, it must be as firmly positive an attitude as the thing against which it is a reaction. This is to say that negation itself must become a value.

The negation which helped to give energy and health to the literature of the Twenties became such a value. But the negation which is merely a form of spiritual nothingness cannot. The nothingness in which all things are unimportant has no value. It is, in fact, a condition in which values have never existed. It is impossible, therefore, for a writer to give it dramatic significance, since to be dramatic a thing must possess a value by which we recognize and accept it as worth while. The best a writer can do if he finds himself dedicated to spiritual nothingness—and he will be if he is at all sensitive to the condition of our time—is to seek in raw violence and direct sensation that drama of shock which will always have a value to all men in all times.

Paul Bowles is acutely sensitive to the condition of our time. His novel *The Sheltering Sky* is a book-length metaphor of the modern world, particularly of the new postwar world in which all morality is relative and life is gray and destined to become grayer as more of the blacks and whites are canceled out. The novel is, in fact, so perfect an image of this world, the quality of the life finds so exact an equivalent in the quality of the art, that all the defects of the life carry over into the art and become defects of the novel.

Kit and Port Moresby, doomed exiles in the contemporary wasteland, move without motive from sensation to sensation through the heat and squalor of Africa. They have no history and no destination. Their names on their passports are their only proof of life, the labels on their luggage their only record of their passage through time. Their sole function in life is, as Hemingway would have put it, *nada;* their sole function in art is to symbolize that condition of spirit in which life, deprived of values, has ceased to exist. They cannot, therefore, by themselves give meaning to the material Bowles has prepared for them. Because they live without values as people, they are without dramatic value as characters.

Fortunately the African setting in which they are placed provides an atmosphere of violence in which their meaning as characters becomes less important than the bizarre actions which they are driven to commit, or which are committed upon them, by their surroundings. The Arab world with its filth, disease, and poverty is an innately destructive world dominated by an ancient spirit of evil. Because of its mixture of races, creeds, and castes, it has no fixed center of moral or religious law. It becomes, therefore, the perfect external equivalent of the spiritual emptiness and moral anarchy of the Moresbys and, through them, of all modern civilization. Like the Pamplona fiesta in *The Sun Also Rises,* it provides the key or parallel in action for the inner breakdown of the characters. But unlike the fiesta and far more importantly, it provides the sole excuse for that breakdown. Because the Moresbys are so completely infused with the complex and richly colored life of Africa, we are led to attribute its complexity and color to them and to find in it a substitute for the motivation we cannot find within their personalities.

The novel consists entirely of a series of violent and sensational actions, of which some are instigated by the Moresbys and others are perpetrated upon them. But in each case it is Africa and not the Moresbys that furnishes the dramatic meaning and impact. Port's experience with the dancing girl Marhnia is the first of these and sets the pattern for the others. As he is guided through the Casbah toward Marhnia's tent, Port is driven by a compulsion which neither he nor we can formulate. He has just come from an odd and inconclusive talk with Kit during which a vague sexual suspicion between them has been hinted at but never made meaningful. He does not particularly want a girl, and we are given no reason for his needing one; yet he allows himself to be led by the Arab Smaïl to Marhnia. The obscurity of his motives is soon disguised, however, by the intrusion upon him of emotions and fears which are not obscure and which, because they are not, serve to divert our minds from everything about him that is. He begins suddenly to suspect that he is being made the victim of some conspiracy in which Smaïl, Marhnia, and all the natives of Africa are involved. Smaïl is evasive about the location of the girl's tent; the streets seem to run endlessly into nowhere; and the section of the city through which they pass seems to conceal a secret horror in its silence. A short time later, as he is making love to Marhnia, this feeling is actualized in concrete violence.

The two arms stole up again, locked themselves about his neck. Firmly he pulled them away, gave them a few playful pats. Only one came up this time; the other slipped inside his jacket and he felt his chest being caressed. Some indefinable false movement there made him reach inside to put his hand on hers. His wallet was already between her fingers. He yanked it away from her and pushed her back on the mattress. "Ah!" she cried, very loud. He rose and stumbled noisily through the welter of objects that lay between him and the exit. This time she screamed briefly. The voices in the other tent became audible. . . .°

The scene that follows is a nightmare of confusion and terror. Port runs wildly away from the tent, imagining, as he does so, that men are converging upon him from all sides. In the darkness he stumbles, falls, and is hurt. But he manages to drag himself up a long staircase leading out of the Arab valley and, at the top, to dislodge a massive boulder and hurl it down the staircase upon the men who he thinks are close behind him. He blunders up a hill through the tombstones of a Moslem graveyard. Finally, exhausted and delirious with fear, he reaches safety on high ground above the city.

The episode, coming as it does near the beginning of the novel, should be expected to illuminate the theme and characters and to accelerate the action. Instead, it serves to replace all three. During its progress, the true action remains suspended, the theme is sacrificed to melodrama, and the character and motives of Port are lost in the raw violence of Africa.

In the episodes that follow, the failure of motivation becomes more obvious as the violence and melodrama become less effective. This is particularly true of those that have to do with the relations of Kit and Tunner. Although Kit is presumably in love with Port at the beginning of the novel and is described as becoming more completely so as the novel progresses, she becomes just as completely involved with Tunner, even though she finds him distasteful as a person and unattractive as a man. The scenes of their love-making, therefore, are totally unjustified thematically and are acceptable at all only because Bowles makes them sensa-

° From *The Sheltering Sky* by Paul Bowles, published and copyright, 1949, New Directions, New York.

tional. The circumstances of Kit's first submission to Tunner on the night of their train trip are illustrative.

There is, first of all, Kit's nervousness which she always has on trains but which is extremely acute on this occasion because Port, in a moment of anger, has put a curse on the trip by saying he hoped there would be an accident. To Kit, a curse of any kind amounts to an open invocation of disaster, so she takes immediate steps to charm herself against it. The champagne Tunner has brought along for quite a different purpose becomes the magic potion which is going to save her, and she drinks a great deal too much of it too quickly. The result is that when she leaves the compartment for the washroom she loses her way and wanders into the fourth-class car which is crowded with Arabs. It is here that the sensational element is introduced; for as she pushes through the crowd of men toward the rear of the car, she is shocked first by the discovery of a yellow louse on the nape of her neck, next by the sight of a man eating quantities of red locusts, and finally by a "wild-faced man holding a severed sheep's head, its eyes like agate marbles staring from their sockets." Then, coming out on the rear platform into a heavy rain, she finds herself "looking directly into the most hideous human face she had ever seen. . . . Where the nose should have been was a dark triangular abyss, and the strange flat lips were white. . . ."

She had the impression of living a dream of terror which refused to come to a finish. She was not conscious of time passing; on the contrary, she felt that it had stopped, that she had become a static thing suspended in a vacuum. Yet underneath was the certainty that at a given moment it would no longer be this way—but she did not want to think of that, for fear that she should become alive once more, that time should begin to move again and that she should be aware of the endless seconds as they passed.

Like Port's premonition of conspiracy during the Mahrnia episode, this impression of Kit's is unexplainable in terms of her character as it has previously been revealed to us. It is perhaps vaguely associated with her latent atavism and it probably fore-shadows her subsequent breakdown after Port's death and her flight into the desert. But in its immediate context it is justified only because it is presented right after the nightmare experience she has just undergone and seems to have been precipitated by it. We are led to assume that her willingness, a few moments later, to let Tunner make love to her is also the result of that experience. The bizarre violence that has gone before has prepared an atmos-phere of unreality in which the act in all its pointlessness is safely removed from the logic by which we must judge it as pointless.

As one might suspect, there comes a time in the narrative when motivation breaks down completely and Africa takes over alto-gether. This begins to occur during the bus trip when Port falls ill, and it is later fully realized in his death and Kit's disappearance. The first symptom is a sudden and unexplained change in Kit's behavior and status as a character. Where previously she had been little more than a shadow in Port's background, she now emerges as the central figure of the novel. As Port loses consciousness and drifts toward death, she comes to life and begins to reveal aspects of herself which we have not been told she possesses. Although she is on the surface a model of solicitude in her concern over Port's suffering, it is evident that there are new impulses awaken-ing within her and that she is finding it increasingly difficult to hold onto her old loyalty to him. It is as if the mysterious evil that is condemning him to die has infected her also and already begun to erase the stamp of his existence from her mind. For as she rides beside him in the bus, she begins to feel, for the first time since she came to Africa, a strong fascination with the wild primitivism of the countryside. The men standing beside the road seem to possess a vital and magnetic attractiveness. She cannot help noticing the admirable figure of a young Arab as he stands erect in his flowing white garment, although "to efface her feeling of guilt at having thought anything at all about him, she felt compelled to bring him to Port's attention." In all her past relations with men, even with Port and Tunner, Kit has been uniformly passionless. But now she is slowly leaving behind all that she was and preparing herself for a destiny of which she has never before been capable.

Unfortunately, in preparing her for this destiny, Bowles not only takes great liberties with Kit's character but inserts a kind of meaning into her relationship with Port that the relationship as it has been portrayed does not justify. Her flight into the desert is ostensibly motivated by three impulses: first, her need to purge herself of the guilt she feels at having deserted Port at the moment of his death; second, her desire to assert life completely and violently now that his death has freed her from the detachment his inertia imposed upon her; and third, her irrational compulsion to give in to the destructive evil which has hitherto manifested itself to her in signs and omens and to become an active, suffering part of it. The weakness of all three is that they have no basis in existing evidence. At no time in the book has Kit shown any real devotion to Port; her affair with Tunner at the outset effectively cancels out all possibility of devotion. There is no more reason, therefore, for her to feel guilty about deserting Port than about spending the night of his death with Tunner. There has, furthermore, been nothing to indicate that she ever felt confined by Port's detachment or that she ever wanted to break free of it. She has, in fact, shown every sign of being entirely committed to his view of life. Her superstitious fears are briefly described near the beginning of the novel and they figure in the train-trip episode, but they are not mentioned again until *after* the desert episode. They cannot, therefore, take on the significance which Bowles now wishes them to have. Because they are consigned to the periphery of the action in the beginning, they must remain there to the end.

As soon as we see Kit's motives for what they are, the entire section devoted to her experience alone in the desert becomes ridiculous. Out of context it would be perfectly suitable as material for an old-time movie thriller, especially if the leading roles could be played by Theda Bara and a dozen Rudolph Valentinos. There are innumerable picturesque rapes performed upon the desperately willing Kit by savage tribesmen during the long Arabian nights; endless comings and goings on camelback among the moonlit sand dunes; exotic revelations of secret harem ceremonies; tense moments of suspense when the heroine pits her Caucasian cleverness against the age-old wisdom of the Orient; and, finally, an exciting escape sequence with the heroine, exhausted and dazed from her Olympian feats of passion, stumbling blindly back into the civilized world.

Yet it is fitting that the novel should end this way. In fact, when we look back to all that has gone before, we can scarcely imagine a different ending. Bowles tries from the beginning to transform the meaningless lives of his people into drama by surrounding them with all the bizarre props of an African setting. At every step of the way he is forced to add a little more violence, a little more suspense, until finally he has no choice but to end with a supreme grotesqueness, one powerful enough to outshine everything that has led up to it. But in spite of all his tricks—the excursions into shock, the sex thrills, and the startling morbidity of some of his descriptions—the clear evidence of his failure to write a truly meaningful book still shows through.

To be sure, there are moments when it seems that Bowles is close to something more profound than mere sensationalism. Once during a brief conversation between Port and Kit and again when Kit returns from the desert, he makes a distinct effort to introduce symbolism into the book. As she goes out to the plane that is to take her back to Algiers, Kit begins to feel once more the sense of overpowering guilt that originally drove her into the desert; and because she remembers that earlier conversation with Port, she identifies the feeling with the sky.

Before her eyes was the violent blue sky—nothing else. For an endless moment she looked into it. Like a great overpowering sound it destroyed everything in her mind, paralysed her. Someone once had said to her that the sky hides the night behind it, shelters the person beneath from the horror that lies above. Unblinking, she fixed the solid emptiness, and the anguish began to move in her. At any moment the rip can occur, the edges fly back, and the giant maw will be revealed.

The horror that the sky conceals is the horror of oblivion in an empty universe. Perhaps it also suggests the vengeance of a primitive god, the kind of god that a person like Kit, with her belief in signs and omens, would fear, the kind, too, that all men who suffer from the modern guilt sickness are continually seeking to escape. But the idea fails as a symbol because it is never brought to terms with the action of the novel. It is true that the Moresbys live always in the shadow of guilt, but it is a guilt that neither they can name nor Bowles can dramatize. It may be all that remains of some uncompleted purpose, some moral design, perhaps, which Bowles tried to build into the novel and which the spiritual void of his characters would not allow him to complete. But as symbolism it stands like the mountain in *The Naked and the Dead,* as a monstrous impurity on a plateau of nothingness.

CHAPTER XIII

Capote and Buechner

The Escape into Otherness

PAUL BOWLES carries to an extreme and, in a sense, concludes by default a tendency which has dominated the work of nearly all the new writers—the struggle to find values in the public world that will make possible the creation of a successful public literature in our time. His novel represents a clear attempt to give dramatic meaning to characters who lack those values through the sensational use of the bizarre setting of Africa. It is, in many ways, the ultimate exploitation of the journalistic method, the supreme admission of failure to find any significance beyond the sheer violence of events. Its aborted symbolism of evil and guilt is also part of this failure; for unless there exists in society a code of morality to which evil and guilt can be meaningfully opposed, a writer, particularly a writer of journalism, cannot give them meaning in his work.

Perhaps as an expression of impatience with the difficulty of producing a public literature under present conditions, a few of the new writers have turned to fantasy, allegory, myth, and more generally private kinds of writing that do not depend on a direct reportage of social manners and that are therefore less affected by the failure of social values. This writing has usually, but not always, been characterized by a certain excess of style and thinness of substance, so that there may be stylistic richness imposed on characters and situations that have little or no meaning in themselves and that would scarcely exist at all if it were not for the author's excessive ornamentation of them. There is also in this

194

writing, as in journalism, a frequent exploitation of the sensational and grotesque; and it is in this respect that the two methods show themselves to be simply two different ways of coping with the same dilemma. For if the journalist tries to substitute shocking and bizarre events for the dramatic value he cannot find in his material, the prose purist tries to charge his material with drama by bringing to it the richness and variety of a bizarre and shocking style. In the one there is a dependency on the values of sheer events, and in the other a dependency on events made valuable by sheer style.

There has, however, been one significant development in the work of the prose purists. In turning away from the world of social manners they have, it is true, greatly narrowed the range of their work. But they have also escaped the problem of giving significance to evil and guilt within the context of a valueless society. They have been able to create a separate and private moral context for each of their books and to find a meaning for the moral dilemma of their characters within that context. It should not matter if the meaning they find lacks reference in the social world. By making their books something other than reflections of that world, they should, by rights, have relieved themselves of all obligation to it. But in even the most perfect novel of privacy there always comes a time when purely contextual meaning ceases to be enough and one begins to wish for a kind of significance that will expand beyond itself and illuminate the universal issues of life.

There are several illustrations of this development in the work of these writers. In addition to Truman Capote's *Other Voices, Other Rooms,* Frederick Buechner's *A Long Day's Dying,* and John Horne Burns's second novel, *Lucifer with a Book,* all of which were mentioned briefly in an earlier chapter as novels in which style nearly crowds out substance, there are Capote's short stories, Jean Stafford's *The Mountain Lion,* Shirley Jackson's *The*

Lottery, Walter Van Tilburg Clark's *The Track of the Cat,* Mary McCarthy's *The Oasis,* Howard Nemerov's *The Melodramatists,* and some others.

Capote's stories are full of characters who are merely private projections of a contextual evil. They do not impress us with the insight they give into human nature. They serve at best simply to evoke in us feelings of horror, perhaps to fascinate us momentarily with the ingenuity of their grotesqueness. James Harris, the ghostly protagonist of several of Miss Jackson's stories, is a demon lover who thrives on the frustrations of lonely women Yet he is neither a Freudian fantasy nor a true sexual symbol. Like Capote's creations he is the embodiment of a horror we can never quite define. The townspeople in the famous title story from *The Lottery* illustrate the savage frenzy that can take possession of simple minds when stimulated by superstition and folk ritual. The story is a perfect image of a relentless and terrifying violence, made more terrifying by the innocence with which it is enacted. Yet it too is basically indefinable. Its meaning never extends beyond its own borders to illuminate the life we know.

Both Miss Stafford and Mr. Clark make use of the figure of the mountain lion as a symbol, respectively, of sexual guilt and primitive evil, and then go on to construct an entire system of moral motivation around it. But in each of their novels the symbol is contextual. Instead of enlarging our understanding of the dilemma of man, it serves merely as an arbitrary focal point for the thoughts and actions of the characters. In Miss McCarthy's novel the ideal morality around which the intellectuals strive to build a cooperative community is vitiated by the pettiness of the problems it is used to solve. Its significance, while presumably meant to extend over most of the great issues of our time, is never made clear in terms of significant actions. Mr. Nemerov sets out with an equally cosmic purpose, with his eye on the great question of crime and punishment, then manages to bring together simply a collection of bizarre episodes that contain his theme but do not give it enough weight to do it justice.

All these writers have turned to the cultivation of their private gardens in the midst of a world that is clearly too much for them. In their isolation they have achieved tight little triumphs of form and technical precision. Their novels are as pure, neat, and carefully refined as symbolist poems, and they can be so because they never come to grips with the complex, disorganized, and highly contradictory experience which is modern life.

Truman Capote and Frederick Buechner are only two or three years younger than the majority of the new writers. They were both twenty-three when their first novels were published; and most of the others were between twenty-five and thirty. Yet one cannot help feeling that they belong to a much younger generation, that the few years separating them from the others also separate them from the experience and attitudes which the others seem to share. One reason for this feeling is, of course, that their books do not have to do with the issues through which the others have habitually reflected their experience and attitudes; they have not, that is, written war novels, veterans'-return novels, race novels, or New York novels. In fact, if one can set aside Stafford, Clark, and McCarthy as belonging to an older literary group and Jackson and Nemerov as existing somewhat apart from the group that came out of the war, it is possible to say that Capote and Buechner are the only writers of the new generation who have departed significantly from the journalistic tradition and explored a genre that does not depend on the reportage of social manners, in the sense that we ordinarily use the term, or of events of strictly topical interest.

Yet the atmosphere of isolation and purity that surrounds their work cannot be explained away as simply the product of their deliberate choice of a different kind of literary material. It is truly as if these writers had grown up in another age, one in which there were no depressions, no wars, no financial problems, no physical or mental hardships, and, above all, no sicknesses of the heart. Their childhoods seem to have been spent in a vacuum of hygienic tranquillity or, one imagines in Capote's case, in just enough picturesque decay to make an interesting oddity of the boy and a writer of the youth. It is hard to believe that they ever experienced adolescence, that they were ever hopelessly and idiotically in love, or that they ever read, imitated, or shouted drunkenly into the night the magnificent dithyrambs of Thomas Wolfe.

One suspects that they were charming and precocious children who were taken by their nurses to the park on sunny afternoons or allowed to sit in the drawing room with their paintboxes and encyclopedias on rainy ones. At the age of nine or ten they were probably entertaining their elders at parties with sleight-of-hand tricks or polite pantomimes of absent friends. At eleven, having sipped their first cocktails and found them bitter, kissed their first girls and found the kissing dull, and analyzed their parents and found them witless, they undoubtedly retired to their rooms and, out of a sense of having been unpleasantly soiled by life, began writing the effete and tremulous books by which they now are known.

The writing of those books was obviously neither a very painful nor a very compulsive undertaking. There could have been for them none of the usual vacillations, false starts, struggles to select and separate truth from illusion, the emotional coloring from the thing remembered. They must simply have looked back to their childhoods, Capote to the sensitive boy locked in the genteel privacy of his other room, Buechner to the prosperous adults whose moneyed foolishness he was privileged to observe, and written down what they saw. And when they decided it was time they became professional novelists, one imagines them sending out engraved cards announcing their availability and then leaning back in careless languor to await the vulgar pounding of the world at the door.

The treatment both these writers have received at the hands of their publishers has done nothing to diminish the impression of fragile aestheticism one draws from a reading of their novels. Capote, in particular, has been so thoroughly exploited as a personality that he has already become as bizarrely legendary in his way as Hemingway and Byron ever were. Up until quite recently one saw those photographs of him everywhere. First there was Joel Knox Capote lying in lush elegance on an antique sofa, eyes peering distastefully out upon the world from beneath the Napoleonic haircut, fingers delicately spread over the famous checked waistcoat. A little later, with the publication of *Tree of Night*, there was Nice American Boy Capote dressed in a sloppy sweater and leaning against a garden wall over which white flowers trailed. Somewhere in between there was Young Nijinski Capote posing demurely in black tights in fifth ballet position. Finally, without benefit of photographs, there was Young Literary Man Capote conducting a series of staged quarrels with Gore Vidal over which of them was the more precocious.

About Buechner it is still too early to tell. He has been touted by his publishers as only *just about* the most promising young writer to appear in the last decade or two; and that, in these times, is not much more than we have come to expect as standard treatment for an interesting first novelist. Presumably he will not become a legend for some time, at least not until more people become fascinated with the remarkable resemblance he bears in his photographs to the young hero of his novel, Leander Poor. But Capote began to be a legend at the very beginning of his career; his personality was a commodity with a grotesquely inflated value from the moment he published his first stories, particularly *Miriam*, and had his picture in *Life*. As a result, the effects upon him are already plain, and the course of his future development is perhaps possible to predict.

The Capote legend, like the Hemingway legend, was initially the product of the kind of world he created as a writer. It was Hemingway's world of violence and war that first gave credence to Hemingway the soldier and big-game hunter; and it was Capote's world of delicate fantasy that first charmed the public into an acceptance of the effete young man of the photographs. At the outset this was perfectly natural and healthy for both writers; for it was a positive indication that their work had captured the imagination of their readers. But as time went on and their personalities rather than their work began to be exploited, something happened that was not so healthy. Hemingway became so hypnotized by the legend that it and his function as a writer became confused in his mind. He got so he wasn't sure when he was supposed to be the writer and when he was supposed to be the legend. After a while the legend began writing his books for him and the writer began spending more and more of his time fishing for marlin off the Florida Coast. *The Green Hills of Africa, Death in the Afternoon,* and *To Have and Have Not* were all written by the legend and, as a result, almost everything in them read like cheap Hemingway parody. Capote has of course not yet had the opportunity to be parodied by his legend; but there is reason to believe that he eventually will. In the last two years he has had to become more and more completely the public embodiment of his literary personality. He has, in fact, so thoroughly sold that personality to the public that most of his readers know it better and admire it more than they know and admire the books out of which it evolved. The ultimate result is, of course, obvious. Now that his legend exists, Capote is committed to keeping it alive; his professional standing depends on it. And since the legend grew out of his special treatment of a special subject matter, this means that he must continue writing in his old vein even if he tires of it, exhausts it, or matures beyond it. And if all goes according to schedule, he should arrive at a time, probably in his middle thirties, the age of menopause for most American writers, when the vision of the child that is so necessary to the creation of his world will have faded into the panic of the man. When this happens, all that he writes must begin to sound like Capote trying with all his might but no longer with all his heart to write like Capote.

Capote is, in this respect, in a far worse position than Hemingway. For one thing, he is much younger than Hemingway was when he began publishing, and his legend has developed much more quickly. Also, his subject matter is far more restricted. Hemingway could at least move on to another war, another act of violence, and even though the formula was the same, the circumstances were usually different enough to give his writing an effect of freshness. But Capote dedicated himself at the outset to a child's world, and it becomes a question just how long he can remain a child. The best he can do is think up new and more bizarre names for his characters and place them in new and more bizarre situations. But the method will be the old one, the characters will be changed only in name, and the margin of safety they once gave him by virtue of their charming novelty will simply not exist.

More completely than any of their contemporaries Capote and Buechner exist today on reputations largely created for them by the secondary agencies of literature. Their personal idiosyncrasies, their exceptional youth, and the superficial effects of style and atmosphere which have drawn readers to their books have been exalted over all questions of their real worth as writers. And since the serious critics tend to avoid them completely, as they have lately avoided all writers who are new and untried, the chances are that we shall be deprived for some time to come of any more accurate estimate of them than can be obtained from their publishers' blurbs. One is of course free at any time to go to their books and to find there the makings of a critical judgment of one's own. But such is the state of things that for a critic, particularly a new and untried critic, to do that before those books have been officially recognized, approved, classified, documented, explicated, and footnoted by other critics would be tantamount to professional heresy and suicide.

Like Joseph Conrad's *Victory*, Capote's *Other Voices, Other Rooms* is a totally created novel. This is to say that what is literally reported and what is metaphorically implied are fused into a single image which is as much an image of a world as it is the novel itself. Yet one crucial difference between the two novels enables us to call Conrad's great and Capote's merely brilliant. Where the private world of Axel Heyst took on life and meaning as the novel progressed until it became a symbol of the public modern world, the private world of Joel Knox remains inert and unchanged. Heyst, Lena, Jones, Ricardo, and the others were never merely themselves. From the moment we encountered them, they began to expand outward and upward—Heyst became a symbolic Christ, Lena the embodiment of faith, Jones and Ricardo a modern-dress Satan and his sadistic henchman. But Capote's Joel, Idabel, Randolph, and Edward Sansom, while superbly and grotesquely effective in themselves, illuminate nothing beyond themselves. Their meaning is confined within the world they have created; and when they seem most charged with meaning they seem so because they have been juxtaposed or ironically contrasted with one another—or some environmental image has been contrasted with them—metaphorically, and not because they have succeeded in transcending the limits of their world symbolically. They are acceptable, therefore, only so long as we take them in context, as the baroque furnishings of the private other room into which Capote leads us, and then only if we are careful to bolt the door against the intrusion of the life outside.

The theme of the novel is a boy's search for a father; but it is not Telemachus's search for Ulysses, Stephen Dedalus's for Bloom, or even Eugene Gant's for W. O. It is literally and permanently Joel Knox's search for one Edward R. Sansom or, as it turns out, for some suitable substitute. The sooner we accept this fact the sooner will we be prepared to accept the novel for what it is and for all that it is and not for what we should like it on every page to become. For viewed within these limits the novel comes alive with metaphorical suggestiveness, and it is possible to appreciate the skill with which Capote has expanded his theme through metaphor rather than through symbol into a complex pattern of psychological and moral action.

Joel's search for Edward Sansom, the blood-father whom he has never seen, is a parallelism of his struggle to grow out of the dreamworld of childhood and to enter the real world of manhood. His discovery of Sansom, lying paralyzed in the center of the paralysis of Scully's Landing, and his subsequent rejection of Sansom as unreal, as literally not existing, is a parallelism of his rejection of the real state of manhood and prepares the way for his acceptance of Cousin Randolph as a homosexual father-substitute. Randolph, with his nightmare history, his obsession with dolls and dead bluejays, and his female impersonations, is as unreal as the fantastic creations of Joel's dreamworld—Mr. Mystery and Annie Rose Kuppermann. But once he has rejected his true father as unreal, Joel is left with no alternative but to accept Randolph, and through him homosexuality, as real.

It is necessary that we understand this paradox; for the entire thematic development of the novel is based upon it. Before Joel came to Scully's Landing the boundaries separating the real from the unreal were as clear and definite as they are for most people. The real world was made up of movies, ice-cream sodas, popcorn,

Sunday school, and secret meetings of the St. Deval Street Secret Nine. The unreal world was a world of his own imagining, a day-dream world inhabited by grotesque figures—"other voices" out of "other rooms." Back home in New Orleans this world was a luxury for Joel. It served him as a refuge into which he could withdraw whenever real life pressed too close around him. But at the Landing he finds himself in the midst of nightmare where the line separating the real from the unreal grows blurred and indistinct. What really happens is that the two worlds become transposed in Joel's mind: life at the Landing is so grotesque that it seems unreal; the dreamworld, by comparison, seems real.

Joel has never seen his father Edward Sansom, but he has come to the Landing to meet him, and he already has a mental picture of what he will be like. He will be tall, strong, rich, and, above all, real, not strange and ghostly like Miss Amy and Cousin Randolph. And not only will he restore life to its proper balance, but he will release Joel from the prison of his childish fantasies and lead him over the threshold of the real world into manhood. This belief, while never overtly stated, clearly sustains Joel during the early part of his stay at the Landing.

But the days go by and Edward Sansom does not appear. Instead, Joel accidentally discovers him; and when he does, he closes the door to manhood forever. For Sansom is not the father whose image Joel has created and worshiped in his mind. He is a helpless invalid, totally paralyzed except for his hands, with which he is able to release red tennis balls when he wants attention, and the restless movement of his eyes. To Joel, Sansom in this condition seems as unreal as all the other inhabitants of the Landing. But by rejecting him as such, Joel has paradoxically rejected his last hope of reality and manhood. For now he must cling more desperately than ever to his dreamworld and find in it a reality he cannot find in his father. But that world is, after all, literally as unreal as the life surrounding him; and there must inevitably come a time when his hold upon it will loosen, when, through fatigue, fright, or sickness, he will have to give in to the unreality of the Landing and accept it as the only reality there is. And when that time comes he must also accept, in place of the man he hoped to become, the child he must permanently remain, and in place of the real father he hoped to find, the homosexual Randolph disguised as a beautiful lady with piled white curls.

The novel is divided into three parts, each part corresponding to a crucial phase in Joel's development toward this moment of acceptance. Part I has to do with his arrival at the Landing and his efforts to escape its influence; Part II with the gradual reduction of his power to escape; and Part III with his surrender to Randolph. In each part the change being effected in Joel is demonstrated in terms of concrete events; and all the parts are tied together with key metaphors that define the various shifts in theme and setting. Thus, when in Part I Joel takes leave of the real world, represented by the garishness of Noon City, and enters the unreal world of the Landing, the transition is shown to be from daylight to darkness, with Joel falling asleep at dusk in the back of Jesus Fever's wagon and entering the house as if in a dream. Then in Part III, after Joel has tried and failed to escape, the process is reversed: he loses his sense of the unreality of the Landing while lying in a coma; and when he awakens he discovers that the unreal has become the real. The transition this time is from darkness (the night of the Carnival episode) to daylight (morning in the sickroom several weeks later).

The bluejay which Miss Amy kills in Joel's room on the morning after his arrival functions in much the same way. As it flutters against the window in a frantic effort to escape, it becomes a metaphor of Joel struggling to shake off the influence of the Landing. And by the time it reappears, at the end of Part II, as merely a lifelike arrangement of feathers on Randolph's worksheet, Joel has arrived at a point where he is no longer capable of escape. Like the bird, he has been changed from a living thing with a free existence in a real world into a dead prisoner in an unreal world.

A similar device is the old bell that lies in the garden outside the house. At the end of Chapter II Joel catches his first glimpse of Randolph standing at an upstairs window in his disguise of the beautiful lady. In his astonishment Joel staggers back against the bell; and it emits "one raucous, cracked note" as if in derision at what is taking place. Then at the end of the book while Joel is waiting in the same spot in the garden he sees the figure of the lady once again, knows it for what it is, and responds to its beckoning. This time there is "a sound, as if a bell had suddenly tolled, and the shape of loneliness, greenly iridescent, whitely indefinite, seemed to rise from the garden. . . ." Now the sound of the bell is imagined; but it seems loud and serious, as if it were tolling the news of a victory; for Joel has finally put the real world and his hope of manhood behind him and accepted the comfort and love of Randolph.

The events of the narrative itself naturally form a literal record of all that happens to Joel. Yet most of them function at the same time as figuratively as these other devices. In fact, so thoroughly is the material of the novel suffused with thematic meaning that it becomes impossible, and probably pointless, to separate metaphor from event. In Part I, Joel's struggle to escape is centered in three events, each of which has a figurative significance.

The first occurs during Jesus Fever's Sunday service shortly after Joel's arrival. As the excitement of the weird ceremony reaches a climax, Zoo, who has been dancing, discards the red ribbon she wears around her throat and reveals the scar left by Keg Brown's razor.

It was as though a brutal hawk had soared down and clawed away Joel's eyelids, forcing him to gape at her throat. Zoo. Maybe she was like him, and the world had a grudge against her, too. But christamighty he didn't want to end up with a scar like that. . . . He leaped off the stump, and made for the house, his loosened shirt-tail flying behind; run, run, run, his heart told him, and wham! he'd pitched headlong into a briar patch. . . .°

Joel's identification of himself with Zoo is important for two reasons: he sees in her an intimation of what is to happen to him if he remains at the Landing (they are both destined to be its victims), and because of his fright at seeing the physical evidence of her suffering he is rendered less capable than he might have been of taking action to free himself.

The second incident occurs on the evening of the same day as Joel is questioning Randolph and Miss Amy about the ghostly lady he has seen at the window. Miss Amy, knowing of Randolph's penchant for this particular disguise, is on the verge of giving away the secret when Randolph kicks her under the table. The effect on the neurotic woman is instantaneous and, to Joel, terrifying:

. . . she jerked back as though lightning had rocked the chair and, shielding her eyes with the gloved hand, let out a pitiful wail: "Snake a snake I thought it was a snake bit me crawled under the table bit me foot you fool never forgive bit me my heart a snake!" repeated over and over the words began to rhyme, to hum from wall to wall where giant moth shadows jittered. . . .
Joel went all hollow inside, he thought he was going to wee wee right there in his breeches, and he wanted to hop up and run, just as he had at Jesus Fever's. Only he couldn't, *not this time* [italics my own].

After the nightmare events of the day, Joel is too paralyzed to move. Already he has begun to slip into that state of passive receptivity which is later to send him to Randolph; although at this point he is still able to distinguish between the real and the outlandish.

The third incident is a logical development of the first two: as

° From *Other Voices, Other Rooms* by Truman Capote, published and copyright, 1948, Random House, New York.

they have paralyzed Joel emotionally, so this one makes it clear that he is paralyzed physically. He has written letters to his Aunt Ellen expressing his hatred of the Landing and asking her to help him get away. He has put the letters in the mailbox and then gone to visit Idabel and her sister. Upon his return he stops at the box and discovers that the letters are gone. The postman has not taken them because the postage money is lying in the dust under the box. Joel realizes for the first time that he is being kept a prisoner at the Landing and has been cut off from all contact with the real world outside. As he starts back to the house, he hears the sound of gunfire as someone shoots at the chicken hawks circling overhead. Like the bluejay and like himself, they are free beings who must be drawn down into the paralysis of the Landing and destroyed. They are also, like his letters, potential agents of interference which constitute a threat to the security of those who depend on the imprisonment of others.

In Part II the emphasis shifts from Joel's struggle to preserve himself from the Landing to his struggle to preserve his masculinity. Interestingly enough, although it is in this section that his masculinity becomes identified with the idea of his father and its loss with his rejection of his father, Joel's conflict is really with the tomboy Idabel. With an evil innocence comparable to that of Henry James's terrible children, she begins to undermine the confidence on which Joel's manhood rests some time before he brings himself to commit the act of denial that is to release him to Randolph.

The process begins shortly after Joel has seen his father for the first time and realized that the hopelessly paralyzed invalid can be of no help to him. As if to erase the shock of the encounter from his mind, he goes with Idabel to fish and swim in the creek. There, as they lie in self-conscious nakedness on the bank, Idabel confesses her loneliness, and Joel suddenly sees that her tough exterior is merely a defense and that beneath it she is really very much like himself. Overcome with tenderness for her, he kisses her on the cheek. Instead of responding to his mood, Idabel reverts at once to her old self, grabs him by the hair, and throws him on the ground. As they struggle together, he falls back on her dark glasses and crushes them. At this Idabel's anger quickly subsides, and when she speaks again, it is as if nothing had happened. "And, indefinably, it was as if nothing had: neither of course would ever be able to explain why they had fought."

The reason is obvious, however, if we relate the incident to all that has led up to it. Idabel has fought to regain the defenses which she let down in her moment of confession and which she must have if she is to dominate her environment and survive within it. Joel has fought to regain his masculine position which was threatened, first, by Randolph, second, by the paralysis of his father, and now by Idabel. The breaking of the glasses ends the struggle for Idabel because the glasses have been an essential part of her defenses—"everything looks a lot prettier" through them—and she is temporarily lost without them. It ends the struggle for Joel not only because the broken bits of glass have cut him but because he realizes that, by having caused the breakage, he has somehow seriously wronged Idabel and, by having fought with her, has somehow defeated himself.

A similar incident occurs a short time later. Joel is reading to his father when he hears Idabel whistle for him to come outside. Although he is supposed to go on reading, he has become so convinced of his father's unreality—"Certainly this Mr. Sansom was not his father. This Mr. Sansom was nobody but a pair of crazy eyes."—that he leaves him and, stopping just long enough to buckle on the sword Zoo has given him, hurries down to Idabel Perhaps because she has lost her glasses, Idabel seems oddly feminine—"all the rough spirit seemed to have drained from her voice. Joel felt stronger than she, and sure of himself as he'd never been with that other Idabel, the tomboy." With her defenses gone, she has lost her dominion over her environment: at home she has had trouble with her sister Florabel, and her father has threatened to shoot her dog Henry because "Florabel . . . says Henry's got a mortal disease. . . ." As they walk toward the creek, she proposes that they run away, and Joel is struck once again by the change in her—"if it had been anyone but Idabel, Joel would've thought she was making up to him." For the first time their relationship seems almost normal, and Joel has a sense of masculine power he has not had since just before their fight on the creek bank. But it is to last only for a moment. As they start across the creek on an old board with Joel leading the way, they suddenly see directly in front of them a huge snake lying coiled and ready to strike. Once again Joel is too paralyzed to move or even speak. He stands there wavering, holding his sword helplessly in his hand, the imagined sting of the snake's bite already hot on his body. But Idabel acts. She pulls the sword out of his hand, swings it, and "the cottonmouth slapped into the air, turned, plunged, flattened on the water: belly up, white and twisted, it was carried by the current like a torn lily root."

The scene is important for several reasons. It is, first of all, another instance of humiliation for Joel. Secondly, it makes explicit the identification of his manhood with his father: the snake's eyes are like Mr. Sansom's; and it is because of this that Joel is so frightened, for the eyes remind him of his sin. He has deserted his father to come with Idabel; and he has gradually come to deny the existence of his father as his attraction toward Randolph has grown stronger. Thirdly, there is the metaphorical use of the sword and snake images. Because of his failure to use the sword, Joel has disgraced not only his own manhood but that of his ancestor, the original owner of the sword. And because Idabel has killed the snake in the midst of his fear, she has figuratively killed his manhood and, as is later evident, all maleness in her world.

Ironically enough, the final act in the drama of Joel's humiliation takes place on the night he and Idabel attempt to escape
from the Landing. He has said good-by to his father for the first
and last time; and as he and the girl hurry through the darkness
down the road toward Noon City, he begins to feel something of
his old affection for her. She, in turn, seems to have changed her
mind about him—"I thought you was a mess just like Florabel;
to be honest to God, I never did much change-mind till today."
But then they come upon a scene that destroys their mood completely.

Behind the foliage, a bull-toned voice, and another, this like a guitar,
blended as raindrops caress to sound a same rhythm; an intricate wind
of rustling murmurs, small laughter followed sighs not sad and silences
deeper than space. Moss cushioned their footsteps as they moved
through the leafy thickness, and came to pause at the edge of an opening: two Negroes, caught in a filmy skein of moon and fern, lay un-
clothed and enfolded, the man's caramel-colored body braceleted with
his darker lover's arms, legs, and his lips nuzzling her nipples: oo-we,
oo-we, sweet Simon, she sighed, love shivering her voice, love rolling
through her like thunder; easy, Simon, sweet Simon, easy honey, she
crooned, and tensed then, her arms lifting as if to embrace the moon;
her lover sank across her, and there together, limbs akimbo, they made
on the bloom of moss a black fallen star.

To Joel, the lovers epitomize sexual passion at its purest, the
final triumph over loneliness and isolation. They also momentarily reaffirm in him his faltering manhood and make him realize
that his escape from the Landing may also be an escape into nor-
mality. But to Idabel the lovers are frightening and obscene; they
remind her of the terrible attraction that draws the sexes together and forces the woman into a role of passive inferiority. This
is, for her, the unspeakable sin of life; and she has fought bitterly
to preserve herself from it. Unfortunately, her reaction dominates
and cancels Joel's:

He wanted to walk with Idabel's hand in his, but she had them doubled like knots, and when he spoke to her she looked at him mean and angry and scared; it was as if their position of the afternoon had somehow reversed: she'd been the hero under the mill, but now he had no weapon with which to defend her, and even if this were not true he wouldn't have known what it was she wanted killed.

What she wants killed is, of course, maleness; but what neither of them knows is that, in Joel at least, it is dead already.

Viewed in these terms the climaxing scene of the novel—the Carnival episode and the encounter with Miss Wisteria—can be taken as a dramatic presentation of the sexual paralysis Idabel has induced in Joel. The Carnival itself, with its whirling ferris-wheel lights and bursting rockets, is a nightmare catalyst that destroys Joel's sense of reality and prepares him to accept as real the world of the Landing and Randolph; while the midget Miss Wisteria is the embodiment of female temptation, Joel's last chance to find reality in a normal sex relationship. Significantly, it is his vision of Randolph standing beneath the ferris wheel that prevents Joel from responding to Miss Wisteria's advances; just as it is the violent rainstorm coming a moment later that separates him from Idabel and prevents their escape.

In the deserted house in which he has sought shelter from the storm, Joel has a brief insight into his predicament. It is not Randolph alone that he fears, he tells himself, but Randolph in the person of "a messenger for a pair of telescopic eyes." Once again it seems to Joel that the eyes of his father are everywhere, accusing him of shameful desertion and even, perhaps, of patricide. But what he does not realize is that his fear of Randolph as a "messenger" and his sense of having, at least mentally, destroyed his father are one and the same thing. The very fact that it was the image of Randolph and not the image of his father who came for him is evidence that Randolph has won out over his father in the struggle for Joel's love. And because Randolph has won, because Joel has *chosen* him to win, he must appear as a messenger of his father's anger; for his appearance is made possible only after the father has been forsaken.

And now that he has finally accepted Randolph, Joel finds it impossible to respond to the pathetic entreaties of Miss Wisteria as she searches for him through the rooms of the empty house.

"Little boy," she said, swerving her flashlight over the bent, broken walls where her midget image mingled with the shadows of things in flight. "Little boy," she said, the resignation of her voice intensifying its pathos. But he dared not show himself, for what she wanted he could not give: his love was in the earth, shattered and still, dried flowers where eyes should be, and moss upon the lips, his love was faraway feeding on the rain, lilies frothing from its ruin.

To Joel the door leading to the real world, to manhood and the love of woman is closed forever. He has been arrested in childhood, led back into the secret "other rooms" of the Landing where the unreality of dream life and the reality of life lived in a dream merge and become indistinguishable.

Joel's second entry into the world of the Landing immediately following the Carnival episode is, as I have already pointed out, the exact opposite of his first. On the earlier occasion he fell asleep in the real world and awoke in the midst of unreality. But now, after discovering the real world to be unreal and lying ill and unconscious for some time, he awakens, as if from nightmare, and finds that the Landing is the real world, warm and familiar, and that Randolph is there to love him.

The awakening scene opens Part III and prepares us for two discoveries that have ironic bearing on Joel's development through the preceding episodes. The first is that Zoo, the daughter of the ancient Negro Jesus Fever, who had left the Landing right after her father's death to find a new life in Washington, D.C., has returned during Joel's illness. When he sees her again, he hardly recognizes her for the gay and optimistic person who was kind to him when he first came to the Landing.

How small she seemed, cramped, as if some reduction of the spirit had taken double toll and made demands upon the flesh: with that illusion of height was gone the animal grace, arrowlike dignity, defiant emblem of her separate heart.

Zoo, during her brief excursion into the outside world, has had an experience as destructive and humiliating as Joel's with Idabel and Randolph. On her way to Washington she was stopped on the road by several men and brutally raped. Like Joel, she has been crucified at the very moment of salvation; and all the hope and illusion that sustained her while she waited for her father to die has been crushed out of her. Now she too has come back to the Landing and accepted its paralysis as the only possibility left to her.

The second discovery is that Idabel has succeeded in escaping to freedom. In a postcard to Joel she says:

Mrs. Collie ½ sister and hes the baptis prechur Last Sunday I past the plate at church! papa and F shot henry They put me to life here. why did you Hide? write to IDABEL THOMPKINS.

But Joel doesn't believe her: "she'd put herself to life, and it was with Miss Wisteria, not a baptis prechur." This, then, is the supreme irony. Like Joel and Zoo, Idabel has fought for freedom; but even though she, alone of them all, has actually found it, she has allowed herself to become imprisoned in a relationship with Miss Wisteria that is as unnatural as that between Joel and Randolph. Joel in his search for manhood has become pervertedly feminine; Idabel in her search for a dominant womanhood has become pervertedly masculine; and Zoo in her search for the normal love of men has been pervertedly violated by them.

The really important event in Part III, however, is Joel's and Randolph's trip to Cloud Hotel, the home of the hermit Little Sunshine. The hotel, with its fantastic, haunted history and picturesque decay, is a microcosm of the entire world of the Landing.

Like Randolph's house, which is slowly sinking into the earth, it represents the way of life to which all the characters, either willingly or unwillingly, are committed. Randolph, Miss Amy, Mr. Sansom, Jesus Fever, and Little Sunshine have nearly always belonged: years before they turned away from the real world of the present and found refuge in the phantasmal world of the past— Randolph in his lost love for Pepe Alvarez, Miss Amy in the baroque manners of a dead culture, Mr. Sansom in the literal cessation of time that accompanies paralysis, Jesus Fever and Little Sunshine in misty memories of their years of aristocratic service. Joel, Idabel, and Zoo have all learned, or have been forced, to belong. The Landing has conquered them as decay has conquered the hotel. It has even turned their struggles for freedom to its own advantage, so that they have been not only imprisoned but maimed in the process.

And as Joel follows Randolph and Little Sunshine through the hotel, seeing the crumbling furniture—"Swan stairs soft with mildewed carpet curved upward from the hotel's lobby; the diabolic tongue of a cuckoo bird, protruding out of a wall-clock, mutely proclaiming an hour forty years before, and on the room clerk's splintery desk stood dehydrated specimens of potted palm" —imagining the scenes of long ago when the huge old rooms were alive with "the humming heel-clatter of chattering girls, the bored snores of fat fathers, . . . the lilt of fans tapped in tune, and the murmur of gloved hands as the musicians, like bridegrooms in their angel-cake costumes, rise to take a bow," it seems to him that the moment for which all his experience at the Landing has prepared him has finally arrived.

. . . all day, after the weeks in bed, it had been as if he were bucking a whirlpool, and now lullabyed to the bone with drowsy warmth, he let go, let the rivering fire sweep him over its fall. . . .

The last of his resistance has now slipped away, the struggle for freedom has ended, and the Landing and the hotel have become

the world, all the world there will ever be. And when, after they return to the Landing, Randolph appears once again at his window
in the disguise of the beautiful lady, Joel is waiting to respond
to his beckoning:

> She beckoned to him, shining and silver, and he knew he must go:
> unafraid, not hesitating, he paused only at the garden's edge where,
> as though he'd forgotten something, he stopped and looked back at the
> bloomless, descending blue, at the boy he had left behind.

I suggested earlier that Capote's achievement, for all its bril-
liance, is an achievement in the skilled use of metaphor rather
than symbol; and I implied that such an achievement is necessarily of smaller scope than, for instance, Conrad's in *Victory*. It
seems to me that we have a right to ask of a novel that it stand in
some meaningful relation to recognizable life; we have a right,
that is, to ask that the characters resemble or in some way illuminate human beings and that their situation in some way connote or
enlarge upon the human situation. It is, of course, true that Capote's
novel is, by its very nature, the product of the disappearance of
those common assumptions of value by which writers have traditionally been able to get such illumination into their books. It
is no longer possible for a writer to take it for granted that his
audience will share his view of life or even that his audience will
comprehend his view of life. But it was beginning to be no longer
possible when Conrad wrote *Victory*, Joyce wrote *Ulysses*, and
Forster wrote *A Passage to India*. Yet these men were able to
infuse their novels with a significance that persistently transcended
the specific characters and situations about which they wrote. We
read *Victory* and we read a chapter from the moral history of
modern man; we read *Ulysses* and we read an ironic satire on the
petty heroism of modern man; we read *A Passage to India* and we
read a tragedy on the evil that is in all men; and we are reading,
at the same time, the stories of Axel Heyst, Leopold Bloom, and
Dr. Aziz. It was not black magic that enabled these writers to get

such meaning into their books. It was the highly organized use of symbolism upon material specifically created to be symbolically suggestive. And it is the absence of such material in *Other Voices, Other Rooms* that renders it simply the exquisitely written, metaphorically reinforced story of Joel Knox.

We cannot say that Conrad, Joyce, and Forster were appreciably nearer to value than Capote is; but we can say that they were infinitely nearer to life, and that, being nearer, they were able to make full use of all the equipment they could muster to give it meaning. All of them had to create a private world just as Capote has had to do; but they took great pains to see that it did not remain private—even if, to make sure, they had to go back in time to ancient Greece or as far from contemporary London and Paris as Chandrapore and Samburan. Their achievement, founded on the deepest insight into life and thus fortified by myth and distance, communicated this insight and took on the universality of myth; while Capote's achievement, founded on a technical skill largely divorced from insight, communicates no insight beyond that which it affords into its own parts.

The difference between the two is essentially the difference between symbol and metaphor. A symbol ordinarily refers to a thing, a person, or, most often, an idea that exists in a context other than its own as do the symbols in *Victory*. A character in a novel may symbolize mankind, evil, sin, or death, but he may not symbolize another character in the same novel. He may, however, serve as a metaphor of another character, and through ironic juxtaposition or contrast enrich or enliven that character as he, in turn, is enriched and enlivened, a type of metaphorical interaction to be found all through *Other Voices, Other Rooms*. A metaphor, this is to say, functions only within a given context; its meaning spreads horizontally through the area in which it is created, not vertically above or beneath it; and it remains in action as a live agent of meaning only so long as the material of which it is a part is in the process of carrying out and completing the idea or theme which originally set it in motion. Once the immediate requirements of the narrative have been satisfied, it ceases to function. A symbol, on the other hand, only begins to fulfill its true function after the action has ceased. It begins, then, to build outward and downward toward all those varieties of meaning which the action, in its passage, has suggested.

As I have attempted to point out in my analysis, the characters in *Other Voices, Other Rooms* repeatedly function as metaphors of one another. Idabel, Zoo, and Miss Wisteria are metaphors of Joel; Jesus Fever and Little Sunshine of Randolph and Miss Amy; Jesus Fever and Idabel's father of Mr. Sansom; and, of course, in each case the relationship is reciprocal, so that the metaphor and the person metaphorized are mutually enhanced. The various other devices such as the bluejay, the hawks, the snake, the hanged mule, and Cloud Hotel are also metaphors. The first four are *like* Joel; they demonstrate his predicament. Cloud Hotel is *like* the Landing and the people of the Landing; it is a physical representation of the decayed past to which Randolph, Miss Amy, and the others are dedicated.

But even though, taken together, the characters and the devices produce a world, they do not produce a world of external significance. They belong eternally to the special illusion Capote has created; outside it, they do nothing and are nothing. If we refuse to accept them on these terms, if for a moment we shake off the dream and open our eyes, then the spell is broken and the real world rushes in upon us. The real world should, by rights, be part of the illusion; but it is not and cannot be. The tennis balls, the beautiful lady, the hanged mule, the bluejay, the dwarfed Miss Wisteria, the neurotic Idabel are the phantasmal contents of the nightmare in which, for a little while, we allow ourselves to be lost. But having once awakened and looked about us, we see that, for all its intensity and horror, the thing was never there at all.

The quality that seems to me most distinctive of the work of Capote and Buechner is isolation. I do not mean the sort we ordinarily associate with Joyce, laboring in Paris to reconstruct his youth in Dublin, or even with Proust, laboring in his cork-lined chambers to reconstruct a past for himself that would justify the death with which he was about to climax it. For both these men isolation was a necessary phase of the creative act. It enabled them to retreat momentarily from the literal business of life so that they could get down to the imaginative business of reentering life through art. The important thing was that they were performing a task of synthesis and interpretation. They had always before them the image of life as they had lived it; in isolation and through a kind of suffering we cannot hope to understand, they elevated that image to the highest level of artistic creation.

In Capote and Buechner one feels not that life has been lived and then laboriously achieved but that life has been somehow missed. Capote's world seems to be a concoction rather than a synthesis. It has a curious easiness about it, as if it had cost nothing to make, as if, really, the parts had all been made separately at some anonymous factory and might have been put together by just anyone. Its purity is not the purity of experience forced under pressure into shape, of painstaking selection and rejection amid a thousand possibilities. Rather, it is the sort that can be attained only in the isolation of a mind which life has never really violated, in which the image of art has developed to a flowerlike perfection because it has developed alone.

Buechner's world derives from an isolation that is equally profound if considerably less pure. Like the new generation of poets with whom he has so much in common, Buechner has found his literary sources in the university classroom. There he has learned all the newest and most enlightened methods of putting a novel together; and he has learned them not from practicing novelists but from teacher-critics who merely write and lecture about the novel. He has been taught that, to be truly acceptable, a novel which pretends to come to grips at all with the contemporary world should make liberal use of the resources of myth and symbol, and that it should be written in a language which will suggest, in its tone, imagery, and structure, the full implications of the theme the author intends to evoke.

The authority for the first requirement is T. S. Eliot, the critic, in collaboration with whom T. S. Eliot, the poet, put the principle to brilliant use in *The Waste Land;* and the authority for the second is, among others, the critic Mark Schorer. Writing of *Ulysses* some years ago in *The Dial,* Eliot remarked that "in using the myth [of the *Odyssey*], in manipulating a continuous parallel between contemporaneity and antiquity, Mr. Joyce is pursuing a method which others must pursue after him. . . . It is simply a way of controlling, of ordering, of giving a shape and a significance to the immense panorama of futility and anarchy which is contemporary history." And Schorer, writing on the technique of the novel in a recent issue of the *Hudson Review,* remarked that, properly speaking, all the resources of language are part of technique—"language as used to create a certain texture and tone which in themselves state and define themes and meanings; or language, the counters of our ordinary speech, as forced, through conscious manipulation, into all those larger meanings which our ordinary speech almost never intends."

Now it seems to me that these two statements, when taken in context, represent just about the most penetrating insights into the nature of the novel that we have had in a great many years. *Ulysses* is all the proof we need to have of the validity of the first; and *Ulysses,* along with a dozen other novels that are easily the best this century and the last have produced,* bears witness to the validity of the second. But notice that they both derive from

* Schorer specifically mentions *Moll Flanders, Wuthering Heights, Tono Bungay, Sons and Lovers,* and *Portrait of the Artist as a Young Man.*

observations of works that have already been written and that they treat myth and symbolic language as *tools* by means of which the full significance of those works has been achieved. They clearly do not advocate the use of either of these tools as an *end* of art or upon material which does not specifically warrant such modification or enlargement. This, it seems to me, is a crucial distinction, and one that Buechner and his teachers might profitably have made.

Joyce resorted to the Homeric myth for the same reason that he resorted to interior monologue—to give the maximum scope and structure to the expression of what he already had to express. Through the myth he was able to manipulate "a continuous parallel between contemporaneity and antiquity" in such a way that the present was illuminated at all points where it impinged upon the past, and vice versa. The myth allowed him to build his novel on at least two main levels of meaning. Without it, he would have had to content himself with building it on only one. The same motive led some of the other writers whom Schorer mentions to exploit to the full all the resources of symbolic language: they were after the most effective means of presenting the material which they had already chosen to present. In each case the precise use to which myth or language was put was conditioned by the working requirements of the writer; in each case, myth or language was the result and not the cause of the writer's work.

In Buechner's hands, however, the process is reversed: myth and symbolic language become not means by which material is presented and justified but ends toward which material is consciously directed and which material is required to justify. *A Long Day's Dying* represents an attempt to apply both methods literally and for their own sake to the writing of a novel; and apparently it was undertaken for no other reason than that Buechner thought such an application fashionable at this time. The result is a novel written in strict observance of all the rules but in which the game for which the rules were devised never gets around to being played.

It is truly as if Buechner had written it to fulfill an assignment in a Creative Writing course. Not only does he seem to have memorized a list of the exact ingredients that must go into a "significant" modern novel, but he seems to have gone to the library and set out consciously to collect them. He appears, furthermore, to have been exceedingly careful to choose only those which are in particularly special favor at the moment and of which his instructor would be absolutely certain to approve. Thus, instead of building his novel around just any myth, he has built it around the myth of Philomela, a story that has been sanctified not only by past writers like Matthew Arnold but by T. S. Eliot himself, who used it in *The Waste Land*. Instead of writing it in the manner of just any established modern novelist (he has cleverly avoided imitating Joyce because Joyce is not now in the ascendancy), he has written it in the later manner of Henry James, who very definitely is in the ascendancy. Then, facing still more deliberately into the prevailing intellectual wind, he has imposed on the whole concoction the great religious theme of sin and retribution, which act, if metaphorically strenuous, must nevertheless have warmed the hearts of all good Anglo-Catholics from here to Little Gidding. By following out his assignment to the letter, he has thus produced a novel that makes proper use of that manipulated parallel between "contemporaneity and antiquity," that is written in the language of an approved master, and that evokes one of the most crucial of contemporary themes. Such a novel satisfies academic requirements in precisely the same way that the average historical novel satisfies public requirements; and if for the myth we substitute lust, for the approved language fruitily exotic imagery, and for the contemporary theme a degenerate moment in the history of seventeenth-century England, we shall be able to see that Buechner and the historical novelist have arrived at their respective products by the same road. But where we might well accept the latter as the huckster of a product which may at least help to amuse us, we can do little more than reject the former as the huckster of a product which, on its merits as a classroom exercise, should have received the grade of A, but which, on its merits as a novel, should never have been published.

The use to which Buechner puts the Philomela myth is illustrative of the main weakness of his whole attempt. When Eliot used it as an adjunct to his primary myth, the legend of the Fisher King rendered impotent by a curse, he achieved a connection he could not otherwise have achieved between the theme of spiritual sterility and the theme of sexual violation. The people of *The Waste Land* were dead not only because the life-giving sources of faith had been lost to them but because sex had lost its life-giving, spiritualizing function and become merely lust. By projecting his references back through time to the earliest forms of religious ritual (the sacrifice of the fertility god) and to an ancient story of virginal sacrifice, Eliot was evoking the whole history of human sacrifice, transforming it with fresh insight, and applying it in new terms to the contemporary dilemma described in his poem. At no time was antiquity merely antiquity or contemporaneity merely contemporaneity: all the past was contained in the present as all the present was contained in the past. But in Buechner's novel the myth remains a static story detached from its ancient setting and applied merely as a story to a contemporary setting. It does not serve to enhance the meaning of the dilemma described in the novel but is simply a borrowed framework on which the characters and their problems are hung and through which Buechner obviously hoped to create an illusion of their significance.

In the mythical story, King Tereus, ruler of an ancient and fabulous land, is persuaded by Procne, his queen, to voyage to her home country and bring her beautiful sister Philomela to live with them. On the return trip, Tereus falls in love with the girl; and when she refuses to accept his attentions, he ravishes her. Then, to make certain that she will never betray him, he has her tongue cut out. When they reach his own country again, Tereus sends her into exile and tells Procne that her sister fell ill and died on the return trip. Philomela manages, however, to weave the story of her violation into a tapestry and to have it taken to Procne, who understands instantly all that has happened and arranges to have her sister brought secretly to the palace. There the two women take revenge on Tereus by killing his son Itys and serving the boy's body to his father for dinner. After the king has eaten, the sisters tell him what they have done; whereupon he tears down from the wall a huge sword and pursues them across the land. When they can run no farther, the two women fall to their knees and pray to the gods to deliver them. Their prayers are heard; and, before the king quite reaches them, all three are transformed into birds— Tereus into a hawk, Procne into a sparrow, and Philomela into a nightingale.

In Buechner's contemporary application of the story, Elizabeth Poor, a wealthy and attractive widow, accepts the invitation of George Motley, a famous novelist, to accompany him on a visit to the university where Elizabeth's son Leander is a student. There she meets Steitler, Leander's English instructor, is strongly attracted to him, and speedily finds herself spending the night in bed with him. Motley, who is himself in love with Elizabeth, suspects her of the indiscretion and reports it to Tristram Bone, an enormous and pontifical gentleman who is also in love with her. After endless divagations Bone brings himself to confront Elizabeth with Motley's charge; and she, in an attempt to conceal her guilt, denies it by accusing Steitler of having a homosexual relationship with her son Leander. But after Steitler and Bone have a conversation, it becomes evident to Bone that Elizabeth has lied. Immediately following this, however, Elizabeth's ailing mother Maroo arrives and saves her daughter from having to face the anger of those she has accused; although by then the damage has been done and she needs no punishment beyond that which she has already inflicted upon herself and the others. For as a result of her lie, her comfortable relationship with Bone and Motley has ended as has the friendship between Steitler and Leander; Bone's pet monkey and alter ego has accidentally committed suicide in a ghastly burlesque of the spiritual suicide of the others; and that misfortune along with the disruption of Bone's delicate relations with his faithful cook Emma and with Elizabeth has effectively ruined the pattern of the fat man's life. That the story should end with Maroo's death is no more than justified; for Maroo has been a sort of moral center for them all; and it is in her disintegration that theirs is made complete.

In tracing the parallels between the myth and the novel it is first necessary to understand that Buechner changes the sex of nearly all the mythical characters in his application of the story and that he makes minor departures from the facts of the relationship they had with one another. To understand this does not require any great amount of ingenuity; for Buechner is so anxious to impress us with his own ingenuity and to avoid Joyce's fate of having his best meanings discovered only after his death that he makes his alterations abundantly clear. Early in the novel he brings Bone and Elizabeth together for apparently no other purpose than to enable Bone to plant the necessary clue.

"In the palace there lived a king," he continued, "of great power and influence. Do you know the story?"

"I don't know," answered Elizabeth. "Who was the king?"

"A very unusual woman."

"Not a queen?"

"No. A king."

"All right then. I don't know the story."

"In that case I shall continue. This case, I beg your pardon, this *king* had two suitors, and the suitors were sisters actually though they only suspected each other's existence and had never met. In fact the king knew only one of them himself (or herself). No one was quite sure. The king also had a son who was, after a fashion, also the son of one of the suitors. . . ." °

Here the narrative abruptly loses itself in the ellipsis of Bone's speech and is never completed. But when it is taken with the literal account of the myth which Motley gives a little later in his lecture, it becomes sufficiently clear evidence of Buechner's intention.

Elizabeth is King Tereus made female. Motley, in the beginning, is Procne made male; for it is he who brings Elizabeth and Steitler (Philomela made male) together. But as soon as Motley reports his suspicions of Elizabeth to Bone, Bone becomes Procne, the outraged wife turned suitor, and Motley takes on the function of the tapestry that brought the news of Philomela's violation to -Procne. Elizabeth's affair with Steitler of course constitutes his violation; and the lie she tells Bone about him not only parallels Tereus's lie to Procne but amounts to a figurative cutting out of his tongue to prevent him from telling the truth.

The meeting of Bone and Steitler to discuss Elizabeth's accusation parallels the meeting of Procne and Philomela to plan the death of Itys; and even though the two men decide not to tell Leander of his mother's lie, it is Elizabeth's fear that they will that brings on her anger. Her reaction to Bone's note telling her of the meeting makes this as well as the identification of her dilemma with the myth explicit:

What she had said of Leander and Steitler she imagined, in retrospect, to have been said in justifiable revenge. Steitler had had no right to do whatever he had done [she suspects him of having revealed her indiscretion], and her own uncertainty strengthened rather than diminished her hate. Tristram himself had been unforgivable enough to have hounded her with the matter when escape was impossible, and then to pursue it even farther still, to see the arch betrayer and write her of it, saying that he hoped it would put her at greater ease, knowing

° From *A Long Day's Dying* by Frederick Buechner, published and copyright, 1950, Alfred A. Knopf, Inc., New York.

the falseness and horror of his own words, was too much. If this was their revenge, somehow she must take after them with weapons of her own, she must pursue them across fields as windy and ringing as those behind the atrocious bird-house, slay them with the axe of her torment and wrath, avenge her son whom they might as well have slain with their cunning prattle and malice. Let them kneel and pray for mercy to see her adamant, tyrannical only in her own defense. Weak, helpless, hapless Tristram she could fell with no more than a look or a word, and, as for Steitler, she had only to continue hinting at what she could call her suspicions to ruin him most irrecoverably. Let them beware.

Elizabeth is here reenacting imaginatively Tereus's pursuit of Procne and Philomela; and it is probable that had it not been for the sudden arrival of Maroo she would shortly have reenacted it literally. Maroo thus thwarts Elizabeth's urge for revenge exactly as the gods thwart Tereus's; and as the gods transform him and the two sisters into birds, so it seems to the dying Maroo that Elizabeth, Bone, and Steitler are transformed.

Of the four who have stood at her side, three now were gone or almost gone, flown up and off it seemed, yet circling still, wings spread, around, around, through what appeared a sky, high, high and blue above.

There is, however, at this point an important deviation from the myth: where Itys was murdered by the vengeful sisters, Leander remains safe. It seems to Maroo that he has survived because of her:

Only her grandson, who stood nearest her, his brown tweed jacket and red tie the only surfaces of plausibility and warmth, appeared to her a living unit. He was hers, she thought. If he were anyone's, he was then hers; or, more accurately, she thought, he was what he was, he was himself, because of her. Nor was he aware of this, which was as she had wanted it. So successfully had her hopes for him been realized, she understood, that he was invulnerable not only as far as the subtle perils of being alive were concerned, perils of which she had written him with quaint indirection in her letters, but as far as the source of his invulnerability, as far as herself, was concerned too.

What she does not know, of course, is that it is Bone and Steitler and not herself who have made it possible for Leander to remain safe. Unlike Procne and Philomela, they have chosen not to avenge the wrong that has been done them and to say nothing about Elizabeth's lie.

Since this is the only major departure Buechner makes from the actual story of the myth, we can safely assume that it contains a clue to the main idea which he intended the novel to set forth. And when we look closely at the character of Bone, who really has more to do with keeping the truth from Leander˙than Steitler has, we can see that this is true. From the moment of his first appearance Bone functions as a distinctly religious symbol. In the opening scene of the novel his huge figure seated majestically in the barber's chair and covered with a great white robe is likened to that of a priest. Later, while on a visit with Elizabeth and Motley to the Cloisters, he accidentally lodges his hand in a recess in the wooden image of a saint and, during his frantic efforts to free it, is overcome with terror at the thought that he has committed sacrilege. Still later, he arranges to meet Steitler at the Cloisters.

He had suggested the Cloisters as their meeting-place not only because they would be undisturbed there, but because the scale of the surroundings tended in a sense, he thought, to justify both the immensity of his person and of all that he had in him to say. There was also an unpaid debt to the monastery involving the earlier unpleasantness in the chapel and making it neat and right that he do this kind of penance, find out from Steitler what he could, sure of being pained whatever his discovery, in full view of the ancient walls, perhaps even of the particular saint, and surely of the unicorn whose agonies would be portrayed about him. They would witness just this much more of Tristram Bone, and then he might go his way to that extent absolved.

The difference, Buechner seems to be trying to say through Bone, between the pagan world of the myth and the modern world of the novel is the difference between blind primitive vengeance and an awareness of universal human guilt. Bone, like Maroo, is a moral agent in whom the consciousness of personal guilt demands.

absolution in an act of goodness. Through that act Leander is saved and the intrigue set in motion by Elizabeth's lie is brought to an end before it has fully run its course.

But Bone's function as a religious symbol, and, therefore, the function of the theme on which the whole novel rests, is vitiated by his lack of personal power as a man. Apart from his acute moral sense, he is as empty of spiritual conviction and substance as the others. His life, as it is portrayed, is so pointless that the most trivial happenings take on a grotesquely inflated importance; and he is so impoverished in resources that the death of his pet monkey can mean the end of the world for him. Like the petty little intrigue in which he and the others are so strenuously involved, he exists in the novel only by virtue of Buechner's talent for inflating to immense size the thinnest of material.

And once we see Bone for what he is—"weak, helpless, hapless," as Elizabeth said—it is inevitable that we should be dissatisfied with the whole novel; for its importance depends entirely on the high moral coloring Bone the priest is intended to give to it. Taken apart from that coloring, the other characters are as pointless, unmotivated, and underdramatized as he. In spite of the fact that Buechner explores in infinite detail the subtlest workings of their minds, they remain wooden and lifeless. There is no passion in either Elizabeth or Steitler to justify the attraction they are supposed to feel toward one another. They go to bed together; but it is obviously only because the requirements of the story compel them to. Leander, although much is made of his salvation, reveals nothing to indicate that he is worthy of salvation. Maroo figures briefly in one or two static scenes in the early part of the book and then, in the closing section, is given a major role to play. But since the exact nature of the influence she has previously had over the others remains a mystery, the exact function of the role also remains a mystery. Whole chapters are devoted to the activities of Bone's monkey and his cook Emma; yet except for the slight ironic contrast which they serve to point up between Bone's dilemma and the monkey's and between Elizabeth's and Emma's, they do little to justify the space they occupy.

What, then, can be said for the elaborate pains Buechner has taken with the novel? Why has he imposed on such a trivial substance such a weight of complication? Why has he gone to all the trouble of working out the mythical parallels, the involved symbolism, the ambivalent names for his characters, and the sensitive, carefully polished, meticulously allusive, and oftentimes quite excellent style? The answer would seem to be that he has attempted by means of these devices to come to terms with the problem which the novels of nearly all his contemporaries have been attempts to solve—the problem of ordering and making dramatically meaningful the experience of a valueless time. Through the myth he has tried to bring to bear on his material the form and richness of an ancient truth; through symbolic language he has tried to extend the implications of that truth to the outermost limits of his material so as to make of the whole novel a complete, consistent, and self-contained world of maximum meaning.

But like Capote, who made the same attempt by resorting to very similar means, and like the journalists, who made a similar effort by resorting to other means, Buechner could not avoid, so long as he wrote in the novel form, making use of human experience; and the moment he did so he could not avoid becoming the victim of the peculiar limitations which have been imposed upon the use of human experience in the novel in our time. Try as he might, he could not, even with the help of myth and religious symbolism, make the dilemma of his characters either moral or significant. To do that he would have had to discover a system of moral value on which to project it; and this he could not do, for no such system exists. The simple fact was that it was a trivial dilemma centering around a trivial act and perpetrated by trivial people who had nothing inside them; and all that he imposed upon it could not make it otherwise.

CHAPTER XIV

The Young Writer in America

I SUGGESTED in the Preface to this book that the writing of novels is basically a process of assigning value to human experience in the social world. The novel, so long as we require of it a narrative form and function, must always have to do with the actions of men within the framework of a particular society; and it must also, so long as we require of it the validity of serious art, endow those actions with meaning. To satisfy these requirements, the novelist begins always with the meaning which he, as a unique sensibility, brings to the experience he has chosen as his material. This amounts to no less than everything he is or has become up to the moment of writing, and that part of everything he is which he is able to communicate in language to the reader. But no matter with what intensity and skill this kind of meaning is communicated, it will not be enough in itself to constitute the total meaning which the novel, to be truly successful, must have. It will remain a private thing, a vision without an object, a nightmare without a cause, unless it can be linked with and somehow made complementary to a larger body of meaning in which the writer and his readers can share and through which the writer's private meaning can be made public.

The attitudes, customs, assumptions, and beliefs held in common by the members of a society will normally constitute such a body of meaning. Taken together, they will add up to everything which sets a society apart from all others and invests its experience with special value. And since the writer working in a society

231

must deal with its experience, these common assumptions will also invest his material and, therefore, his art with the value necessary to make it something more than private. They will form a sort of hierarchy of meaning in terms of which he will be able to select his material (the act of selection depends on the assignment of value) and make it dramatic (drama depends on the value of the material selected); and they will make it certain that the material he selects as important enough to write about will seem to his audience important enough to read about.

It should be clear from this that the relationship between a writer and his society is a vital and reciprocal one, that the very existence of the writer depends on the existence within his society of a stable order of values. Also, it should follow from this that when such an order breaks down and disappears altogether from a society not only must the society itself but literature, as we normally think of it, cease to exist. If we look back to the changes that have occurred in our own society in the last hundred years (unless we wish to trace them back four hundred years to the English Renaissance), we shall be able to see that such a breakdown has been in the process of gradually taking place. Nearly all the old primary assumptions which men once took for granted—the idea of one god and of a very few fixed doctrines suitable to his worship, of a fixed code of sexual and social morality, of a fixed dichotomous universe divided between the two irreconcilable forces of Good and Evil—have been slowly but relentlessly eroded away by the advancement of natural science, philosophy, and, particularly, psychiatry; or, to put it more precisely, they have been dissected and atomized until they have lost the authority of a single, integrated body of belief and been scattered into countless fragments of comfortless superstition, vague longing, and abortive guilt. The change, in short, has been from a stable and secure absolutism, in which what was possible was certain, to an unstable and insecure relativism, in which everything is possible because nothing is certain.

The history of the period from 1890, roughly, to 1940 might therefore have been the history of the disappearance of the novel as an art form in our society. All the forces of the modern age seem, in those years, to have conspired to separate the writer from his audience by depriving him of those common assumptions of value on which narrative communication with any audience depends. Yet, as even the most casual reading in the literature of the period must make clear, there has seldom if ever before been a time when more novels of distinction as well as novels of more distinction have been produced or when writers have been more intent on exploring and extending the possibilities of the novel as an art form.

One explanation is that at the precise moment when the novel seemed destined to die as narrative, it was being transformed, in the work of a few writers of genius, into something more than narrative, into something, that is, which depended less on direct contact between the writer and his audience through the medium of shared assumptions than on the ability of the writer to impress his own assumptions upon his audience. For a moment in history it was possible for writers like Conrad, Woolf, and Joyce to turn the forces that were operating against the novel to the service of the novel and to exploit the methods of the new science, philosophy, anthropology, and psychiatry in the creation of a new novel of the single consciousness, a consciousness expressed with such thoroughness and dramatic intensity that it came to stand as its own frame of reference and to replace with its own value the social values that were disintegrating.

This is not to say, of course, that the work of these writers was without narrative content. As novelists, they could not have avoided dealing with the actions of men in society nor, indeed, would they have wished to. It was simply that in dealing with them they placed them in a new context, one in which their consequences as actions in society became less important than their moral and psychological consequences in the mental scheme of the protagonist. That scheme was usually the organizing principle of the entire novel, so that what was made meaningful in its terms automatically became meaningful in the novel's terms. Joyce's Dublin, for example, is not the real Dublin: if it were, Joyce would have been obliged to justify it to Dubliners; and his task would have been a task of making recognizable what was already familiar. It is, rather, an abstraction and a hallucination of the real Dublin, not as seen by Dubliners but as seen by Leopold Bloom and Stephen Dedalus; and it is, therefore, meaningful and valuable in proportion as it has meaning and value to their minds. But this kind of achievement would have been beyond Joyce, as it would have been beyond Conrad and Woolf, if they had not all had the good fortune to come of age at a time when the new techniques of science had been developed to a point where they were readily translatable into new techniques of fiction. The findings of Einstein, Jung, Freud, and the others could be used in the novel to explore the stream of consciousness, to create a whole inner world of consciousness, and to give that world a value with which to save the novel when the disintegration of social and moral standards was rapidly making the novel obsolete.

Yet at the same time that Joyce, Conrad, and Woolf were exploiting their private worlds, another group of writers were facing squarely into the social chaos and deriving from it a kind of power that enabled them to present it successfully in their novels. If Joyce and the others found a way of making the value of the single consciousness stand as a substitute for the values that had been lost in society, Lawrence and Huxley in England and Hemingway, Dos Passos, and Fitzgerald in America found a way of making a value of the loss itself. They too imposed their personal biases upon an audience that had no biases; but they expressed them not through the creation of a personal world of private value but through a set of attitudes which suffused their work and gave it value. Basically, these were negative attitudes—rebelliousness, disillusionment, irreverence, and mockery—and they were made possible by the happy circumstance that the loss of values was accompanied and accelerated by a hearty desire, at least on the part of the enlightened portions of society, to be rid of them. If it had not been for this desire, it is doubtful if these writers would have been able to function as writers; for it afforded them just about their only means of seeing and formulating their society in perspective and of achieving a kind of art that was capable of expressing cultural disintegration without succumbing to it.

The thing that gave the younger Huxley the power to write two good novels was the horrified amusement he was able to bring to the spectacle of a whole British leisure class crumbling between the twin futilities of a Victorianism that had lost its faith in God because of science and a Modernism that had lost its faith in science because it had lost its faith in God. The reason, on the other hand, that the older Huxley could write only mediocre novels was his failure to remain amused as he came to identify himself increasingly with the object of his horror. Lawrence was at his best when he was adapting the teachings of Freud to his new scheme of religious sexuality and attempting through it to rejuvenate a culture made barren by machinery and brains. If sex had not urgently needed to be championed at the moment he began writing and if Lawrence had not been able to give it the dignity of a religious faith as well as of an artistic doctrine, it is probable that he would be remembered today as merely a Messianic madman.

Hemingway's first and best two novels were, like Huxley's, primarily descriptions of a society that had lost the possibility of belief. They were dominated by an atmosphere of Gothic ruin, boredom, sterility, and decay. Yet if they had been nothing more than descriptions, they would inevitably have been as empty of meaning as the thing they were describing. What saved them as novels was the values which Hemingway was able to salvage out of the ruin of his characters and transform, through the medium of style and tone, into a kind of moral network that linked them together in a unified pattern of meaning. The famous code of forbearance, primitive loyalty, and silent suffering, which was the direct product of the disappearance of all traditional codes, was a weapon that served for a little while to protect Hemingway's characters from the worst consequences of a life without meaning. It also served to protect Hemingway himself from the worst consequences of writing about that life; for the unceasing conflict between the code and the life created the dramatic tension that lifted his work above mere reportage and gave it the stature of art. It is interesting to note, however, that there was in the major characters of those early novels a vestigial respect for the old values, particularly for the value of religion. Jake Barnes had what amounted to an ancestral memory of God which caused him to frequent cathedrals. The same memory made it impossible for Frederick Henry to join his fellow officers in baiting the priest. Yet the problem for Frederick, and the thing which contributed, along with the code, to the dramatic tension of his story, was that he could not give himself completely either to faith or to doubt. The priest believed in God; Catherine believed in the sanctity of love; Frederick believed in both and neither. Like the age he symbolized, Frederick was lost between two worlds, the world of tradition and belief and the world of modern war in which tradition and belief had become merely empty forms. It is because of this that *A Farewell to Arms* has the depth and complexity of meaning and design that allows it to be read on a number of levels—as a story of love in wartime, as a story of spiritual exile, as a religious story about godlessness, as a godless story about religion. It is also because of this that the dilemma of Frederick and Catherine continues to have value. In their suffering Hemingway found a subject that fittingly dramatized the collapse of a moral order.

Fitzgerald shared with Frederick and his creator that vantage point located squarely between the crumbling old order and the new world struggling to be born. In his first novels he did little more than report, to a generation of outraged elders, the social and biological sins of his contemporaries. As a young modern fresh out of Princeton, he was delighted with the life he was exposing and gave lavishly of his time, money, and talent to make it more delightful than it was. But as a young Midwestern Catholic fresh out of St. Paul he was shocked by that life and uneasily, if dimly, aware of its sinister implications. At first the paradox made him popular. It gave his books the quality of a combined public slander, confessional, and self-flagellation. But as time went on, Fitzgerald's sense of personal damnation began to grow stronger than the enchantment he had felt for the damnation of others; and when that happened, he began to project the horror of his own collapse upon the life around him and to see that too as collapse. The result was a novel like *Tender Is the Night,* a story like *Babylon Revisited,* and an essay like *The Crack-Up,* all much less popular works than the earlier books, but carrying beneath their surfaces the buried traces of that legend Paul Rosenfeld always hoped Fitzgerald would one day write, "the legend of a moon which never rose."

The thing that gave Fitzgerald his initial stimulus as a writer was the profound change that occurred in American morals and manners after the end of the first war. But the thing that made him into a great writer was the weakness I have spoken of, the one which finally caused him to identify his own spiritual tragedy with the cultural tragedy he saw behind that change. In the neurotic union of himself with the dark currents of his time, Fitzgerald found his true theme—the legend of the simple Midwestern boy struggling to hold onto his illusions amid the corruption of Eastern wealth. The tragedy lay, of course, in the depth of the boy's eventual disenchantment and in the suffering of such men as Jay Gatsby and Dick Diver. But it lay, first and foremost, in Fitzgerald himself because he too had believed and been disenchanted.

The virtues of an older and simpler age, the frontier virtues of honesty, dignity, industry, and thrift, were essential to the creation of the kind of writer Fitzgerald was. They gave breadth and substance to his early infatuation with the rich; and they gave intensity and depth to his later renunciation of them. But they were also essential to the creation of that whole group of writers who produced the best literature of the period between the two wars. They are the same virtues that were behind Hemingway's vision of the red barn back in Michigan, Wolfe's tortured dream of the great lost Gant down in Old Catawba, Lewis's memories of a Sauk Center boyhood, Farrell's obsession with his early life in the Chicago slums, and Dos Passos' imaginary U.S.A., which could only have grown out of the lost idealism of an immigrant's grandson. All these writers were provincials; and what they caught in their books was that moment in history when provincialism was dying, when for a little while they could see and record its passing in perspective, before they and the values they had been born to became part of the vanished past.

The writers who have come after them, the best young writers of the second war and its aftermath, have not had the advantage of either the perspective or the values of another and more stable age. They have come to maturity at the end of the period of transition and loss when the wreckage of the old order has been made complete and the energy of rebellion has been dissipated. Perhaps the most unfortunate aspect of their dilemma is that, although they have been denied the energy, they have inherited the wreckage and are obliged to face it nakedly and coldly without resources.

There is no longer for them the possibility of a literature of consciousness, such as Joyce, Woolf, and the others evolved, nor of a literature that draws its power from disillusion, shock, and social change. The techniques of science that were exploited so brilliantly by the founders of the literature of consciousness are not the bright new instruments they were when they were discovered. They no longer promise to open fresh and unexplored fields to the novelist. They would seem, rather, to offer only to lead him back over old ground to the kind of material which Joyce and Woolf explored thoroughly and for all time. Besides, since the new writers cannot possibly use those techniques with the same sense of defiant discovery, they would probably use them badly and with a paralyzing realization of their triteness. For much the same reason they cannot follow in the paths of Lewis, Fitzgerald, Dos Passos, and Hemingway. The basic social changes brought about by the rise of modern America in the first three decades of the century have been largely completed. The social patterns have been set. The Babbitt class is no longer new; it has, in fact, been so thoroughly absorbed into American life that no standard exists by which it can be satirized. Fitzgerald's golden dream of Paradise died in the Depression; and even though there has been a pathetic attempt to revive it, we should be able to see by now that it does not belong to the America of today. The workers are winning their fight without the help of new Dos Passoses; besides, the cause of labor is an unfashionable, if not a downright dangerous, one for writers today. The problems which concerned the writers of the 1930's might just as well have never existed. Steinbeck's Okies have been absorbed into the California countryside; and no one cares to hear any more about the sweaty struggles of young Studs Lonigans. Because of this, the new writers are faced with the task of maintaining themselves as writers at a time when there are no strongly prevailing attitudes or issues to help give value to their work.

The result is that, whether they have sought to maintain themselves through the simple reporting of facts and events, the exploitation of such shock value as they can find in race problems or sexual maladjustment, or the creation of a private world of pure prose, these writers have been constantly handicapped by the emptiness of the characters and situations about which they have been obliged to write. Since they have inherited a world without values and since they have had no choice but to find their material in that world, they have had to deal with valuelessness; and that can never form the basis of a successful literature.

The absence of a set of attitudes and values, both in themselves and in their society, has left its mark on the work of nearly all the new writers I have discussed in this book. It is behind the failure of that portion of *The Naked and the Dead* which has to do with the philosophical evil of war; and it is clearly epitomized in the emptiness of the central character, Lieutenant Hearn. In *The Gallery* it is behind the failure of the "Portraits" to dramatize fully Burns's undramatized assertions in the "Promenades"; and once again the dilemma of the novel is represented in the dilemma of a character—the neurotic Lieutenant Hal. The absence of genuine values led Shaw in *The Young Lions* to concoct false values and to superimpose them upon his material. Miller in *That Winter* was guilty of much the same offense, although in a large part of the book he avoided the problem of values simply by falling back on the skillful manipulation of trivia. The weakness of all of Vidal's novels between *Williwaw* and *A Search for the King* is that the material presented in them is not valuable enough to dramatize successfully the issues which Vidal wished to set forth. The emptiness of Jim Willard in *The City and the Pillar* vitiates the tragedy of his homosexual dream; the emptiness of Bill Giraud in *The Season of Comfort* vitiates the drama of his struggle against his mother. The same emptiness in Kit and Port Moresby in *The Sheltering Sky* made it impossible for Bowles to motivate or dignify their destruction; and in *Other Voices, Other Rooms* and *A Long*

Day's Dying the metaphorical complexities and mythical parallels serve merely to disguise the triviality of the characters and situations.

Yet it would be a mistake to assume, as I may seem to have assumed, that the failure of values is a mechanical and lifeless formula which can be applied in laboratory isolation to the work of the new writers. If I have applied it in isolation and as a formula, I have done so purely in the interests of analysis and in order to compress a great many ideas and observations into a single working principle. Actually, the failure of values is only part of the total problem facing these writers. There are other issues which have as much bearing on their dilemma and which are more concretely the results of their circumstances as writers and the intellectual climate of their age.

The war years gave many of the new writers an opportunity to leave the country, stay away for a time, and come back again. They were able, as few Americans are, to watch the fading of their old attitudes and to prepare their minds for a fresh perspective. Returning from Europe and the Pacific, they were, in a sense, returning exiles, more knowledgeable and less provincial than they had been. If what they found at home had offered them a new contact with experience, they might have been afforded what Louis Bromfield has called "the sense of criticism and of valuation" needed for fresh writing. But the country they returned to was much the same country they had left; and it was not greatly different from the country which had been responsible for the vehement exile of the Lost Generation.

Businessmen still made up the bulk of the population. People were still paying homage to the machine, still scrambling after goods and wealth to the neglect of their sensibilities. The average citizen retained his inscrutable apathy toward matters of social injustice, morals, art, and affairs abroad. People who were old enough to have been outraged by Sinclair Lewis were living as if *Babbitt* and *Main Street* had never been written. Life in America was as aesthetically starved as ever, still without a true culture and a standard of adult values. The ingredients for another all-out war of artistic secession were there, but the will to revolt was not. The most aborting truth was that it had all been done before.

Social protest had been for the generation of Mencken and Lewis what negation and loss had been for the generation of Hemingway, Fitzgerald, and Dos Passos—a frame of art, a means of ordering the material of life into the material of art. In the years after 1910, protest depended upon the recollection of a time when values were relatively secure and the immediate apprehension of a time when values were in transition—when machine ethics and machine culture was vulgarizing Main Street and provincialism was giving way to a cheap and artificial urbanity. For the writers who attacked the American way of life in *Civilization in the United States* in 1921, it depended upon a belief in aesthetic values over the values of mass production, the European way over the American. But by the end of the second war, the transitional phase was over; the machine age was a going concern; and the values of the machine had become such an integral part of the national culture that not only was protest redundant but the perspective necessary for protest had ceased to exist.

And as American life was formulated, so also was American literature. The literary movements that sprang up in Chicago and Greenwich Village before 1920 were energized by a sense of new beginnings. Writers were consciously breaking with the past and asserting the unique experience of life in the modern age. If the best books and poems of the time protested the evils of industrialism and the paralysis of industrial man, it was because writers were at last discovering the truth of industrialism and beginning to sense the dominant sickness of the age. They were experimenting with new forms and techniques, new ideas and a new language, because the world was new; and they were held together by their common devotion to the cause of art because not only was that cause threatened but the impact of artistic change was moving them all in the same direction toward the same goal. By the middle 1940's, however, the age of awakening had become the age of somnolence. There had been the brief concern for the Depression victims of the 1930's; but the literature of economics and the people had been short-lived and had failed to leave an important mark on new writing. The "experimentalists" of the 1920's were the true literary forefathers of the present generation; but their experiments were now established; and young writers seemed unable to make new ones.

Lacking the focus of negation and loss, a new world to discover, and a single perspective for protest, the new writers are deprived as well of group solidarity. They form no distinct generation in the old sense; they champion no cause; they share no common aim; they are impelled by no awareness of a common artistic mission. It is the sum of their rejections that even though they have never known the values that were lost for them thirty years ago, they cannot make a new or substitute value of their art. For them the religion of art belongs with all the other dead faiths. It was good for a time when writers functioned on the periphery of life, when there was a side for art and a side for life. But it is of no use in a time when the position of the writer, if it is defined at all, is somewhere near the bottom of the list of artisans and almost at the top of the list of tradesmen. Besides, they have seen the religion of art become in their time a blind alley, a coterie dogma with restrictive by-laws that threaten to smother the thing they were invented to preserve; they have seen pedantry, obscurantism, and snobbery sprout like anemic flowers from the dead health of Stein and Joyce. They have learned that after the innovators come the specialists and after the specialists the imitators and that after a movement has spent itself there can only come the incestuous, the archaeologists, and the ghouls.

But perhaps more than anything else they have learned that they no longer need the protection of one another. The revolt of their predecessors required the strategy of a complex military maneuver. They were attacking the past by invading the present; and there were enemies in both camps. There was poverty in the beginning—the persistent affliction of the young of Grub Street and Greenwich Village in all ages; the reactionary element in power; the philistinism of the press and the popular magazines; the babbittry of the folks back home; comstockery; prohibition; and the general public resistance to change. Today the anti-literary elements have been to a great extent overridden; or perhaps they have simply faded into the background for lack of opposition. A young writer can produce his novel today without first having to defend himself for being a writer; and he can stay at home to do it. His greatest disadvantage is that, being alone, he is denied access to the free interplay of ideas that can only be had through association with other writers; and he is likely to find it hard in isolation to preserve his singular function amid those other functions which are carried on around him and which, because of their difference of aim, are necessarily opposed to his.

It might even be said that the young writer's very freedom from adversity today makes his situation more difficult. Like the factors which might have compelled him to revolt and exile, he has himself been absorbed into American life and, in many cases, made the ward of the culture with which, perhaps to be wholly effective, he ought to be at odds. Young men who, if they had come to maturity in the Twenties, would have followed the expatriate vanguard to Paris are able today to find jobs allied to their literary interests—in publishing, advertising, Hollywood, on the radio and the editorial staffs of *Time* and *Life*—or they are studying at universities. The universities alone are doing much to prevent the outbreak of another exile movement, at the same time that they are, as Stephen Spender said, "subsidizing American contemporary literature." They are attracting talented beginners with lucrative writing fellowships and offers of a congenial atmosphere and the company of other writers. Instead of starving in Montparnasse, the young man of ability can take up residence on the campus, work under the tutelage of such writer-scholars as Wallace Stegner at Stanford, Robert Penn Warren at Minnesota, Mark Schorer at California, R. P. Blackmur at Princeton, and Lionel Trilling at Columbia, and even prepare himself for jobs like theirs so that if his writing should not pay off he will always be assured of a steady income.

At first glance, such an arrangement seems attractive indeed. But it carries with it many dangers, both for the beginning writer and the professional who takes an "in residence" or a teaching job. Perhaps the greatest danger for the beginner inheres in the kind of life with which the university provides him. By its very nature, the university exists somewhat outside the main current of human experience; it is secure, sheltered, and intellectually concentrated in a way that ordinary life is not. It is therefore, at least in this respect, an artificial environment, one in which more ideas are conceived than are ever put to use, more passions are analyzed than are ever felt. If the young writer belongs to a regular writing program, as he would at Bread Loaf, Iowa, or Stanford, he is likely to find that he is absorbing excellent ideas and theories *about* writing, that he is being constantly stimulated, even overstimulated, by his contacts with his talented associates, but that he is not learning *how* to write nor experiencing enough of life to give him anything to write about. He is also likely to find that the literary standards of his instructors, for all their theoretical soundness, are not the same as those he will have to meet as a professional and that they tend to force him into a premature concern with such problems as the divisibility of technique and subject matter and the proper use of symbol and myth. These problems must be taken seriously by every conscientious student of literature; but they can be fatal to the young writer who takes them seriously. They can force him away from his proper function as a creator and into the subsidiary function of criticism; or they can make him so deliberately conscious of his own processes that he will turn out novels of the sort Frederick Buechner has written, novels that fulfill all the classroom requirements, that are full of symbols and mythical references, but that are without human significance and life.

There is another kind of danger for the young writer who, while studying at a university, profits too much from his courses and wins a sudden and premature success through publication. Perhaps he is awarded a fellowship in a Prize Novel contest or has a story accepted by the O'Henry Memorial Committee. At once he finds himself, or fancies himself, in the professional class with professional obligations to the market. He has no time or inclination now to learn to write, to decide whether he really has anything to say: he is already a writer and, as such, he must begin thinking about his next book or stories and wondering how he can best please those who liked his first. Quite naturally, there is no room in his situation for experiment nor for a deep and honest evaluation of his time. He is likely to be committed to serving up a light transcript of reality, a paper-thin reflection of popular clichés, and a slightly more than ordinary version of the ideas most people want to hear. To be sure, the universities are turning out many good writers (although few truly outstanding ones) and the prize contests and literary fellowships are discovering and subsidizing many more. But their good fortune is bought too often at the price of that indispensable period of gestation and growth during which, in the privacy of exile and obscurity, writers have always made their first discoveries and had the time for greatness.

For the writer "in residence" or the promising young novelist turned part-time instructor the dangers of the university are perhaps less severe; but their effects are much more permanent. Like the beginner, the professional writer on the campus is imprisoned in an artificial atmosphere; and he has the irritating advantage over his nonwriting colleagues of being at all times aware of the fact. He lives and works with his senses and his intuitive responses to life; they work with their intellects and their logical responses to facts and formulas; and in his terms they do not live at all. He asks nothing of them but that they leave him alone and let him do his work; they constantly draw invidious comparisons between his lot and theirs, sit in perpetual judgment on his actions and quirks, and openly denounce his classroom practices as seductive and unethical. Yet because he belongs, however uneasily and temporarily to their world, he must accept them. He must appease them, convince them that he is in no way different from them, by attending their dull parties (only he will know how dull they really are), joining in with their pathetic attempts at ribaldry (only he will have lived enough to know what true ribaldry is), enduring their petty gossip about one another (only he will understand the terrible fear and loneliness behind it). But even as he is performing the ritual of acceptance and being accepted, he must continually perform within the secrecy of himself the far more complicated ritual of self-preservation. He must learn to keep alive the unique and delicate thing which is his singular function as a writer; and he must do this in the midst of just about the most anti-literary environment to be found in the civilized world.

If he does not learn this, if for a moment he opens himself to the spite, jealousy, and pettiness surrounding him, he will be in immediate danger of becoming something else. Like the beginner who absorbs too much theory, he will become self-conscious about his work and begin to suspect vaguely that there is something adolescent and irresponsible about being a writer. In his isolation he may begin to feel that there are no other writers in the world, that he is the last of the line, and that he might just as well stop trying to preserve a vision and way of life which no longer has meaning or relevance. Finally, if he follows his logic through, he will probably arrive at a time when he will be willing to compromise, when the pressure to conform will at last have grown too great to bear, and he will be glad to settle for something safer and more acceptable. Finally, he may decide to give up his writing altogether and devote his best energies to teaching others to write; or, what is more likely, he may decide to become a critic.

Criticism is the present-day substitute for the old community of art, the last haven for those many writers who have gone to the universities in search of that most paradoxical of current nirvanas, a literary atmosphere that offers both stimulation and security. It is the natural by-product of an overexposure to university habits of life and thought, just as it is the unavoidable answer at a time when it is no longer possible for young writers to ally themselves with a specific movement or to follow the fluctuating rate of exchange in self-conscious abandon across Europe. One can write criticism today when one does not feel a strong enough impulse to write anything else; and one can write it in the safety of a teaching job without first having to organize and conduct a dangerous and perhaps fatal revolt against established authority. It is also one of the few remaining ways of acquiring a literary reputation, of pursuing a literary life, without lowering oneself to the levels of Hollywood, the book clubs, and *The Saturday Review of Literature*. But most importantly of all, it is the respectable form of writing (at least among the people whose respect one values), the one which it is most possible and proper for the university mind to produce, the one for which there is the readiest and most consistently honorable market.

The market for new and serious creative work, on the other hand, has declined sharply in this country in the last several years, particularly in the years since the end of the second war. "If one wished," said Stephen Spender, "to publish a poem or story in America which would meet with the attention of an American intelligentsia, one would be puzzled where to publish it." The larger popular serious magazines such as *Harper's* and *The Atlantic Monthly,* which in the past at least professed an interest in new writing and current literary problems, are devoted today almost exclusively to discussions of economic and political opinion. The few stories and poems they do publish are seldom new and certainly not experimental. Rarely are the stories in these two magazines vigorous, challenging, or even particularly memorable; while the poems are likely to be easily clever, perhaps slightly satirical, but carefully restrained and tailored to the requirement that a poem should not disturb. Even *The Saturday Review of Literature,* which began in the 1920's as a serious outlet for literary opinion and which still bears the terrible responsibility of being the only literary magazine of large circulation in the country, has become a sounding board for opinions on every conceivable subject except literature. Crammed in with the cartoons, the record, film, and book reviews, the double-crostics, the limp wisecracks of Bennett Cerf, and the schoolmarmish editorial euphemisms of Harrison Smith will be articles on Russia, Occupied Germany, criminology, feminism, and the Kinsey Report. When a literary article does appear, it is almost certain to be another of those nice, hopeful surveys of the current literary situation (in which, one gathers, only nice, hopeful novelists are writing anything worthwhile) or a diatribe against the "new criticism" (meaning the work of Eliot, Tate, Ransom, and others who have been writing authoritative criticism for at least the last twenty-five years) or the "fascism" to be found in the thirty-year-old work of Ezra Pound and, by implication, T. S. Eliot (the most influential poets and critics of the modern tradition). Lately, as the policy has been increasingly compromised to please the tastes of the many, as the reviews have grown more and more superficial, as less and less space has been given to new fiction, the name of *The Saturday Review* has lost the last of the authority and prestige which once surrounded it.

As for the new "little" magazines which could always be counted on in the past to support fresh and experimental writing, we might just as well lament their passing. Since the war no magazine has appeared to do for this generation what the old *Dial, Broom,* and *transition* were able to do for the generation of Hemingway. There has, to be sure, been an attempt in Paris to revive *transition;* and in Italy and North Africa, the new expatriate Holy Lands, there have even been new magazines founded. But, for the most part, these have been febrile efforts, motivated, like the new exile itself, more by an anxiety to recapture the glory of the past than to discover the truth of the present. A few of them, such as the North African *Zero,* have been launched without confidence or hope, often with a prefatory note asserting the futility of all literary endeavor in a valueless time like ours, and then given over, with a suggestion of the old defiance, to stories and poems that are not so much expressive of the contemporary neurosis (although they are often that) as of the pathetic lack of talent of their authors. Others, such as *Wake,* have been devoted almost entirely to poor translations of little-known foreign writers (who, it would appear, have just cause for being little known) and to mediocre, castoff stories by new minor masters like Paul Bowles. What little fresh material is in them is often startlingly crude and naïve, as if the writers still entertained the quaint notion that scatology is synonymous with realism and technical oddity a substitute for something to say. Most often, however, it is merely innocent, as when very young poets affirm, as if for the first time, the primacy of the Poetic Spirit and the religiosity of the Poetic Life.

The young writer is thus faced with the cold fact that no significant publication exists today through which his work will reach an enlightened audience and he will be assured of an opportunity to develop a reputation as a writer. Because of this, he is reduced to one of two alternatives: either he can spend his apprenticeship writing novels and hope that he will win a position at least of notoriety before the public begins to be aware of the immaturities he is forcing upon them, or he can postpone his creative career and try for a reputation as a critic. If he attempts the former, he is likely to find himself in the predicament of having to turn out too many novels too quickly (as Gore Vidal has done) and of having to build his reputation afresh with each novel. If he attempts the latter, he is, of course, running the risk of sealing off his talent for good. But he is at least placing himself within range of a fairly large and steady market. For by deciding to become a critic, he is automatically asserting his candidacy for membership in the strongest and most highly organized literary society in existence today, the society of the small established critical journals.

If the young writer succeeds in winning a place for himself in the exclusive, even hierarchical company of critics who write for the journals, he can be assured that his critical work will reach an enlightened audience and that it will be judged by the most rigid standards. He will also be freed of that most insidious compulsion of the popular market, the compulsion to make his criticism continually provocative, gossipy, and simple. He will no longer have to hold suspended in his mind the subtle distinctions between a review and an analysis, a "trend" article and a comprehensive evaluation. He will no longer have to struggle to minimize the difficulty of his ideas for the sake of the readers of *Harper's, The Saturday Review,* and *The New Republic,* at the same time that he is struggling to make them worthy of the readers of the *Sewanee, Kenyon,* and *Partisan Reviews* (only Malcolm Cowley has been able to do both with equal success). He will be writing now for his peers, for men of integrity and judgment, whose only demand upon him will be that he write with thoroughness, discrimination, and complete honesty.

Yet largely because they represent the last stronghold of sound literary value in this country, the journals have certain limitations. For one thing, they have had, in recent years, to go more and more on the defensive. To combat the growing influence and hostility of more popular competitors, they have had to set up all sorts of protective barriers, among them a distinction between "good" writing and "commercial" writing—writing for art and writing for hire—and another between the intellectual and the mass audience. The result has been a double standard of literary excellence: the journals have become consistently more private and precious as the popular magazines have become consistently more vulgar.

Even within their chosen province of criticism, the journals have set up barriers. As the gap between the general public and the intellectuals has widened, the journal critics, most of whom are professors of English, have grown increasingly specialized. An overwhelming majority of them have devoted themselves entirely to the analysis of poetry—seventeenth-century and modern—and other criticism. Of the best journal critics—John Crowe Ransom, Allen Tate, Cleanth Brooks, R. P. Blackmur, Robert Penn Warren, Yvor Winters, I. A. Richards, and Kenneth Burke—only Blackmur, Warren, and Tate have made more than an exploratory attempt to deal critically with fiction. And even of these three, only Warren has ventured any distance outside the field of the approved masters—Dostoevski, Joyce, James, Kafka, Proust—and into what is still considered the contemporary field of Hemingway and Faulkner.

It is probably here, in their treatment of fiction, that these critics have revealed their most serious limitations. Even though they have nearly all individually acknowledged their failure to treat it adequately and have even predicted that they will shortly be left with no choice but to begin treating it adequately, they have still shown no inclination to take note of the fiction which is now being produced around them. Apparently, they are just beginning to consider it safe, at least for others, to acknowledge the existence of novels by Hemingway, Wolfe, Dos Passos, and Fitzgerald (who has just been officially ordained by Arthur Mizener); but they obviously do not consider it safe for anyone to acknowledge the existence of novels by Capote, Vidal, Mailer, Shaw, and the other new writers. They prefer, at least for the moment, to leave these writers to the mercy of the reviewers and the literary columnists who, while they have never been noted for powers of penetrating evaluation, can presumably afford to make mistakes.

The result of such timidity in our best critics is that the new writers are deprived of the benefit of sound critical attention at the time in their careers when they need it most desperately. Not only do they have no periodical in which they can publish their experimental work and develop the beginnings of a reputation but they have no authority to whom they can turn for guidance and encouragement, or simply for understanding, as Fitzgerald turned to Wilson and Bishop, and Hemingway to Pound and Ford and later to Cowley. In the Twenties, when the Lost Generation writers were about as far along in their careers as the new writers now are, Wilson in *Hound and Horn,* Ford and Pound in the *transatlantic review,* Cowley in *Broom,* and Bishop in *Vanity Fair* were giving detailed attention to their work, not two years or five years after they had proved themselves, but virtually at the moment of their first tentative appearances in apprentice novels and stories. The benefits these writers derived from such attention are evident not only in the quality of the work they produced but in their own grateful acknowledgments of them in their essays and letters.

Today Bishop and Ford are dead, Pound is confined in a sanitarium, Wilson has gone into semiretirement, and Cowley, who, alone of them all, continues to expand and deepen his critical interests and capacities, has lately concerned himself with the earlier American writers and taken to commenting only desultorily on the contemporary scene. The kind of critical service which they performed for their generation seems to have passed with the passing of their youth; and no one has come along to take their place. If one were asked to prepare a list of the new young critics (those, that is, born between 1918 and 1924) who are working today in the literature of their own generation, one would be forced to submit a blank page. Yet the new generation of writers is already formed, many of its members have already produced their second and third novels, and all of its members are in need of the kind of attention which only their contemporaries, who are living in their own world and sharing in their own experience, can give them. If they do not get it, they will survive; but they will survive in isolation, and there will be less between them and the emptiness which surrounds them and which has placed such a heavy price on their survival.

Yet the state of criticism, like the failure of values and the absence of a community of art, is only a symptom of the general debility of the times as a whole. Since the end of the war there has been, in all parts of the world, a gradual dwindling of creative vitality and impulse. The moral and political chaos of Europe has led, in Germany, to a virtual cessation of all activity in both the sciences and the arts, in France, to a paralysis of nerve and a literature of nervelessness, in England, to an irreparable weakening of creative fiber in the entire younger generation. The atmosphere of tension and distrust generated in this country by the fear of Communism and the threat of another war has led to a frantic search for financial and spiritual security and created a state of mind in which the ideal of creative independence and rebellion not only has no place but is viewed with active hatred. The writers and artists who are trying to stay alive and develop their talents have had to struggle continually against their own inertia and sense of purposelessness at the same time that they have had to intensify their struggle against the inertia and hostility of the public. As a result, the work they have produced has been, for the most part, labored, consciously contrived, and lacking in that free play of imaginative energy which can only be achieved in a stable, tolerant society.

The last few seasons on Broadway have been remarkable for the absence of strong new plays. Only Tennessee Williams has brought fresh promise to the postwar American theater; and even he, if the paucity of his themes is an indication, is already beginning to show signs of bankruptcy. Out of the many new young painters, all of whom seem to have been born with technical facility, there may possibly be two or three with enough individuality and drive to go beyond the promising stage and develop into good minor painters. In music the situation is much the same: there is facility in abundance; but one would have to look far to find a young composer with even an intimation of the daring, originality, and insight of a Stravinsky or even of a Gershwin.

It is of course much more difficult to be new and original today than it was in those years when the modern tradition in all the arts was still being discovered and originality was synonymous with just about any interesting departure from custom. Today young artists are infected with the approved modern techniques almost from the moment they begin their training; and these techniques are so excellently suited to what they have to say that they spend their careers perfecting them instead of developing new ones. Yet it is always true in an artistically healthy age that the act of perfecting old techniques will sooner or later evolve into an act of such infinite skill and subtlety that it will become in itself an act of innovation: the impress of the increasingly new interpretation on the old form causes the interpretation to become paramount and the form to become extinct. But for this to occur, almost the same elements must be present that are required for creation—a high order of technical skill, idiosyncrasy, and imagination—and these seem to be lacking today. Our young artists are learning the old forms meticulously well; but instead of building upon them, they seem able only to imitate them.

Perhaps the main reason for this, apart from the general confusion of the times, is that the artist today has no distinct attitude either toward his experience or toward the medium in which he works. He is unable to ally himself with a specific school or movement, for none exists. He is unable simply to look into his heart because he no longer knows where his heart is or whether he has one. He has been so thoroughly dissected and atomized that when he sits down to probe his conscience he has to summon into consultation a thousand disparate fragments of himself. He has been taught so many secrets about his own inner workings that he is scarcely able to practice his art without experiencing a moment of humiliation at the thought of the shoddy, vulgar, or adolescent motive behind it. He is, in short, a man who knows too much to be knowing, who is too convinced of his own lack of conviction to be convincing, and who, therefore, lacks the basic requirement of the healthy artist—a dogmatic belief in his supreme power as an individual and a complete contempt for everything which stands in the way of its exercise.

The absence of such a belief is largely responsible for the emptiness one senses in so much of the new fiction. It accounts for the mask of phony wisdom which writers like Merle Miller and Irwin Shaw put up between themselves and their readers. It is implicit in all the novels of Gore Vidal; for Vidal simply does not know what he believes or ought to believe about himself, his characters, or the act of writing. Both Capote and Buechner have created in their novels a world of such perfect artistry that any suggestion in them of an overt attitude of the author would seem an impurity; and yet the lack of an attitude makes for another kind of impurity. It has caused the characters of Joel Knox and Tristram Bone to come through as empty shells; and they are two characters who cannot afford to be empty.

What we need today to give us a literature of vitality and significance, in spite of the prevailing inertia and confusion, is a few writers of genius, men who would be able to go on day in and day out, year in and year out, patiently creating out of their own spiritual resources master works of art. They would have to be as strong as Proust and Joyce in order to survive in the midst of isolation and paralysis. They would have to be big enough and dedicated enough to withstand all our efforts to kill them, frighten them, buy them off, or send them to prison. But if we had them and they were able to survive, they might succeed in envisioning for us the reality we seek and cannot find for ourselves. And then all the small, confused, and misguided talents whose troubles concern us now might be impelled to draw close around them and discover, in their example, the means and the desire to create a literature that would be worthy of our time.

Index

The pages of the main discussion of an author, or of important topics, are italicized.